A Random Walk
Down Wall Street

FOURTH EDITION

A Random Walk Down Wall Street

FOURTH EDITION

BURTON G. MALKIEL

DEAN, YALE SCHOOL OF ORGANIZATION AND MANAGEMENT

W · W · NORTON & COMPANY
NEW YORK   LONDON

Printed in the United States of America.

This book is composed in Baskerville. Composition by JGH Composition Inc. Manufacturing by The Maple-Vail Book Group.

FOURTH EDITION

Library of Congress Cataloging in Publication Data
Malkiel, Burton Gordon.
  A random walk down Wall Street.
  Bibliography: p.
  Includes index.
1. Investments.   2. Stocks.   3. Random walks
(Mathematics)   I. Title.
HG4521.M284   1985   332.6'78   84-29476

ISBN 0-393-01999-3
ISBN 0-393-95460-9 {PBK.}

W. W. Norton & Company, Inc., 500 Fifth Avenue, New York, N.Y. 10110
W. W. Norton & Company Ltd., 37 Great Russell Street, London WC1B 3NU

67890

To

Jonathan

and

Rugby

Contents

PART TWO   *How the Pros Play the Biggest
            Game in Town*   **101**

Preface to the Fourth Edition

This new edition represents a complete revision. To take account of the breathtaking pace of financial innovation during the early 1980s and the changed investment climate of the mid-1980s, a complete rewriting of Part IV covering investment strategies has been required. Materials are included on such new financial instruments as zero coupon bonds, money-market deposit accounts, government-security money funds, adjustable rate mortgages, universal and variable life insurance policies, and GNMA investment funds. The extraordinary financial innovations of the 1980s, as well as the new tax laws encouraging personal savings, have created uncommon opportunities for investors.

The institutional chapters are not the only ones to have been reworked. Revised and expanded, the analytical sections reflect the considerable body of work completed through 1984. Added materials range from arbitrage pricing models of stockprice valuation to empirical studies showing higher returns available on securities with low price-earnings multiples and small capitalizations.

Even the historical sections have been amended to include the most recent market history. This new edition should be useful both for individual investors and for students in courses on financial markets, investment management, and personal finance. Despite the inclusion of the major academic findings of recent years, the book retains its nontechnical character and is easily accessible to readers with no mathematical training.

I have been fortunate to have been able to continue to count on the help of many of those who assisted in the earlier editions. In addition, I want to express my gratitude for the absolutely essential assistance of John Bogle and Melissa McGinnis of the Vanguard Group of Investment Companies; Frank Wisneski of Wellington Management Company; H. Bradlee Perry of David L. Babson & Co.; George Putnam of Putnam Funds; George S. Johnston of Scudder, Stevens & Clark; and George Smith of Baker, Fentress & Company. Steve Feinstein provided invaluable research assistance, and Linda Wheeler and Patricia Taylor offered exceedingly skillful editorial assistance. Barbara Johnson faithfully typed and kept track of various drafts of the manuscript, and Bernice Parent pitched in by accurately typing final drafts of some chapters. Donald Lamm and my editor Robert Kehoe continued to make my association with W. W. Norton a most pleasant one. Joan Ryan and Claire Bien were extremely helpful in preparing new and updated charts. Michele Petersen also assisted in many ways. Finally, Rugby was particularly cooperative in agreeing to chew shoes and pillows instead of this manuscript. Because of her essential contribution, she has been added to the dedication.

Burton G. Malkiel
New Haven, Connecticut
January 1985

Acknowledgments for the First Edition

My debts of gratitude to people and institutions who have helped me with this book are enormous in both number and degree. My academic colleagues and friends in the financial community who have contributed to various drafts of chapters are too numerous to mention. I must acknowledge explicitly, however, the many who have read through the entire manuscript and offered extremely valuable suggestions and criticisms. These include Peter Asch, Leo Bailey, Jeffrey Balash, William Baumol, G. Gordon Biggar, Jr., Lester Chandler, Barry Feldman, William Grant, Sol Malkiel, Richard Quandt, Michael Rothschild, H. Barton Thomas, and Robert Zenowich. It is particularly appropriate that I emphasize the usual *caveat* that the above-named individuals are blameless for any errors of fact or judgment in these pages. Many have warned me patiently and repeatedly about the madness of my heresies, and the above list includes several who disagree sharply with my position.

Many research assistants have labored long in compiling information for this book. Especially useful contributions were made by Barry Feldman, Paul Messaris, Barry Schwartz, Greg Smolarek, Ray Soldavin, and Elizabeth Woods. Helen Talar and Phyllis Durepos not only faithfully and accurately typed several drafts of the manuscript, but also offered extremely valuable research assistance as well. Elvira Giaimo provided most helpful computer programming. Many of the supporting studies for this book were conducted at Princeton's Financial Research Center.

A vital contribution was made by Patricia Taylor, a professional writer and editor. She read through two complete drafts of the book and made innumerable contributions to the style, organization, and content of the manuscript. She deserves much of the credit for whatever lucid writing can be found in these pages.

I am also grateful to Arthur Lipper Corporation for permission to use their mutual fund rankings, Wiesenberger Investment Services for the use of their data in many of my tables, Moody's Investors Service for permission to reproduce several of their stock charts, Consumers Union for their estimates of life insurance costs, College Retirement Equities Fund for making available to me James Farrell's performance studies, and Smith, Barney & Co., Inc. for allowing me the run of their investment library.

My association with W. W. Norton & Company has been an extremely pleasant one, and I am particularly grateful to my editor, Starling Lawrence, for his invaluable help.

Finally, the contribution of my wife Judith Malkiel, was of inestimable importance. No perfunctory uxorial reference of "cheerful encouragement" can do justice to her contribution. She painstakingly edited every page of the manuscript and was helpful in every phase of this undertaking. This acknowledgment of my debt to her is the largest understatement of all.

Burton G. Malkiel
Princeton, New Jersey
April 1973

PART ONE

Stocks and Their Value

CHAPTER ONE

Firm Foundations and Castles in the Air

> What is a cynic? A man who knows the price of everything, and the value of nothing—Oscar Wilde, *Lady Windermere's Fan*

In this book I will take you on a random walk down Wall Street, providing a guided tour of the complex world of finance and practical advice on investment opportunities and strategies. Many people say that the individual investor has scarcely a chance today against Wall Street's pros. Nothing could be further from the truth. You can do just as well as the experts—perhaps even better.

This book presents a succinct guide for the individual investor. It covers everything from insurance to income taxes. It gives advice on shopping for the best mortgage and planning an Individual Retirement Account. It tells you how to buy life insurance, how to avoid getting ripped off by banks and brokers, and even what to do about gold and diamonds. But primarily it is a book about common stocks—an investment medium that not only has provided generous long-run returns in the past but also appears to represent excellent possibilities for the years ahead.

What Is a Random Walk?

A random walk is one in which future steps or directions cannot be predicted on the basis of past actions. When the term is applied to the stock market, it means that short-run changes in stock prices cannot be predicted. Investment advisory services, earnings predictions, and complicated chart patterns are useless. On Wall Street, the term "random walk" is an obscenity. It is an epithet coined by the academic world and hurled insultingly at the professional soothsayers. Taken to its logical extreme, it means that a blindfolded monkey throwing darts at a newspaper's financial pages could select a portfolio that would do just as well as one carefully selected by the experts.

Now, financial analysts in pin-striped suits do not like being compared with bare-assed apes. They retort that academics are so immersed in equations and Greek symbols (to say nothing of stuffy prose) that they couldn't tell a bull from a bear, even in a china shop. Market professionals arm themselves against the academic onslaught with one of two techniques, called fundamental analysis and technical analysis, which we will examine in Part Two. Academics parry these tactics by obfuscating the random-walk theory with three versions (the "weak," the "semi-strong," and the "strong") and by creating their own theory, called the "new investment technology." This last includes a concept called "beta," and I intend to trample on that a bit. As you can see, there's a tremendous battle going on, and it's fought with deadly intent. That's why I think you'll enjoy this random walk down Wall Street. It has all the ingredients of high drama — fortunes made and lost — and classic arguments about their cause.

But before we begin, perhaps I should introduce myself and

state my qualifications as guide. In writing this book I have drawn on three aspects of my background; each provides a different perspective on the stock market.

First is my employment two decades ago as a market professional with one of Wall Street's leading investment firms. It takes one, after all, to know one. In a sense, I remain a market professional in that I currently sit on the finance committee of an insurance company that invests close to $100 billion in assets and on the boards of several of the largest investment companies in the nation. This perspective has been indispensable to me. Some things in life can never fully be appreciated or understood by a virgin. The same might be said of the stock market.

Second is my current position as an economist and dean at a leading management school. Specializing in securities markets and investment behavior, I have acquired detailed knowledge of academic research and findings on investment opportunities. I have relied on many new research findings in framing recommendations for you.

Last, and certainly not least, I have been a lifelong investor and successful participant in the market. How successful I cannot say, for it is a peculiarity of the academic world that a professor is not supposed to make money. A professor may inherit lots of money, he may marry lots of money, and he may spend lots of money, but he is never, never supposed to earn lots of money; it's unacademic. Anyway, teachers are supposed to be "dedicated," or so politicians and administrators often say—especially when trying to justify the low academic pay scales. Academics are supposed to be seekers of knowledge, not of financial reward. It is in the former sense, therefore, that I shall tell you of my victories on Wall Street.

This book has a lot of facts and figures. Don't let that worry you. It is specifically intended for the financial layperson—and offers practical, tested investment advice. You need no prior knowledge to follow it. All you need is the interest and the desire to have your investments work for you.

Investing as a Way of Life Today

At this point, it's probably a good idea to explain what I mean by "investing" and how I distinguish this activity from "speculating." I view investing as a method of purchasing assets in order to gain profit in the form of reasonably predictable income (dividends, interest, or rentals) and/or appreciation *over the long term*. It is the definition of the time period for the investment return and the predictability of the returns that often distinguish an investment from a speculation. An excellent analogy from the movie *Superman* comes to mind. When the evil Luthor bought land in Arizona with the idea that California would soon slide into the ocean, thereby quickly producing far more valuable beach-front property, he was speculating. Had he bought such land as a long-term holding after examining migration patterns, housing-construction trends, and the availability of water supplies, he would probably be regarded as investing — particularly if he viewed the purchase as likely to produce a dependable future stream of cash returns.

Let me make it quite clear that this is not a book for speculators: I am not going to promise you overnight riches. Indeed, a subtitle for this book might well have been *The Get Rich Slowly but Surely Book.* Remember, just to stay even, your investments have to produce a rate of return equal to inflation. Even if the inflation rate proceeds at a rate just over $5\frac{1}{2}$ percent — a rate lower than we had in the 1970s and early 1980s — the effect on our purchasing power would still be devastating. The table below shows what an average 5.8 percent inflation has done over a recent period. My morning newspaper has risen 500 percent. My afternoon Hershey bar has risen even more and it's actually smaller than it was in 1962, when I was in graduate school. If inflation continued at the same rate, today's Hershey bar would cost over $4.00 by the year 2000. It is clear that if we are to cope with even a mild inflation, we must undertake investment strategies that maintain our real purchasing power; otherwise, we are doomed to an ever-decreasing standard of living.

The Bite of Inflation

	Average 1962	Average 1984	Percentage Increase	Compound Annual Rate of Inflation (%)
Consumer Price Index	90.60	310.7	243	5.8
Hershey Bar	$.05	$.40	700	9.9
New York Times	.05	.30	500	8.5
First-Class Postage	.04	.20	400	7.6
Gasoline (Gallon)	.31	1.16	274	6.2
Hamburger (McDonald's Double)	.28[a]	1.35	382	7.4
Chevrolet (Impala)	2529.00	9985.00	295	6.4
Refrigerator freezer	470.00	620.00	32	1.3

Source: *Forbes*, Nov. 1, 1977, for 1962 prices, and various government and private sources for current prices.
[a] 1963 data.

Investing requires a lot of work, make no mistake about it. Romantic novels are replete with tales of great family fortunes lost through neglect or lack of knowledge on how to care for money. Who can forget the sounds of the cherry orchard being cut down in Chekhov's great play? Free enterprise, not the Marxist system, caused the downfall of Chekhov's family: they had not worked to keep their money. Even if you trust all your funds to an investment advisor or to a mutual fund, you still have to know which advisor or which fund is most suitable to handle your money. Armed with the information contained in this book, you should find it a bit easier to make your investment decisions.

Most important of all, however, is the fact that investing is *fun*. It's fun to pit your intellect against that of the vast investment community and to find yourself rewarded with an increase in assets. It's exciting to review your investment returns and to see how they are accumulating at a faster rate than your salary. And it's also stimulating to learn about new ideas for products and services, and innovations in the forms of financial investments. A successful investor is generally a well-rounded individual who puts a natural curiosity and an intellectual interest to work to earn more money.

Investing in Theory

All investment returns—whether from common stocks or exceptional diamonds—are dependent, to varying degrees, on future events. That's what makes the fascination of investing: it's a gamble whose success depends on an ability to predict the future. Traditionally, the pros in the investment community have used one of two approaches to asset valuation—the "firm-foundation theory" or the "castle-in-the-air theory." Millions have been gained and lost on these theories. To add to the drama, they appear to be mutually exclusive. An understanding of these two approaches is essential if you are to make sensible investment decisions. It is also a prerequisite for keeping you safe from serious blunders. During the 1970s, a third theory, born in academia and named the "new investment technology," became popular in "the Street." Later in the book, I will describe that theory and its implications for investment analysis.

The Firm-Foundation Theory

The firm-foundation theory argues that each investment instrument, be it a common stock or a piece of real estate, has a firm anchor of something called "intrinsic value," which can be determined by careful analysis of present conditions and future prospects. When market prices fall below (rise above) this firm foundation of intrinsic value, a buying (selling) opportunity arises, because this fluctuation will eventually be corrected — or so the theory goes. Investing then becomes a dull but straightforward matter of comparing something's actual price with its firm foundation of value.

It is difficult to ascribe to any one individual the credit for originating the firm-foundation theory. S. Eliot Guild is often given this distinction, but the classic development of the technique and particularly of the nuances associated with it was worked out by John B. Williams.

In *The Theory of Investment Value*, Williams presented an actual formula for determining the intrinsic value of stock. Williams based his approach on dividend income. In a fiendishly clever attempt to keep things from being simple, he introduced the concept of "discounting" into the process. Discounting basically involves looking at income backwards. Rather than seeing how much money you will have next year (say $1.05 if you put $1 in a savings bank at 5 percent interest), you look at money expected in the future and see how much less it is currently worth (thus, next year's $1 is worth today only about 95¢, which could be invested at 5 percent to produce $1 at that time).

Williams was actually serious about this. He went on to argue that the intrinsic value of a stock was equal to the present (or discounted) value of all its future dividends. Investors were advised to "discount" the value of moneys received later. Because so few people understood it, the term caught on and "discounting" now enjoys popular usage among investment people. It received a further boost under the aegis of Professor Irving Fisher of Yale, a distinguished economist and investor.

The logic of the firm-foundation theory is quite respectable and can be illustrated best with common stocks. The theory stresses that a stock's value ought to be based on the stream of earnings a firm will be able to distribute in the future in the form of dividends. It stands to reason that the greater the present dividends and their rate of increase, the greater the value of the stock. Thus, differences in growth rates are a major factor in stock valuation. And now the slippery little factor of future expectations sneaks in. Security analysts must estimate not only long-term growth rates but also how long an extraordinary growth can be maintained. When the market gets overly enthusiastic about how far in the future growth can continue, it is popularly held on Wall Street that "stocks are discounting not only the future but perhaps even the hereafter." The point is that the firm-foundation theory relies on some tricky forecasts of the extent and duration of future growth. The foundation of intrinsic value may thus be less dependable than is claimed.

The firm-foundation theory is not confined to economists alone. Thanks to a very influential book, Graham and Dodd's *Security Analysis*, a whole generation of Wall Street security analysts was converted to the fold. Sound investment management, the practicing analysts learned, simply consisted of buying securities whose prices were temporarily below intrinsic value and selling ones whose prices were temporarily too high. It was that easy. Of course, instructions for determining intrinsic value were furnished and any analyst worth his salt could calculate it with just a few taps of the calculator or personal computer.

The Castle-in-the-Air Theory

The castle-in-the-air theory of investing concentrates on psychic values. Lord Keynes, a famous economist and outstandingly successful investor, enunciated the theory most lucidly in 1936. It was his opinion that professional investors prefer to devote their energies not to estimating intrinsic values, but rather to analyzing how the crowd of investors is likely to behave in the future and how during periods of optimism they tend to build their hopes into castles in the air. The successful investor tries to beat the gun by estimating what investment situations are most susceptible to public castle-building and then buying before the crowd.

According to Keynes, the firm-foundation theory involves too much work and is of doubtful value. Keynes practiced what he preached. While London's financial men toiled many weary hours in crowded offices, he played the market from his bed for half an hour each morning. This leisurely method of investing earned him several million pounds for his account and a tenfold increase in the market value of the endowment of his college, King's College, Cambridge.

In the depression years in which Keynes gained his fame, most people concentrated on his ideas for stimulating the economy. It was hard for anyone to build castles in the air or to dream that others would. Nevertheless, in his book *The General Theory of Employment, Interest and Money*, he devoted an entire chapter to the stock market and to the importance of investor expectations.

With regard to stocks, Keynes noted that no one knows for sure what will influence future earnings prospects and dividend payments. As a result, Keynes said, most persons are "largely concerned, not with making superior long-term forecasts of the probable yield of an investment over its whole life, but with fore-seeing changes in the conventional basis of valuation a short time ahead of the general public." Keynes, in other words, applied psychological principles rather than financial evaluation to the study of the stock market. He wrote, "It is not sensible to pay 25 for an investment of which you believe the prospective yield to justify a value of 30, if you also believe that the market will value it at 20 three months hence."

Keynes described the playing of the stock market in terms readily understandable by his fellow Englishmen: it is analogous to entering a newspaper beauty-judging contest in which you have to select the six prettiest faces out of a hundred photographs, with the prize going to the person whose selections most nearly conform to those of the group as a whole.

The smart player recognizes that personal criteria of beauty are irrelevant in determining the contest winner. A better strategy is to select those faces the other players are likely to fancy. This logic tends to snowball. After all, the other contestants are likely to play the game with at least as keen a perception. Thus, the optimal strategy is not to pick those faces the player thinks are prettiest, or those the other players are likely to fancy, but rather to predict what the average opinion is likely to be about what the average opinion will be, or to proceed even further along this sequence. So much for British beauty contests.

The newspaper-contest analogy represents the ultimate form of the castle-in-the-air theory of price determination. An investment is worth a certain price to a buyer because he expects to sell it to someone else at a higher price. The investment, in other words, holds itself up by its own bootstraps. The new buyer in turn anticipates that future buyers will assign a still-higher value.

In this kind of world, there is a sucker born every minute — and he exists to buy your investments at a higher price than you paid for them. Any price will do as long as others may be willing to pay more. There is no reason, only mass psychology. All the smart investor has to do is to beat the gun — get in at the very beginning. This theory might less charitably be called the "greater-fool" theory. It's perfectly all right to pay three times what something is worth as long as later on you can find some innocent to pay five times what it's worth.

The castle-in-the-air theory has many advocates, in both the financial and the academic communities. Keynes' newspaper contest is the same game played by "Adam Smith" in *The Money Game*. Mr. Smith also espouses the same view of stock price determination. On the academic side, Oskar Morgenstern was a leading champion. The views he expressed in *Theory of Games and Economic Behavior*, of which he was coauthor, have had a significant impact not only on economic theory but also on national security decisions and strategic corporate planning. In 1970 he coauthored another book, *Predictability of Stock Market Prices*. Here, he and his colleague, Clive Granger, argued that the search for intrinsic value in stocks is a search for the will-o'-the-wisp. In an exchange economy the value of any asset depends on an actual or prospective transaction. Morgenstern believed that every investor should post the following Latin maxim above his desk:

Res tantum valet quantum vendi potest.
(A thing is worth only what someone else will pay for it.)

How the Random Walk Is to Be Conducted

With this introduction out of the way, come join me for a random walk through the investment woods, with an ultimate stroll down Wall Street. My first task will be to acquaint you with the historical patterns of pricing and how they bear on the two different theories of pricing investments. It was Santayana who warned that if we did not learn the lessons of the past we would be doomed to repeat the same errors. Therefore, in the pages to come I will describe some spectacular crazes — both long past and recently past. Some readers may pooh-pooh the mad public rush to buy tulip bulbs in seventeenth-century Holland and the eighteenth-century South Sea Bubble in England. But no one can disregard the new-issue mania of 1959–61, the conglomerate wave of the middle 1960s, the boom and bust of the so-called concept stocks during the 1967–70 period, the "Nifty Fifty" and gambling stock crazes of the 1970s, and the 1980s version of a new issue craze.

These more recent speculative "bubbles" all involved the savvy institutions and investment pros. All too many investors are lazy and careless — a terrifying combination when greed gets control of the market and everyone wants to cash in on the latest craze or fad.

Then I throw in my own two cents' worth of experience. Even in the midst of a period of speculation, I believe, it is possible to find a logical basis for security prices. In Chapter Four I present some rules that should be helpful in giving investors a sense of value and in protecting you from the horrible blunders made by many professional investment managers.

Theories are fine in their place, but it's important to look behind them and see how professional investment people actually practice their calling. In Part Two I rely on my Wall Street experience and current academic research to analyze various systems used by market professionals in their attempt to beat the market.

The pros have traditionally used two general methods: fundamental analysis and technical analysis. Fundamental analysis is the technique used by those believing in the firm-foundation theory. It involves a study of the fundamental valuation factors — earnings growth, dividend payments, risk — upon which the firm-foundation theory is built. Technical analysis is more often used by those subscribing to the castle-in-the-air view of the market. It involves an attempt to measure the psychology of the crowd and its propensity to build castles in the air. Unfortunately, both types of analysts have feet of clay. Using these methods, the Street has touted such sure winners as Four Seasons Nursing Centers of America, which sold at over $90 per share in 1968 and traded in the mid-1970s at 2¢. The sad fact is that you are likely to be just as well off picking stocks by letting your fingers take a random walk down the Wall Street stock pages as by following their advice. I'll back up that statement, too.

Part Three is devoted to a description of the academic theories of securities valuation. Beginning in the 1950s and 1960s, economists and statisticians armed with computers not only attacked the traditional methods of security analysis but also constructed their own new valuation theories. By the 1980s, academic jargon on "portfolio theory" and "asset pricing theory" had been picked up by Wall Street and investment professionals. Most major Wall Street firms now employ a quantitative ("quant") group as an integral part of their research department. In the name of the new investment technology, these people throw around expressions that include Greek symbols, such as alpha and beta, with carefree abandon. Even firms not embracing the new investment technology have felt it necessary to have at least a token quant around the house.

No book on security valuation would be complete without a full description of the meaning of these new techniques as well as a discussion of the serious problems associated with them. I have attempted to discuss this work without using mathematics. But although the theories are described without the normal mathematical apparatus, they are presented in a way that makes their meaning and logic clear and that enables the investor to understand both their uses and their misuses.

Finally, in Part Four, I attempt to make order out of chaos. I show that the lessons of history, the record of professionals, and the significant academic work do suggest answers to the questions of what you should do with your money and what sound investment strategies are available to you. Even in a random-walk market there are important opportunities available to increase your returns.

While my recommendations are often substantially different from the conventional wisdom, they are presented in easy-to-follow, step-by-step fashion, in the tradition of the many how-to-do-it books. This is the golden age of the how-to-do-it book. For a judicious investment of three or four dollars at the corner paperback bookstore, one can purchase a detailed guide on how to overhaul automobile engines, paint with the skill of a Rembrandt, eat anything you want and lose weight, and even how to get your body to look like Jane Fonda's. Admittedly, this volume promises less than books of the genre *How I made a Million Dollars in the Stock Market in My Spare Time and Found God While High on Inflation; or, How to Profit from Armageddon*. Nevertheless, it is intended to develop sensible rules to guide the conduct of individual investors. I think you will find our walk both enjoyable and profitable.

CHAPTER TWO

The Madness of Crowds

October. This is one of the pecularly dangerous months to speculate in stocks in. The others are July, January, September, April, November, May, March, June, December, August and February. — Mark Twain, *Pudd'nhead Wilson*

Greed run amok has been an essential feature of every spectacular boom in history. In their frenzy for money, market participants throw over firm foundations of value for dubious but thrilling assumption that they too can make a killing by building castles in the air. Such thinking can, and has, enveloped entire nations.

The psychology of speculation is a veritable theater of the absurd. Several of its plays are presented in this chapter. The castles that were built during the performances were based on Dutch tulip bulbs, English "bubbles," and good old American real estate and blue-chip stocks. In each case, some of the people made some money some of the time, but only a very few emerged unscathed.

History, in this instance, does teach a lesson: While the castle-in-the-air theory can well explain such speculative binges, out-guessing the reactions of a fickle crowd is a most dangerous game.

"In crowds it is stupidity and not mother-wit that is accumulated," Gustave Le Bon noted in his 1895 classic on crowd psychology. It would appear that not many have read the book. Skyrocketing markets that depend on purely psychic support have invariably succumbed to the financial law of gravitation. Unsustainable prices may persist for years, but eventually they reverse themselves. Such reversals come with the suddenness of an earthquake; and the bigger the binge, the greater the resulting hangover. Few of the reckless builders of castles in the air have been nimble enough to anticipate these reversals perfectly and escape without losing a great deal of money when everything came tumbling down.

The Tulip-Bulb Craze

The tulip-bulb craze was one of the most spectacular get-rich-quick binges in history. Its excesses become even more vivid when one realizes that it happened in staid old Holland in the early seventeenth century. The events leading to this speculative frenzy were set in motion in 1593 when a newly appointed botany professor from Vienna brought to Leyden a collection of unusual plants that had originated in Turkey. The Dutch were fascinated with this new addition to the garden — but not with the professor's asking price (he had hoped to sell the bulbs and make a handsome profit). One night a thief broke into the professor's house and stole the bulbs, which were subsequently sold at a lower price but at greater profit.

Over the next decade or so the tulip became a popular but expensive item in Dutch gardens. Many of these flowers succumbed to a nonfatal virus known as mosaic. It was this mosaic that helped to trigger the wild speculation in tulip bulbs. The virus caused the tulip petals to develop contrasting colored stripes or "flames." The Dutch valued highly these infected bulbs, called "bizarres." In a short time, popular taste dictated that the more bizarre a bulb, the greater the cost of owning it.

Slowly, tulipmania sets in. At first, bulb merchants simply tried to predict the most popular variegated style for the coming year, much as clothing manufacturers do in gauging the public's taste in fabric, color, and hemlines. Then they would buy an extra-large stockpile to anticipate a rise in price. Tulip bulb prices began to rise wildly. The more expensive the bulbs became, the more people viewed them as smart investments. Charles Mackay, who chronicled these events in his book *Memoirs of Extraordinary Popular Delusions*, noted that the ordinary industry of the country was dropped in favor of speculation in tulip bulbs: "Nobles, citizens, farmers, mechanics, seamen, footmen, maid-servants, even chimney sweeps and old clotheswomen dabbled in tulips." Everyone imagined that the passion for tulips would last forever and buyers from all over the world would come to Holland and pay whatever prices were asked for them.

People who said the prices could not possibly go higher watched with chagrin as their friends and relatives made enormous profits. The temptation to join them was hard to resist; few Dutchmen did. In the last years of the tulip spree, which lasted approximately from 1634 to 1638, people started to barter even their personal belongings, such as land, jewels, and furniture, to obtain the bulbs that would make them even wealthier.

Part of the genius of financial markets is that, when there is a real demand for a method to enhance speculative opportunities, the market will surely provide it. The instruments that enabled tulip speculators to get the most action for their money were "call options" similar to those popular today in the stock market.

A call option conferred on the holder the right to buy tulip bulbs (call for their delivery) at a fixed price (usually approximating the current market price) during a specified period. He was charged an amount called the option premium, which might run 15 to 20 percent of the current market price. An option on a tulip bulb currently worth 100 guilders, for example, would cost the buyer only about 20 guilders. If the price moved up to 200 guilders, the option holder would exercise his right; he would buy at 100 and simultaneously sell at the then current price of 200. He then had a profit of 80 guilders (the 100 guilders' appreciation less the 20 guilders he paid for the option). Thus he enjoyed a fourfold increase in his money, whereas an outright purchase would only have doubled his money. By using the call option it was possible to play the market with a much smaller stake as well as get more action out of any money invested. The call is one way to leverage one's investment. Leveraging is any technique that increases the potential rewards (and risks) of an investment. Such devices helped to insure broad participation in the market. The same is true today.

The history of the period was filled with tragicomic episodes. One such incident concerned a returning sailor who brought news to a wealthy merchant of the arrival of a shipment of new goods. The merchant rewarded him with a breakfast of fine red herring. Seeing what he thought was an onion on the merchant's counter, and no doubt thinking it very much out of place amid silks and velvets, he proceeded to take it as a relish for his herring. Little did he dream that the "onion" would have fed a whole ship's crew for a year. It was a costly Semper Augustus tulip bulb. The sailor paid dearly for his relish — his no longer grateful host had him imprisoned for several months on a felony charge.

As happens in all speculative crazes, eventually prices had been high for so long that some people decided they would be prudent and sell their bulbs. Soon others followed suit. Like a snowball rolling downhill, bulb deflation grew at an increasingly rapid pace, and in no time at all panic reigned.

Government ministers stated officially that there was no reason for tulip bulbs to fall in price — but no one listened. Dealers went bankrupt and refused to honor their commitments to buy tulip bulbs. A government plan to settle all contracts at 10 percent of their face value was frustrated when bulbs fell even below this mark. And prices continued to decline. Down and down they went until the tulip bulb became almost worthless — selling for no more than the price of a common onion.

And what of those who had sold out early in the game? In the end, they too were engulfed by the tulip craze. For the final chapter of this bizarre story is that the shock generated by the boom and collapse led to a prolonged depression in Holland. No one was spared.

The South Sea Bubble

Suppose your broker has called you and recommended that you invest in a new company with no sales or earnings — just great prospects. "What business?" you say. "I'm sorry," your broker explains, "no one must know what the business is, but I can promise you enormous riches." A con game, you say. Right you are, but 300 years ago in England this was one of the hottest new issues of the period. And, just as you guessed, investors got very badly burned. The story illustrates how fraud can make greedy people even more eager to part with their money.

At the time of the South Sea Bubble, the British were ripe for throwing away money. A long period of English prosperity had resulted in fat savings and thin investment outlets. In those days, owning stock was considered something of a privilege. As late as 1693, for example, only 499 souls benefited from ownership of East India stock. They reaped rewards in several ways, not least of which was that their dividends were untaxed. Also, their number included women, for stock represented one of the few forms of property that females could possess in their own right. The South Sea Company, which obligingly filled the need for investment vehicles, had been formed in 1711 to restore faith in the government's ability to meet its obligations. The company took on a government IOU of almost £10 million. As a reward, it was given a monopoly over all trade to the South Seas. The public believed there were immense riches in such trade, and regarded the stock with distinct favor.

From the very beginning, the South Sea Company reaped profits at the expense of others. Holders of the government securities to be assumed by the company simply exchanged their securities for those of the South Sea Company. Those with prior knowledge of the plan quietly bought up government securities selling as low as £55 and then turned them in at par for £100 worth of South Sea stock when the company was incorporated. Not a single director of the company had the slightest experience in South American trade. This did not stop them from quickly outfitting African slave ships (the sale of slaves being one of the most lucrative features of South American trade). But even this venture did not prove profitable, because the mortality rate on the ships was so high.

The directors were, however, wise in the art of public appearance. An impressive house in London was rented, and the board room was furnished with thirty black Spanish upholstered chairs whose beechwood frames and gilt nails made them handsome to look at but uncomfortable to sit in. In the meantime, a shipload of company wool that was desperately needed in Vera Cruz was sent instead to Cartagena, where it rotted on the wharf from lack of buyers. Still, the stock of the company held its own and even rose modestly over the next few years despite the dilutive effect of "bonus" stock dividends and a war with Spain which led to a temporary collapse in trading opportunities.

Across the Channel, another stock company was formed by an exiled Englishman named John Law. Law's great goal in life was to replace metal as money and create more liquidity through a national paper currency backed by the state and controlled through a network of local agencies. To further his purpose, Law acquired a derelict concern called the Mississippi Company and proceeded to build a conglomerate that became one of the largest capital enterprises ever to exist, even to this day.

The Mississippi Company attracted speculators and their money from throughout the Continent. The word "millionaire" was invented at this time, and no wonder: the price of Mississippi stock rose from 100 to 2,000 in just two years, even though there was no logical reason for the increase. At one time the inflated total market value of the stock of the Mississippi Company in France was more than eighty times that of all the gold and silver in the country.

Meanwhile, back on the English side of the Channel, a bit of jingoism now began to appear in some of the great English houses. Why should all the money be going to the French Mississippi Company? What did England have to counter this? The answer was the South Sea Company, whose prospects were beginning to look a bit better, especially with the December 1719 news that there would be peace with Spain and hence the way to the South American trade would at last be clear. Mexicans supposedly were waiting for the opportunity to empty their gold mines in return for England's abundant supply of cotton and woolen goods. This was free enterprise at its finest.

In 1720, the directors, an avaricious lot, decided to capitalize on their reputation by offering to fund the entire national debt, amounting to £31 million. This was boldness indeed, and the public loved it. When a bill to that effect was introduced in Parliament, the stock promptly rose form £130 to £300.

Various friends and backers who had shown interest in getting the bill passed received as their reward an option with a twist: the individual was granted a certain amount of stock without having to pay for it; it was simply "sold" back to the company when the price went up, and the individual only collected the profit. Among those rewarded were George I's mistress and her "nieces," who all bore a startling resemblance to the king.

On April 12, 1720, five days after the bill became law, the South Sea Company sold a new issue of stock at £300. The issue could be bought on the installment plan—£60 down and the rest in eight easy payments. Even the king could not resist; he subscribed for stock totaling £100,000. Fights broke out among other investors surging to buy. The price had to go up—and the eager buyers were right. It advanced to 340 within a few days. To ease the public appetite, the South Sea directors announced another new issue—this one at £400. But the public was ravenous. Within a month the stock was 550, and it was still rising. On June 15 yet another issue was put forth, and this time the payment plan was even easier—10 percent down and not another payment for a year. The stock hit 800. Half the House of Lords and more than half the House of Commons signed on. Eventually, the price rose to more than 1000. The speculative craze was in full bloom.

Not even the South Sea Company was capable of handling the demands of all the fools who wanted to be parted from their money. Investors looked for other new ventures where they could get in on the ground floor. Just as speculators today search for the next Xerox and the next IBM, so in England in the early 1700s they looked for the next South Sea Company. Promoters obliged by organizing and bringing to the market a flood of new issues to meet the insatiable craving for investment.

As the days passed, new financing proposals ranged from ingenious to absurd—from importing a large number of jack-asses from Spain (even though there was an abundant supply in England) to making salt water fresh. Increasingly the promotions involved some element of fraud, such as making boards out of sawdust. There were nearly one hundred different projects, each more extravagant and deceptive than the other, but each offering the hope of immense gain. They soon received the name of "bubbles," as appropriate a name as could be devised. Like bubbles, they popped quickly—usually within a week or so.

The public, it seemed, would buy anything. New companies seeking financing during this period were organized for such purposes as: the building of ships against pirates; encouraging the breeding of horses in England (there were two issues for this purpose); trading in human hair; building of hospitals for bastard children; extracting of silver from lead; and even for a wheel of perpetual motion.

The prize, however, must surely go to the unknown soul who started "A Company for carrying on an undertaking of great advantage, but nobody to know what it is." The prospectus promised unheard-of rewards. At nine o'clock in the morning, when the subscription books opened, crowds of people from all walks of life practically beat down the door in an effort to subscribe. Within five hours a thousand investors handed over their money for shares in the company. Not being greedy himself, the promoter promptly closed up shop and set off for the Continent. He was never heard from again.

Not all investors in the bubble companies believed in the feasibility of the schemes to which they subscribed. People were "too sensible" for that. They did believe, however, in the "greater-fool" theory — that prices would rise, that buyers would be found, and that they would make money. Thus, most investors considered their actions the height of rationality as, at least for a while, they could sell their shares at a premium in the "after market," that is, the trading market in the shares after their initial issue.

Whom the gods would destroy, they first ridicule. Signs that the end was near were demonstrated with the issuance of a pack of South Sea playing cards. Each card contained a caricature of a bubble company, with an appropriate verse inscribed underneath. One of these, the Puckle Machine Company, was supposed to produce machines discharging both round and square cannonballs and bullets. Puckle modestly claimed that his machine would make a total revolution in the art of war. The eight of spades describe it as follows:

> A rare invention to destroy the crowd.
> Of fools at home instead of fools abroad.
> Fear not, my friends, this terrible machine.
> They're only wounded who have shares therein.

Many individual bubbles had been pricked without dampening the speculative enthusiasm, but the deluge came in August with an irreparable puncture to the South Sea Company. This was self-administered by its directors and officers. Realizing that the price of the shares in the market bore no relationship to the real prospects of the company, they sold out in the summer.

The news leaked and the stock fell. Soon the price of the shares collapsed and panic reigned. Government officials tried in vain to restore confidence, and a complete collapse of the public credit was barely averted. Similarly, the price of Mississippi Company shares fell to a pittance as the public realized that an excess of paper currency creates no real wealth, only inflation. Big losers in the South Sea Bubble included Isaac Newton, who exclaimed, "I can calculate the motions of heavenly bodies, but not the madness of people." So much for castles in the air.

To protect the public from further abuses, Parliament passed the Bubble Act, which forbade the issuing of stock certificates by companies. For over a century, until the act was repealed in 1825, there were relatively few share certificates in the British market.

The Florida Real Estate Craze

The bulbs and bubbles are, admittedly ancient history. Could the same sort of thing happen in sophisticated modern times? Let's turn to more recent and familiar events from our own past and see. America, the land of opportunity, had its turn in the 1920s. And given our emphasis on freedom and growth, we produced two ot the most spectacular booms and two of the loudest crashes civilization has ever known.

Conditions could not have been more favorable for speculative crazes. The country had been experiencing unrivaled prosperity. One could not but have faith in American business, and as Calvin Coolidge said, "The business of America is business." Businessmen were likened to religious missionaries and almost deified. Such analogies were even made in the opposite direction. Bruce Barton, of the New York advertising agency Batten, Barton, Durstine and Osborn, wrote in *The Man Nobody Knows* that Jesus was "the first businessman," and his parables were "the most powerful advertisements of all time."

The euphoric mood of optimism and faith in business that prevailed in the twenties led to widespread enthusiasm about real estate and the stock market. It would appear only natural that Americans, having conquered an entire continent, would succumb to real estate booms. One of the greatest centered on Florida in the middle 1920s. The climate was just right. The population was steadily growing and housing was in short supply. Land values began increasing rapidly. Stories of investments doubling and tripling attracted speculators from all over the country. Easy credit terms added fuel to the speculative frenzy. "This market has no downside risk," the land speculators opined, as Dutchmen undoubtedly said to each other about the tulip-bulb market in an earlier time.

There are reports of Palm Beach land bought for $800,000 in 1923, subdivided, and resold in 1924 for $1.5 million. By the following year the same land sold at $4 million. At the top of the boom there were 75,000 real estate agents in Miami, one-third of the entire population of the city.

Inevitably the boom ended, as do all speculative crazes. By 1926 new buyers could no longer be found and prices softened. Then the speculators dumped their holdings on the market and a complete collapse ensued.

Wall Street Lays an Egg

With this Florida experience so recent, one would have thought that investors would avoid a similar misadventure on Wall Street. But Florida was only a regional prelude to what came next. Beginning in 1928, stock-market speculation became a national pasttime. From early March 1928 through early September 1929, the market's percentage increase equaled that of the entire period from 1923 through early 1928. The price rises for the major industrial corporations sometimes reached 10 or 15 points per day. The extent of the rise is illustrated in the table on the following page.

Not "everybody" was speculating in the market, as was commonly assumed. Borrowing to buy stocks (buying on margin) did increase from only $1 billion in 1921 to almost $9 billion in 1929. Nevertheless, only about a million persons owned stocks on margin in 1929. Still, the speculative spirit was at least as widespread as in the previous crazes and was certainly unrivaled in its intensity. More important, stockmarket speculation was

Security	Opening Price March 3, 1928	High Price September 3, 1929[a]	Percentage Gain in 18 Months
American Telephone & Telegraph	179½	335⅝	87.0
Bethlehem Steel	56⅞	140⅝	146.8
General Electric	128¾	396¼	207.8
Montgomery Ward	132¾	466½	251.4
National Cash Register	50¾	127½	151.2
Radio Corporation of America	94½	505	434.5

[a] Adjusted for stock splits and the value of rights received subsequent to March 3, 1928.

central to the culture. John Brooks, in *Once in Golconda*,* recounted the remarks of a British correspondent newly arrived in New York: "You could talk about Prohibition, or Hemingway, or air conditioning, or music, or horses, but in the end you had to talk about the stock market, and that was when the conversation became serious."

Unfortunately, there were hundreds of smiling operators only too glad to help the public construct castles in the air. Manipulation on the stock exchange set new records for unscrupulousness. No better example can be found than the operation of investment pools. One such undertaking raised the price of RCA stock 61 points in four days. Let me explain how the pools could manipulate the price of a stock.

An investment pool required close cooperation on the one hand and complete disdain for the public on the other. Generally such operations began when a number of traders banded

*Golconda, now in ruins, was a city in India. According to legend, everyone who passed through it became rich.

together to manipulate a particular stock. They appointed a pool manager (who justifiably was considered something of an artist) and promised not to doublecross each other through private operations.

The pool manager accumulated a large block of stock through inconspicuous buying over a period of weeks. If possible, he obtained an option to buy a substantial block of stock at the current market price within a stated period of, say, three or six months. Next he tried to enlist the stock's specialist on the exchange floor as an ally.

Pool members were in the swim with the specialist on their side. A stock-exchange specialist functions as a broker's broker. If a stock was trading at $50 a share and you gave your broker an order to buy at $45, the broker typically left that order with the specialist. If and when the stock fell to $45, the specialist then executed the order. All such orders to buy below the market price or sell above it were kept in the specialist's supposedly private "book." Now you see why the specialist could be so valuable to the pool manager. The book gave information about the extent of existing orders to buy and sell at prices below and above the current market. It was always helpful to know as many of the cards of the public players as possible. Now the real fun was ready to begin.

Generally, at this point the pool manager had members of the pool trade between themselves. For example, Haskell sells 200 shares to Sidney at 40, and Sidney sells them back at $40\frac{1}{8}$. The process is repeated with 400 shares at prices of $40\frac{1}{4}$ and $40\frac{1}{2}$. Next comes the sale of a 1,000-share block at $40\frac{5}{8}$, followed by another at $40\frac{3}{4}$. These sales were recorded on ticker tapes across the country and the illusion of activity was conveyed to the thousands of tape watchers who crowded into the brokerage offices of the country. Such activity, generated by so-called "wash sales," created the impression that something big was afoot.

Now, tipsheet writers and market commentators under the control of the pool manager would tell of exciting developments in the offing. The pool manager also tried to insure that the flow of news from the company's management was increasingly favorable — assuming the company management was involved in the operation. If all went well, and in the speculative atmosphere of the 1928–29 period it could hardly miss, the combination of tape activity and managed news would bring the public in.

Once the public came in the free-for-all started and it was time discreetly to "pull the plug." Since the public was doing the buying, the pool did the selling. The pool manager began feeding stock into the market, first slowly and then in larger and larger blocks before the public could collect its senses. At the end of the roller-coaster ride the pool members had netted large profits and the public was left holding the suddenly deflated stock.

But people didn't have to band together to defraud the public. Many individuals, particularly corporate officers and directors, did quite well on their own. Take Albert Wiggin, the head of Chase, the nation's second largest bank at the time. In July 1929 Mr. Wiggin became apprehensive about the dizzy heights to which stocks had climbed and no longer felt comfortable speculating on the bull side of the market. (He is rumored to have made millions in a pool boosting the price of his own bank.) Believing that the prospects for his own bank's stock were particularly dim (perhaps because of his previous speculation), he sold short over 42,000 shares of Chase stock. Selling short is a way to make money if stock prices fall. It involves selling stock you do not presently own in the expectation of buying it back later at a lower price. It's like hoping to buy low and sell high, but in reverse order.

Wiggin's timing was perfect. Immediately after the short sale the price of Chase stock began to fall, and when the crash came in the fall the stock dropped precipitously. When the account was closed in November, Mr. Wiggin had netted a multi-million-dollar profit from the operation. Conflicts of interest apparently did not trouble Mr. Wiggin. Usually corporate officers are encouraged to own the stock of their company so that they will have an added incentive to put out their best efforts. Wiggin, on the other hand, had provided himself with an incentive (and a very large one at that) to encourage the deterioration of the shares of the financial institution he headed.

There's a sequel to this story. When Wiggin retired in 1932, the Chase Executive Committee thanked him warmly for his many services to the bank and unanimously voted him a life pension of $100,000 per year.

On September 3, 1929 the market averages reached a peak that was not to be surpassed for a quarter of a century. The "endless chain of prosperity" was soon to break; general business activity had already turned down months before. Prices drifted for the next day, and on the following day, September 5, the market suffered a sharp decline known as the "Babson Break."

This was named in honor of Roger Babson, a frail, goateed, pixyish-looking financial adviser from Wellesley, Massachusetts. At a financial luncheon that day he had said, "I repeat what I said at this time last year and the year before, that sooner or later a crash is coming." Wall Street professionals greeted the new pronouncements from the "sage of Wellesley," as he was known, with their usual derision.

As Babson implied in his statement, he had been predicting the crash for several years and he had yet to be proven right. Nevertheless, at two o'clock in the afternoon, when Babson's words were quoted on the "broad" tape (the Dow Jones financial-news ticker, which is an essential part of the furniture in every brokerage house across the country), the market went into a nose-dive. In the last frantic hour of trading, two million shares changed hands—Telephone went down 6 points, Westinghouse 7, and U.S. Steel 9 points. It was a prophetic episode, and after the Babson Break the possiblity of a crash, which was entirely unthinkable a month before, suddenly became a common subject for discussion.

Confidence faltered. September had many more bad than good days. At times the market fell sharply. Bankers and government officials assured the country that there was no cause for concern. Professor Irving Fisher of Yale, one of the progenitors of the intrinsic-value theory, offered his soon-to-be-immortal opinion that stocks had reached what looked like a "permanently high plateau."

By Monday, October 21, the stage was set for a classic stock market break. The declines in stock prices had led to calls for more collateral from margin customers. Unable or unwilling to meet the calls, these customers were forced to sell their holdings. This depressed prices and led to more margin calls and finally to a self-sustaining selling wave.

The volume of sales on October 21 zoomed to over 6 million shares. The ticker fell way behind, to the dismay of the tens of thousands of individuals watching the tape from brokerage houses around the country. Nearly an hour and forty minutes had elapsed after the close of the market before the last transaction was actually recorded on the stock ticker.

The indomitable Fisher dismissed the decline as a "shaking out of the lunatic fringe that attempts to speculate on margin." He went on to say that prices of stocks during the boom had not caught up with their real value and would go higher. Among other things, the professor believed that the market had not yet reflected the beneficient effects of Prohibition, which had made the American worker "more productive and dependable."

On October 24, later called "Black Thursday," the market volume reached almost 13 million shares. Prices sometimes fell $5 and $10 on each trade. Many issues dropped 40 and 50 points during a couple of hours. On the next day, Herbert Hoover offered his famous diagnosis. "The fundamental business of the country . . . is on a sound and prosperous basis."

Tuesday, October 29, was the most catastrophic day in the history of the New York Stock Exchange. Over 16.4 million shares were traded. (A 16-million-share day in 1929 would be equivalent to something like a billion-share day in 1985 because of the greater number of shares now listed on the New York Stock Exchange.) Prices fell almost perpendicularly, and kept on falling, as is illustrated by the following table, which shows the extent of the decline during the autumn of 1929 and over the next three years.

Security	High Price September 3, 1929[a]	Low Price November 13, 1929	Low Price for Year 1932
American Telephone & Telegraph	304	$197\frac{1}{4}$	$70\frac{1}{4}$
Bethlehem Steel	$140\frac{3}{8}$	$78\frac{1}{4}$	$7\frac{1}{4}$
General Electric	$396\frac{1}{4}$	$168\frac{1}{8}$	$8\frac{1}{2}$
Montgomery Ward	$137\frac{7}{8}$	$49\frac{1}{4}$	$3\frac{1}{2}$
National Cash Register	$127\frac{1}{2}$	59	$6\frac{1}{4}$
Radio Corporation of America	101	28	$2\frac{1}{2}$

[a]Adjusted for stock splits and the value of rights received subsequent to September 3, 1929.

Perhaps the best summary of the debacle was given by *Variety*, the show-business weekly, which headlined the story, "Wall Street Lays an Egg." The speculative boom was dead and billions of dollars of share values — as well as the dreams of millions — were wiped out. The crash in the stock market was followed by the most devastating depression in the history of the country.

An Afterword

Why are memories so short? Why do such speculative crazes seem so isolated from the lessons of history? I have no apt answer to offer, but I am convinced that Bernard Baruch was correct in suggesting that a study of these events can help equip investors for survival. The consistent losers in the market, from my personal experience, are those who are unable to resist being swept up in some kind of tulip-bulb craze. It is not hard, really, to make money in the market. As we shall see later, investors who select stocks by throwing darts at the stock listings in the *Wall Street Journal* can make fairly handsome long-run returns. What is hard to avoid is the alluring temptation to throw your money away on short, get-rich-quick speculative binges.

And yet the melody lingers on. I have a good friend who once built a modest stake into a small fortune. Then along came a stock called Alphanumeric. In addition to offering an exciting name, it also promised to revolutionize the method of feeding data into computers. My friend was hooked.

I begged him to investigate first whether the huge future earnings that were already reflected in the price could possibly be achieved given the likely size of the market. (Of course, the company had no *current* earnings.) He thanked me for my advice but dismissed it by saying that stock prices weren't based on "fundamentals" like earnings and dividends. "They are based on hope and dreams," he said. "The history of stock valuation bears me out. This Alphanumeric story will have all the tape watchers drooling with excitement and conjuring up visions of castles in the air. Any delay in buying would be self-defeating." And so my friend had to rush in before the crowd could bid up the price.

And rush in he did, buying at $80, which was close to the peak of a craze in that particular stock. The stock plunged to $2, and with it my friend's fortune — which is now much more modest than what he originally started out with. The ability to avoid such horrendous mistakes is probably the most important factor in preserving one's capital and allowing it to grow. The lesson is so obvious and yet so easy to ignore.

CHAPTER THREE

Stock Valuation from the Sixties into the Eighties

Everything's got a moral if only you can find it. — Lewis
Carroll, *Alice's Adventures in Wonderland*

The madness of the crowd, as we have just seen,
can be truly spectacular. The examples I have just cited, plus a
host of others, have convinced more and more people to put
their money under the care of a professional — someone who
knows what makes the market tick and who can be trusted to
act prudently. Thus most of us find that at least a part (and
often all) of our investable funds are in the hands of institutional portfolio managers — those who run the large pension
and retirement funds, mutual funds, investment counseling
organizations and the like. While the crowd may be mad, the
institution is above all that. The institution is, to borrow a
phrase from Tennyson, "of loyal nature and of noble mind."
Very well, let us then take a look at the sanity of institutions.

The Sanity of Institutions

By 1960, institutions and other professional investors accounted for almost half of the total shares traded on the New York Stock Exchange; surveys in the mid-1980s indicate that this figure may have increased to above three-quarters of stock-exchange volume. Surely, in a market where professional investors dominate trading, the game must have changed. The hard-headed, sharp-penciled reasoning of the pros ought to be a guarantee that the extravagant excesses of the past will be avoided.

And yet in 1969 a company with annual sales of only $16 million was "valued" by the market at $1 billion—the latter value being obtained by multiplying the number of shares outstanding by the price per share. Throughout the past twenty-five years of institutional domination of the market, prices often gyrated more rapidly and by much greater amounts than could plausibly be explained by apparent changes in their anticipated intrinsic values.

In 1955, for example, General Electric announced that its scientists had created exact duplicates of the diamond. The market became entranced at once, despite the public acknowledgment that these diamonds were not suitable for sale as gems and that they could not be manufactured cheaply enough for industrial use. Within twenty-four hours, the shares of G.E. rose 4¼ points. This increased the total market value of all G.E. shares by almost $400 million, approximately twice the then current value of total worldwide diamond sales and six times the value of all industrial diamond sales. Clearly, the price rise was not due to the worth of the discovery to the company, but rather to the castle-building potential this would hold for prospective buyers. Indeed, speculators rushed in so fast to beat the gun that the entire price rise was accomplished in the first minutes of trading during the day following the announcement.

Of course, we should not generalize from isolated instances.

Professional investors, however, did participate in several distinct speculative movements from the 1960s through the 1980s. In each case, professional institutions bid actively for stocks not because they felt such stocks were undervalued under the firm-foundation principle, but because they anticipated that some greater fools would take the shares off their hands at even more inflated prices. It's true these speculative movements were somewhat less dramatic than those covered in the preceding chapter. But the parallels are obvious, and, particularly since they relate to present-day markets, I think you'll find this institutional tour especially useful.

The New "New Era": The Growth Stock/New Issue Craze

In the 1959–61 period, growth was the magic word. It was the corollary to the Soaring Sixties, the wonderful decade to come. Growth stocks (those issues for which an extraordinary rate of earnings growth was expected), especially those associated with glamorous new technologies like Texas Instruments and Varian Associates, far outdistanced the standard blue-chip stocks. Wall Street was eager to pay good money for space travel, transistors, klystron tubes, optical scanners, and other esoteric things. Backed by this strong enthusiasm, the price of securities in these businesses rose wildly.

By 1959 the traditional rule that stocks should sell at a multiple of 10 to 15 times their earnings had been supplanted by multiples of 50 to 100 times earnings, or even more for the most glamorous issues. For example, at the peak of the craze in 1961 Control Data, a new computer company, sold for over 200 times its previous year's earnings. Farrington, a handbag manufacturer that had consistently lost money but hoped to manufacture a new electronics device, rose rapidly in the over-the-counter market. The stock later plummeted to 2 and eventually the company went bankrupt. Even large, well-established growth companies with a technological basis rose to unprecedented heights, as the following table illustrates.

Security	1961		1962	
	High Price	Price-Earnings Multiple[a]	Low Price	Price-Earnings Multiple[a]
IBM	607	80.7	300	34.4
Texas Instruments	206¾	87.6	49	23.0
Microwave Associates	60⅝	85.0	8	12.7
Fairchild Camera	88¼	42.0	31	13.1
Perkin-Elmer	83½	67.3	25	16.7

[a]Price divided by earnings per share for the year.

Growth took on an almost mystical significance, and questioning the propriety of such valuations became, as in the generation past, almost heretical. These prices could not be justified on firm-foundation principles. But investors firmly believed that later in the wonderful decade of the sixties, buyers would eagerly come forward to pay even higher prices. Lord Keynes must have smiled quietly from wherever it is that economists go when they die.

To be sure, many professionals viewed the market with incredulity. One New York investment manager noted: "I think this market is crazy, just plain crazy. There are still good stocks around, companies selling at 10 to 20 times earnings and with good earnings prospects. But people seem to want to buy stocks selling at 60 or 80 times a company's earnings. I don't know why. This just isn't a thinking man's market."

I had just gone to work on Wall Street during the boom and recall vividly one of the senior partners of my firm shaking his head and admitting that he knew of no one over forty, with any recollection of the 1929–32 crash, who would buy and hold the

high-priced growth stocks. But the young Turks held sway. The
sky was the limit and the growth stocks were the ones that were
going up. *Newsweek* quoted one broker as saying that speculators have the idea that anything they buy "will double overnight. The horrible thing is, it has happened."

But more was to come. Promoters, eager to satisfy the insatiable thirst of investors for the space-age stocks of the Soaring Sixties, created new offerings by the dozens. A new-issue
craze (more were offered in the 1959–62 period than at any
other time in history) developed as investors—both individual
and institutional—whipped themselves into a speculative frenzy.
The new-issue mania of the period rivaled the South Sea Bubble in its intensity and also, regrettably, in the fraudulent practices that were revealed.

It was called the "tronics boom," since the stock offerings
often included some garbled version of the word "electronics"
in their title even if the companies had nothing to do with the
electronics industry. Buyers of these issues didn't really care
what the companies made—so long as it sounded electronic,
with a suggestion of the esoteric. For example, American Music
Guild, whose business consisted entirely of the door-to-door
sale of phonograph records and players, changed its name to
Space-Tone before "going public." The shares were sold to the
public at 2, and within a few weeks rose to 14.

The name was the game. There were a host of "trons" such
as Astron, Dutron, Vulcatron, and Transitron, and a number
of "onics" such as Circuitronics, Supronics, Videotronics, and
several Electrosonics companies. Leaving nothing to chance,
one group put together the winning combination Powertron
Ultrasonics. The prices commanded in the market by these
companies were unbelievable.

Jack Dreyfus, of Dreyfus and Company, commented on the
mania as follows:

> Take a nice little company that's been making shoelaces for 40
> years and sells at a respectable six times earnings ratio. Change
> the name from Shoelaces, Inc. to Electronics and Silicon Furth-

Burners. In today's market, the words "electronics" and "silicon" are worth 15 times earnings. However, the real play comes from the word "furth-burners," which no one understands. A word that no one understands entitles you to double your entire score. Therefore, we have six times earnings for the shoelace business and 15 times earnings for electronic and silicon, or a total of 21 times earnings. Multiply this by two for furth-burners and we now have a score of 42 times earnings for the new company.

In a later investigation of the new-issue phenomenon, the Securities and Exchange Commission uncovered considerable evidence of fraudulence and market manipulation. For example, some investment bankers, especially those who underwrote the smaller new issues, would often hold a substantial volume of securities off the market. This made the market so "thin" at the start that the price would rise quickly in the after market. In one "hot issue" that almost doubled in price on the first day of trading, the SEC found that a considerable portion of the entire offering was sold to broker-dealers, many of whom held on to their allotments for a period until the shares could be sold at much higher prices. The SEC also found that many underwriters allocated large portions of hot issues to insiders of the firms such as partners, relatives, officers, and other securities dealers to whom a favor was owed. In one instance, 87 percent of a new issue was allocated to "insiders," rather than to the general public, as was proper.

Another trick was for the underwriter to allocate stock to brokers only on the condition that they trade the stock at rising prices. The investor, in turn, was allowed to purchase some stock at the original offering price only if he would buy more in the market after the initial offering, thus swelling the demand for the shares in the after market.

The following table shows some representative new issues of this period and records their price movements after the shares were issued. At least for a while, the new-issue buyers did very well indeed. Large advances over their already inflated initial offering prices were scored for such companies as Boonton

Electronics and Geophysics Corporation of America. The speculative fever was so great that even Mother's Cookie could
count on a sizable gain. Think of the glory they could have
achieved if they had called themselves "Mothertron's Cookitronics." Ten years later, the shares of most of these companies
were almost worthless.

Security	Offering Date	Offering Price	Bid Price First Day of Trading	High Bid Price 1961	Low Bid Price 1962
Boonton Electronics Corp.	March 6, 1961	$5\frac{1}{2}$[a]	$12\frac{1}{4}$[a]	$24\frac{1}{2}$[a]	$1\frac{5}{8}$[a]
Bristol Dynamics	March 20, 1961	7	16	23	$3\frac{1}{2}$
Geophysics Corp. of America	December 8, 1960	14	27	58	9
Hydro-Space Technology	July 19, 1960	3	7	7	1
Mother's Cookie Corp.	March 8, 1961	15	23	25	7
Seaboard Electronic	July 5, 1961	$5\frac{1}{2}$	$8\frac{3}{4}$	$15\frac{1}{2}$	$2\frac{1}{4}$
Universal Electronic Labs	November 25,	4	$4\frac{1}{2}$	18	$1\frac{3}{8}$

[a]Per unit of 1 share and 1 warrant.

Many underwriters wore a smug smile during this period.
They not only received a handsome underwriting fee for their
role but also usually received warrants from the company to
purchase additional shares of stock at very low prices. The
small investment banking firm of Michael A. Lomasney & Co.,

for example, underwrote an issue of 100,000 shares of B.B.M. Photocopy, which it sold for $3 a share. In addition to an underwriting fee of approximately $20,000 Lomasney also received 20,000 warrants, each warrant entitling him to buy one share of stock at a price of one cent. Within a short period B.B.M. was selling at $40 per share, which gave the warrants a paper value of approximately $800,000. Thus Lomasney was close to a million dollars richer for his efforts, while the company received $280,000 — the $300,000 from the issue of its shares less the $20,000 underwriting commission.

But the public had done well with new issues and many believed they represented a sure road to wealth. The 1961 price gain in the table above told them so and reinforced their general mood of optimism. Speculation in these securities and in space-age stocks was the closest the bull market of the early sixties came to the speculative fever of 1929.

New issues became standard cocktail party chatter, and women's clubs abandoned lectures on art and other cultural pursuits for discussions of the stock market. Tips and rumors were ubiquitous. Brokers reported record crowds in their offices, and the general volume of trading soared dramatically. The jargon and speculative spirit of Wall Street spread to other markets as well — such as the art market.

Robert Sobel, author of *The Big Board*, noted that the *Art Market Guide and Forecaster* urged the purchase of paintings as follows:

32 ARTISTS TO *TRIPLE* IN PRICE

With the Art Market for paintings up 975% since the war — and 65% in the last year alone — you can lose immense profits by failing to keep informed of the *monetary* values of art, present and future. Among the 500 painters whose price trends are under regular study by our organization, many have gone down in price as well as up — ranging from *gains* up to 61,900% to *losses* of 87% (compared to the 975% gain for the whole market as measured by the new *AMG 500-Painters Average*).

Where was the Securities and Exchange Commission all this time? Hadn't it changed the rule from "Let the buyer beware" to "Let the seller beware"? Aren't new issuers required to register their offering with the SEC? Can't they (and their underwriters) be punished for false and misleading statements?

Yes to all these questions and yes, the SEC was there, but by law it had to stand by quietly. As long as a company has prepared (and distributed to investors) an adequate prospectus, the SEC can do nothing to save buyers from themselves. For example, many of the prospectuses of the period contained the following type of warning in bold letters on the cover.

> WARNING: THIS COMPANY HAS NO ASSETS OR EARNINGS AND WILL BE UNABLE TO PAY DIVIDENDS IN THE FORESEEABLE FUTURE. THE SHARES ARE HIGHLY RISKY.

But just as the warnings on packs of cigarettes do not prevent many people from smoking, so the warning that this investment may be dangerous to your wealth cannot block a speculator from forking over his money if he is hell-bent on doing so. The SEC can warn a fool but it cannot prevent him from parting with his money. And the buyers of new issues were so convinced the stocks would rise in price (no matter what the company's assets or past record) that the underwriter's problem was not how he could sell the shares but how to allocate them among the frenzied purchasers.

Fraudulence and market manipulation are different matters. Here the SEC can take and has taken strong action. Indeed, many of the little known brokerage houses on the fringes of respectability, which were responsible for most of the new issues and for manipulation of their prices, were suspended for a variety of peculations.

The staff of the SEC is limited, however; the major problem is the attitude of the general public. When investors are infused with a get-rich-quick attitude and are willing to snap up any piece of bait, anything can happen—and usually does. Without public greed, the manipulators would not stand a chance.

The tronics boom came back to earth in 1962. The tailspin started early in the year and exploded in a horrendous selling wave five months later. On Monday, May 28, the worst day of the decline, the Dow Jones averages of thirty leading industrial stocks fell 34.95 points (this was one of the largest declines ever recorded. On that single day, the decline in the market value of all stocks listed on the New York Stock Exchange amounted to $20.8 billion. Even on October 28, 1929 only $9.6 billion evaporated, because the total value of listed stocks was smaller on that day. "Something like an earthquake hit the stock market," editorialized the *New York Times*. Growth stocks, even the highest-quality ones, took the brunt of the decline, falling much further than the general market. Yesterday's hot issue became today's cold turkey.

Many professionals refused to accept the fact that they had speculated recklessly. Rather they blamed the decline on President Kennedy's tough stand with the steel industry, which led to a rollback of announced price hikes. Former President Eisenhower blamed the decline on Kennedy's "reckless spending programs," and Walter Lippmann chastised Kennedy for not fulfilling his "promise to bring about something near to the full employment of capital and labor and a rising rate of economic growth."

Others did recognize the speculative mania and said simply that the market, and growth stocks in particular, were "too high" in 1961. As far as steel prices were concerned, with strong foreign competition in steel the price rises would probably have been rescinded anyway. Very few pointed out that it is always easy to look back and say when prices were too high or too low. Fewer still said that no one seems to know the proper price for a stock at any given time.

Synergy Generates Energy: The Conglomerate Boom

The market shook off its losses and settled down to ponder its next move. It was not too long in coming.

I've said before that part of the genius of the financial market is that if a product is demanded, it is produced. The product that all investors desired was expected growth in earnings per share. And if growth wasn't to be found in a name, it was only to be expected that someone would find another way to produce it. By the mid-sixties, creative entrepreneurs had discovered that growth was a word and that the word was *synergism*.

Synergism is the quality of having 2 plus 2 equal 5. Thus, it seemed quite plausible that two separate companies with an earning power of $2 million each might produce combined earnings of $5 million if the businesses were consolidated. This magical, mystical, surefire profitable new creation was called a conglomerate.

While antitrust laws kept large companies from purchasing firms in the same industry, it was possible for a while to purchase firms in other industries without interference from the Justice Department. The consolidations were carried out in the name of synergism. Ostensibly, mergers would allow the conglomerate to achieve greater financial strength (and thus greater borrowing capabilities at lower rates); to enhance marketing capabilities through the distribution of complementary product lines; to give greater scope to superior managerial talents; and to consolidate, and thus make more efficient operating services such as personnel and accounting departments. All this led to synergism — a stimulation of sales and earnings for the combined operation that would have been impossible for the independent entities alone.

In fact, the major impetus for the conglomerate wave of the 1960s was that the acquisition process itself could be made to produce growth in earnings per share. Indeed, the managers of conglomerates tended to possess financial expertise rather than the operating skills required to improve the profitability of the acquired companies. By an easy bit of legerdemain, they could put together a group of companies with no basic potential at all and produce steadily rising per-share earnings. The following example shows how this monkey business was performed.

Suppose we have two companies—the Able Circuit Smasher Company, an electronics firm, and Baker Typewriter Company, which makes typewriters. Each has 200,000 shares outstanding. It's 1965 and both companies have earnings of $1 million a year, or $5 per share. Let's assume neither business is growing and that, with or without merger activity, earnings would just continue along at the same level.

The two firms sell at different prices, however. Since Able Circuit Smasher Company is in the electronics business, the market awards it a price-earnings multiple of 20 which, multiplied by its $5 earnings per share, gives it a market price of $100. Baker Typewriter Company, in a less glamorous business, has its earnings multiplied at only 10 times and, consequently, its $5 per share earnings command a market price of only $50.

The management of Able Circuit would like to become a conglomerate. It offers to absorb Baker by swapping stock at the rate of two for three. The holders of Baker shares would get two shares of Able stock—which have a market value of $200—for every three shares of Baker stock—with a total market value of $150. Clearly this is a tempting proposal, and the stockholders of Baker are likely to accept cheerfully. The merger is approved.

We have a budding conglomerate, newly named Synergon, Inc., which now has 333,333 shares* outstanding and total earnings of $2 million to put against them, or $6 per share. Thus, by 1966 when the merger has been completed, we find that earnings have risen by 20 percent, from $5 to $6, and this growth seems to justify Able's former price-earnings multiple of 20. Consequently, the shares of Synergon (née Able) rise from $100 to $120, everybody's judgment is confirmed, and all go home rich and happy. In addition, the shareholders of Baker who were bought out need not pay any taxes on their profits until they sell their shares of the combined company.

---

*There are 200,000 original shares of Able plus an extra 133,333, which get printed up to exchange for Baker's 200,000 shares according to the terms of the merger.

The top three lines of the following table illustrate the transaction thus far.

A year later, Synergon finds Charlie Company, which earns $10 per share or $1 million with 100,000 shares outstanding.

	Company	Earnings Level	Number of Shares Outstanding	Earnings per Share	Price-Earnings Multiple	Price
Before Merger 1965	Able	$1,000,000	200,000	$5.00	20	$100
	Baker	1,000,000	200,000	5.00	10	50
After First Merger 1966	Synergon (Able and Baker Combined)	2,000,000	333,333	6.00	20	120
	Charlie	1,000,000	100,000	10.00	10	100
After Second Merger 1967	Synergon (Able, Baker, and Charlie Combined)	3,000,000	433,333	6.92	20	138⅜

Charlie Company is in the relatively risky military-hardware business so its shares command a multiple of only 10 and sell at $100. Synergon offers to absorb Charlie Company on a share-for-share exchange basis. Charlie's shareholders are delighted to exchange their $100 shares for the conglomerate's $120 shares. By the end of 1967, the combined company has earnings of $3 million, shares outstanding of 433,333, and earnings per share of $6.92.

Here we have a case where the conglomerate has literally manufactured growth. Neither Able, Baker, nor Charlie was growing at all; yet simply by virtue of the fact of their merger, the unwary investor who may finger his *Stock Guide* to see the past record of our conglomerate will find the following figures:

Earnings per Share

	1965	1966	1967
Synergon, Inc.	$5.00	$6.00	$6.92

Clearly, Synergon is a growth stock and its record of extraordinary performance appears to have earned it a high and possibly even an increasing multiple of earnings.

The trick that makes the game work is the ability of the electronics company to swap its high-multiple stock for the stock of another company with a lower multiple. The typewriter company can only "sell" its earnings at a multiple of 10. But when these earnings are packaged with the electronics company, the total earnings (including those from selling typewriters) could be sold at a multiple of 20. And the more acquisitions Synergon could make, the faster earnings per share would grow and thus the more attractive the stock would look to justify its high multiple.

The whole thing was like a chain letter—no one would get hurt as long as the growth of acquisitions proceeded exponentially. Of course the process could not continue for long, but the possibilities were mind-boggling for those who got in at the start. It seems difficult to believe that Wall Street professionals could be so myopic as to fall for the conglomerate con game, but accept it they did for periods of several years. Or perhaps as subscribers to the castle-in-the-air theory, they only believed that other people would fall for it.

The story of Synergon describes the standard conglomerate earnings "growth" gambit. There were a lot of other monkeyshines practiced. Convertible bonds (or convertible preferred stocks) were often used as a substitute for shares in paying for acquisitions. A convertible bond is an IOU of the company, paying a fixed interest rate, that is convertible at the option of the holder into shares of the firm's common stock. As long as the earnings of the newly acquired subsidiary were greater than the relatively low interest rate that was placed on the convertible bond, it was possible to show even more sharply rising earnings per share than those in the previous illustration. This is because no new common stocks at all had to be issued to consummate the merger, and thus the combined earnings could be divided by a smaller number of shares.

One company was truly creative in financing its acquisition program. It used a convertible preferred stock that paid no cash dividend at all.* Instead, the conversion rate of the security was to be adjusted annually to provide that the preferred stock be convertible into more common shares each year. The older pros in Wall Street shook their heads in disbelief over these shenanigans.

It is hard to believe that investors did not count the dilution potential of the new common stock that would be issued if the bond holders or preferred stockholders were to convert their securities into common stock. Indeed, as a result of such manipulations, corporations are now required to report their earnings on a "fully diluted" basis, to account for the new common shares that must be set aside for potential conversions. But most investors in the middle 1960s ignored such niceties and were satisfied only to see steadily and rapidly rising earnings.

Automatic Sprinkler Corporation (later called A-T-O Inc. and later still, at the urging of its modest chief executive officer Mr. Figgie, Figgie International) is a good example of how the game of manufacturing growth was actually played during the 1960s. Between 1963 and 1968, the company's sales volume rose by over 1400 percent. This phenomenal record was due solely to acquisitions. In the middle of 1967, four mergers were completed in a twenty-five day period. These newly acquired companies were all selling at relatively low price-earnings multiples, and thus helped to produce a sharp growth in earnings per share. The market responded to this "growth" by bidding

---

*Convertible preferred stock is similar to a convertible bond in that the preferred dividend is a fixed obligation of the company. But neither the principal nor the preferred dividend is considered a *debt*, so your company can usually skip a payment with greater freedom. Of course, in the example above, the stock paid no cash dividend at all.

up the price-earnings multiple to over 50 times earnings in 1967. This boosted the price of the company's stock from about $8 per share in 1963 to $73⅝ in 1967.

Mr. Figgie, the president of Automatic Sprinkler, performed the public relations job necessary to help Wall Street build its castle in the air. He automatically sprinkled his conversations with talismanic phrases about the energy of the free-form company and its interface with change and technology. He was always ready to talk about the "bottom line" of the income statement (where you get down to what the company earned) and insisted on emphasizing "earnings per share." He did not hesitate to project growth five to ten years out in the future. (After all, who'll remember in ten years what your forecast was?) He was careful to point out that he looked at twenty to thirty deals for each one he bought. Wall Street loved every word of it.

Mr. Figgie was not alone in conning Wall Street. Managers of other conglomerates almost invented a new language in the process of dazzling the investment community. They talked about market matrices, core technology fulcrums, modular building blocks, and the nucleus theory of growth. No one from Wall Street really knew what the words meant, but they all got the nice, warm feeling of being in the technological mainstream.

Conglomerate managers also found a new way of describing the businesses they had bought. Their shipbuilding businesses became "marine systems." Zinc mining became the "space minerals division." Steel fabrication plants became the "materials technology division." A lighting fixture or a lock company became part of the "protective services division." And if one of the "ungentlemanly" security analysts (somebody from CCNY rather than Harvard Business School) had the nerve to ask how you can get 15 to 20 percent growth from a foundry or a meat packer, the typical conglomerate manager suggested that his efficiency experts had isolated millions of dollars of excess costs; that his marketing research staff had found several fresh, uninhabited markets; and that the target of tripling profit margins could be easily realized within two years. To this add talk of breakfast and Sunday meetings with your staff, and the image of the hardworking, competent, go-go atmosphere is complete.

Instead of going down with merger activity, the price-earnings multiples of conglomerate stocks rose higher and higher. Even Textron, which generally disdained gimmickry and retained its terribly maladroit name indicating the company's association with the beleaguered textile industry, finally got its multiple up to 25 times earnings. Price and multiples for a selection of conglomerates in 1967 are shown in the following table.

	1967		1969	
Security	High Price	Price-Earnings Multiple	Low Price	Price-Earnings Multiple
Automatic Sprinkler (A-T-O Inc.)	73⅝	51.0	10⅞	13.4
Litton Industries	120½	44.1	55	14.4
Teledyne Inc.	71½ [a]	55.8	28¼	14.2
Textron, Inc.	55	24.9	23¼	10.1

[a]Adjusted for subsequent split.

The music slowed drastically for the conglomerates on January 19, 1968. On that day, the granddaddy of the conglomerates, Litton Industries, announced that earnings for the second quarter of that year would be substantially less than had been forecast. It had recorded 20 percent yearly increases for almost an entire decade. The market had so thoroughly come to believe in alchemy that the announcement was treated with disbelief and shock. In the selling wave that followed, conglomerate stocks declined by roughly 40 percent before a feeble recovery set in.

Worse was to come. In July, the Federal Trade Commission announced it would make an in-depth investigation of the conglomerate merger movement. Again the stocks went tumbling down. The Securities and Exchange Commission and the accounting profession finally made their move and began to make attempts to clarify the reporting techniques for mergers and acquisitions.

In January 1969, Litton again announced lower earnings. If that company—believed to be the best managed of the group—was unable to maintain earnings growth, how could the others continue to do so? Perhaps weak parts do not a strong whole make. The sell orders came flooding in. These were closely followed by new announcements from the SEC and the Assistant Attorney General in charge of antitrust, indicating a strong concern about the accelerating pace of the merger movement.

It should be quite a while before the conglomerate castle rises again, although given the propensity of institutions to run in packs after any concept suggesting growth one can't be quite that sure. The aftermath of this speculative phase revealed two disturbing factors. First, conglomerates were mortal and were not always able to control their far-flung empires. Indeed, investors became disenchanted with the conglomerate's new math; 2 plus 2 certainly did not equal 5 and some investors wondered if it even equaled 4. Second, the government and the accounting profession expressed real concern about the pace of mergers and about possible abuses. These two worries on the part of investors reduced—and in many cases eliminated—the premium multiples that had been paid for the anticipation of earnings from the acquisition process alone. This in itself makes the alchemy game almost impossible, for the acquiring company has to have an earnings multiple larger than the acquired company if the ploy is to work at all.

The combination of lower earnings and flattened price-earnings multiples implied a drastic decline in the prices of conglomerates. The preceding table indicates the depths to which stock prices sank in 1969 as the players in the game all rushed to grab their seats. Even greater declines were suffered in the 1970 bear market.

It was the professional investors who were hurt the most in the wild scramble for chairs. Few mutual or pension funds were without large holdings of conglomerate stocks. Castles in the air are not reserved as the sole prerogative of individuals; institutional investors can build them too. An interesting footnote to this episode is that by the 1980s deconglomeration came into fashion. Many of the old conglomerates began to shed their unrelated, poor-performing acquisitions in order to boost their earnings.

Many of these sales were financed through a popular innovation of the 1980s, the leveraged buyout (LBO). Under an LBO the purchaser, often the management of the division assisted by professional deal makers, puts up a very thin margin of equity, borrowing 90 percent or more of the funds needed to complete the transaction. The tax collector helps out too by allowing the bought-out entity to increase the value of its depreciable asset base. The combination of high interest payments and larger depreciation charges ensures that taxes for the new entity will remain low or nonexistent for some time. If things go well, the owners can often reap windfall profits. William Simon, a former secretary of the Treasury, made a multi-million-dollar killing on one of the earliest LBOs of the 1980s, Gibson Greeting Cards. Of course if economic conditions turn sour, the high interest costs are likely to place the new entity in considerable financial jeopardy. The late 1980s will undoubtedly witness the financial fallout from the explosion of some of the most poorly considered leveraged buyouts, conceived earlier in the decade.

Performance Comes to the Market: The Bubble in Concept Stocks

Our next speculative mania came into being during the mid-sixties, when there was heightened competition among mutual funds for the customer's dollar. Performance became the new golden calf. It meant that a fund performing better than the others (that is, with stocks in its portfolio that went up in value faster than the stocks in its competitors' portfolios) was far easier to sell to the public than one with a less lustrous record. So, with the public buying, mutual fund salesmen began to clamor for even greater performance.

And perform the funds did—at least over short periods of time. Fred Carr's highly publicized Enterprise Fund racked up a 117 percent total return (including both dividends and capital gains) in 1967 and followed this with a 44 percent return in 1968. The corresponding figures for the Standard & Poor's 500-Stock Index were 25 percent and 11 percent respectively. This performance brought large amounts of new money into the fund, and into other funds that could boast glamorous performances. The public no longer bet on the horse but rather on the jockey.

How did these jockeys do it? They concentrated the portfolio in dynamic stocks. Take the Dreyfus Fund and the growth-oriented Fidelity Funds. Jack Dreyfus, a high-stakes bridge player, got a running start on the performance record by investing heavily in Polaroid during that company's most rapid growth stage. Fidelity, run by Edward Johnson and Gerald Tsai, also held large blocks of stock in a relatively few rapidly growing companies. Johnson and Tsai were not faithful to these companies, however. At the sign of a better story, they would quickly switch. Both funds chalked up impressive successes in the mid-sixties and this led to many imitators. The camp followers were quickly given the accolade "go-go" funds, and the fund managers were often called "the youthful gunslingers." "Nothing succeeds so well as success," Talleyrand once observed, and this was certainly true for the performance funds in their early years—the customers' dollars flowed in.

The fickleness of men like Gerry Tsai extended even to their own relationships. Feeling he could make a better story on his own, Tsai left Fidelity in February 1966. In retrospect his ambitions were modest: he felt he would be able to raise $25 million in an initial offering for his own fund, the Manhattan Fund. His underwriters, Bache & Co., agreed and opened their subscription books for orders. Both found out that Gerry didn't know his own multiple. $274 million was subscribed on the first day. Within a year, Gerry Tsai had more than $400 million to manage. Tsai became the first superstar of the performance game and brokers could sound wise by watching the ticker tape and saying, "Ah, Gerry is buying again."

The performance game was not limited to mutual funds. It spread to all kinds of investing institutions. Businessmen who had to make constantly larger contributions to their workers' pension funds to meet retirement obligations began to ask pointedly whether they might be able to reduce their current expenses by switching more of the fund from fixed-income bonds into common stocks with exciting growth possibilities. Even university endowment-fund managers were pressured to strive for performance. McGeorge Bundy of the Ford Foundation chided the portfolio managers of universities:

> It is far from clear that trustees have reason to be proud of their performance in making money for their colleges. We recognize the risks of unconventional investing, but the true test of performance in the handling of money is the record of achievement, not the opinion of the respectable. We have the preliminary impression that over the long run caution has cost our colleges and universities much more than imprudence or excessive risk-taking.

And so performance investing took hold of Wall Street in the late 1960s. The commandments for fund managers were simple: Concentrate your holdings in a relatively few stocks and don't hesitate to switch the portfolio around if a more desirable investment appears. And because near-term performance was especially important (investment services began to publish monthly records of mutual fund performance) it would be best to buy stocks with an exciting concept and a compelling story. You had to be sure the market would recognize the beauty of your stock now—not far into the future. Hence, the birth of the so-called concept stock.

Xerox was a classic example of a concept stock. The concept was that of a new industry where machines would make dry copies by electrostatic transference. The company, Xerox, with its patent protection and its running head start, could look forward to several years of increased earnings. It was a true story — a believable story, one that would quicken the pulse of any good performance manager.

But even if the story were not totally believable, as long as the investment manager was convinced that the average opinion would think that the average opinion would believe the story, that's all that was needed. The youthful gunslingers became disenchanted with normal security analysts who could tell you how may railroad ties Penn Central had, but couldn't tell you when the company was about to go bankrupt. "I don't want to listen to that kind of security analyst," one of Wall Street's gunslingers told me. "I just want a good story or a good concept."

According to Martin Mayer, an investment manager who ran one of 1968's hottest mutual funds had a framed sign in Gothic lettering hanging on the wall of his office: "Invest Then Investigate." This was the reverse of the stock exchange's long-established slogan and was as apt a symbol as any for the atmosphere of the day. The gunslingers would buy thousands of shares of any security on any good story, and it became perfectly respectable to adopt a concept approach. Mayer quotes another fund manager as saying, "Since we hear stories early, we can figure enough people will be hearing it in the next few days to give the stock a bounce, even if the story doesn't prove out." Many Wall Streeters looked on this as a radical new investment strategy, but Lord Keynes had it all spotted in 1936.

Eventually, it reached a point where any concept would do. Enter Cortess W. Randell. His concept was a youth company for the youth market. He became founder, president, and major stockholder of National Student Marketing. Randell's motto, if he had one, appears to have been borrowed from Shakespeare: "Nothing can seem foul to those that win." First, he sold an image — one of affluence and success. He owned a

personal white Lear Jet named Snoopy, an apartment in New
York's Waldorf Towers, a $600,000 castle with a mock dun-
geon in Virginia, and a 55-foot yacht that slept twelve. Adding
to his image was an expensive set of golf clubs propped up by
his office door. Apparently the only time the clubs were used
was at night when the office cleanup crew drove wads of paper
along the carpet.

He spent most of his time visiting the financial community
or calling them on the sky phone from his Lear, and sold the
concept of NSM in the tradition of a South Sea Bubble promoter. Randell's real métier was evangelism. When he told
meetings of security analysts that NSM was well on its way
toward becoming a $700 million marketing organization, they
listened with faith, respect, and awe.

The concept that Wall Street bought from Randell was
that a single company could specialize in servicing the needs of
young people. NSM built its early growth via the merger route,
just as the ordinary conglomerates of the 1960s had done. The
difference was that each of the constituent companies had
something to do with the college-age youth market. Subsidiary
companies sold magazine subscriptions, books and records,
posters, paper dresses, guidebooks for summer jobs, student
directories, a computer dating service, youth air-fare cards,
sweatshirts, live entertainment programs, and a variety of consumer staples. What could be more appealing to a youthful
gunslinger than a youth-oriented concept stock—a full-service
company to exploit the youth subculture? Youth was in—this
one couldn't miss.

Randell kept up his whirlwind promotional pace, making
new converts as he went along. Glowing press releases issued
forth from company headquarters and Randell's earnings projections for the company became increasingly optimistic.

While there were some thistles among such roses (the earnings growth was produced by the old conglomerate gambit
with the generous support of some creative accounting), the
"concept" investors bought heavily in the company and blithely

ignored all questions. When Gerry Tsai's Manhattan Fund bought 120,000 shares for $5 million, it became clear that Randell had obtained the imprimatur of Wall Street's performance investors. Even some of the most august and conservative firms, including Bankers Trust, Morgan Guaranty, and Boston's venerable State Street Fund, bought stock. Pension funds, including General Mills, bought heavily; and United States Trust Company (the country's largest trust company) bought the stock for many of its accounts. University endowment fund managers, heeding the words of McGeorge Bundy, also bought in the mad scramble for performance. Blocks of NSM were bought by Harvard, Cornell, and the University of Chicago. Bundy himself practiced what he preached, and the previously conservatively managed Ford Foundation Fund also bought a large block.

The following table shows the high prices and enormous price-earnings multiples for National Student Marketing and for a small group of other concept stocks. The number of institutional holders (probably understated) for each security is also shown. Clearly, institutional investors are at least as adept as the general public at building castles in the air.

Security	High Price 1968–69	Price-Earnings Multiple at High	Number of Institutional Holders Year-end 1969	Low Price 1970	Percentage Decline
Four Seasons Nursing Centers of America	90¾	113.4	24	0.20	99
National Environment Corp.	27	103.8	8	⅜	99
National Student Marketing	35¾[a]	111.7	21	⅞	98
Performance Systems	23	∞	13	⅛	99

[a]Adjusted for subsequent stock split.

There were other concepts. Health care, for example, attracted quite a few adherents. Given the increasing numbers of older people and the spread of federal and private health insurance plans, someone was bound to make lots of money. Four Seasons Nursing Centers of America looked just like that someone. The biggest and most aggressive mutual funds bought in. At one point in 1969, institutions owned close to 50 percent of the company's stock.

The company expanded at a feverish pace, financing itself largely through the issuance of debt. These borrowings were sweetened, however, with so-called "equity kickers." This meant that attached to each bond were warrants to buy common stock of Four Seasons at fixed prices. Thus, if the stock price continued to go up, the bondholders could exercise their warrants and make additional profits.

These issues were so popular that customers would swear at their underwriters if they were not given a chance to buy. The institutional buyers who flocked in were not only Americans — even the "shrewd" European bankers bought heavily. European purchasers included such illustrious names as Banque Rothschild, Kreditbank Luxembourgeoise, Crédit Commercial de France, and the European operations of such U.S. firms as American Express Securities, S.A.; Bache & Co.; Burnham & Co.; and Merrill Lynch, Ltd. Four Seasons president Jack L. Clark boasted, "Without the institutions, we couldn't have grown nearly this fast."

As the debt mounted up no one seemed to worry much about the old ideas of prudent debt ratios, for this was a new concept and the rules of the game had changed. On June 26, 1970 the company filed a petition for reorganization under Chapter X of the Bankruptcy Act.

National Environment demonstrates the benefits of a new name. It started out in life as a prosaic construction company. I once asked one of the performance fund managers why a home builder was worth over 100 times earnings. He answered, "You are obviously not into the environment concept. This stock is 'heavy.' It gives me good vibrations."

Once National Environment got its price-earnings multiple up, it started an acquisition program, turning itself into a junior conglomerate. For example, in 1968 it bought a firm called "Uncle John's Restaurants" and promptly changed its name to "Envirofood, Inc." It also added nursing homes, insurance, soft drinks, and wholesale liquor operations, just to be sure it didn't miss any of the current fads. This company was really with it.

Minnie Pearl's concept is our last example of the period. Minnie Pearl was a fast-food franchising firm that was as accommodating as all get out. To please the financial community, Minnie Pearl's chickens became "Performance Systems." After all, what better name could be chosen for performance-oriented investors? On Wall Street a rose by any other name does not smell as sweet. The ∞ shown in the table under "price-earnings multiple" indicates that the multiple was infinity. Performance Systems had no earnings at all to divide into the stock's price at the time it reached its high in 1968. As the table indicates, Minnie Pearl laid an egg — and a bad one at that. The subsequent performance for this and the other stocks listed was indeed truly remarkable — although not quite what their buyers had anticipated.

Why did the stocks actually perform so badly? One general answer was that their price-earnings multiples were inflated beyond reason. If a multiple of 100 drops to the more normal multiple of 15 for the market as a whole, you have lost 85 percent of your investment right there. But in addition most of the concept companies of the time ran into severe operating difficulties. The reasons were varied: too rapid expansion, too much debt, loss of management control, etc. These companies were run by men who were primarily promoters, not sharp-penciled operating managers. In addition, fraudulent practices were common. For example, Performance Systems reported profits of $3.2 million in 1969. The SEC claimed that this report was "false and misleading." In 1972 Performance Systems issued a revision of the 1969 report. Apparently a loss of $1.3 million more accurately reflected 1969 operations. Similarly, the management of National Student Marketing was accused of fraud. NSM's Cortess Randell eventually pleaded guilty to stock fraud; he served eight months in prison and was fined $40,000.

And so when the 1969–71 bear market came, these concept stocks went down just as fast as they went up. In the end it was the pros who were conned most of all. While there is nothing wrong with seeking good performance, the mad rush to outgun the competition week by week had disastrous consequences. The cult of performance and the concept of "concept" stocks were henceforth greeted with disdain when mentioned in Wall Street.

The Nifty Fifty

Like generals fighting the last war, Wall Street's pros were planning not to repeat the mistakes of the 1960s in the 1970s. No more would they buy small electronics companies or exciting concept stocks. There was a return to reason and with it a return to "sound principles" that translated to investing in blue-chip companies with proven growth records. These were companies, so the thinking went, that would never come crashing down like the speculative favorites of the 1960s. Nothing could be more prudent than to buy their shares and then relax on the golf course while the long-term rewards materialized.

There were only four dozen or so of these premier growth stocks that so fascinated the institutional investors. The names were very familiar—IBM, Xerox, Avon Products, Kodak, McDonald's, Polaroid, and Disney, to list a few. They were called the "Nifty Fifty." They were "big capitalization" stocks, which meant that an institution could buy a good-sized position without disturbing the market. And since most pros realized that picking the exact correct time to buy is difficult if not impossible, these stocks seemed to make a great deal of sense. So what if you paid a price that was temporarily too high? Since these stocks were proven growers, sooner or later the price you paid would be justified. In addition, these were stocks which — like the family heirlooms — you would never sell. Hence they were also called "one-decision" stocks. You made a decision to buy them, once, and your portfolio-management problems were over.

These stocks provided security blankets for institutional investors in another way too. They were so respectable. Your colleagues could never question your prudence in investing in IBM. True, you could lose money if IBM went down, but that was not considered a sign of imprudence (as it would be to lose money in a Performance Systems or a National Student Marketing). Like greyhounds in chase of the mechanical rabbit, big pension funds, insurance companies, and bank trust funds loaded up on the Nifty Fifty one-decision growth stocks. Hard as it is to believe, the institutions had actually started to speculate in blue chips. This is a case of classic insanity. The heights to which the stocks rose were unbelievable. In the table below I have listed the price-earnings multiples achieved by a handful of these stocks in 1972. For comparison, the price-earnings multiples at the start of the 1980s are listed too. Institutional managers blithely ignored the fact that no sizable company could ever grow fast enough to justify an earnings multiple of 80 or 90. They once again proved the maxim that stupidity well packaged can sound like wisdom.

Security	Price-Earnings Multiple 1972	Price-Earnings Multiple 1980
Sony	92	17
Polaroid	90	16
McDonald's	83	9
Intl. Flavors	81	12
Walt Disney	76	11
Hewlett-Packard	65	18

Perhaps one might argue that the craze was simply a mani-
festation of the return of confidence in late 1972. Richard
Nixon had been reelected by a landslide, peace was "at hand"
in Vietnam, price controls were due to come off, inflation was
apparently "under control," and no one knew what OPEC was.
But in fact the market had already started to decline in early
1972, and when it did the Nifty Fifty mania became even more
pathological. For as the market in general collapsed, the Nifty
Fifty continued to command record earnings multiples and, on
a relative basis, the overpricing greatly increased. There appeared to be a "two-tier" market. *Forbes* magazine commented
as follows:

> [The Nifty Fifty appeared to rise up] from the ocean; it was as
> though all of the U.S. but Nebraska had sunk into the sea. The
> two tier market really consisted of one tier and a lot of rubble
> down below.
>
>   What held the Nifty Fifty up? The same thing that held up
> tulip-bulb prices in long-ago Holland — popular delusions and
> the madness of crowds. The delusion was that these companies
> were so good that it didn't matter what you paid for them; their
> inexorable growth would bail you out.

The end was inevitable. The Nifty Fifty craze ended like all
other speculative manias. The Nifty Fifty were — in the words
of *Forbes* columnist Martin Sosnoff — taken out and shot one by
one. The oil embargo hit Disney and its large stake in Disney-
land and Disneyworld. Production problems with new cameras
hit Polaroid. The stocks sank like stones into the ocean. A critical cover story in widely respected *Forbes* magazine sent Avon
Products down almost 50 percent in six months. The real problem was never the particular needle that pricked each individual bubble. The problem was simply that the stocks were
ridiculously overpriced. Sooner or later the same money managers who had worshiped the Nifty Fifty decided to make a
second decision and sell. In the debacle that followed, the
premier growth stocks fell completely from favor.

The Gambling-Stock Bingo

Late in the 1970s, Wall Street decided to play bingo in a big way. What better object for Wall Street's floating crap game than the gambling stocks themselves? Atlantic City, known for its shabby turn-of-the-century hotels and a long line of antiseptic beauty princesses, brought Wall Street's tired blood to the bubbling point.

When the state of New Jersey voted to legalize gambling in Atlantic City, Wall Street decided that East Coast casinos were the best thing to happen since Monday-night football. There began one of the greatest speculative binges in market history.

During the first half of 1978, the market value of a small group of gambling stocks appreciated by the staggering amount of $1.5 billion. As Alan Abelson of *Barron's* put it, the craze left "logic, prudence, and skepticism crumbled beyond recognition." Heinz Biel commented in *Forbes* that it was "like the 1960s all over again."

One of the main objects of the market's affection was a company called Resorts International (née Mary Carter Paint Company). Resorts was granted the first casino license in Atlantic City and the prospect of having a monopoly on casino operations for about a year and a half. The stock price increased tenfold, reaching a total market value of almost $1 billion. No one worried about the possibility of future competition as other casinos were licensed, nor was there any concern that the state and municipal governments might decide to squeeze operators with heavy taxes once gambling became firmly established. As in past speculative crazes, enthusiasm simply fed itself, and it appeared that the stock could go nowhere but up. After reaching its high of over $108 per share* in 1978, the stock tumbled to a third of its former value within the next two years.

Bally Manufacturing was another belle of the gambling ball. In the midst of visions of long-legged chorus girls and

*Class B stock adjusted for subsequent stock splits.

rooms filled with gaming tables, Bally boasted that it was the major U.S. manufacturer of pinball and slot machines. It also had plans to build an $80 million hotel/casino complex in Atlantic City. In 1978 and 1979, Bally stock enjoyed an almost perpendicular rise. Even more money was made by purchasers of Bally options. No one scrutinized the assets, potential earnings, and potential debt of the company with a croupier's sharp eye, which might have made it difficult to accept the picture Wall Street was painting. When the stock broke in 1979, many a fortune was lost.

Speculative fever also spread to stocks of companies that had only a peripheral involvement in the gambling industry. This was one of the most pathological manifestations of the gambling craze. Perhaps the most extreme case was that of Allied Leisure, which in 1977 had gone through a Chapter XI bankruptcy proceeding. The company was a Florida manufacturer of coin-operated amusement devices, and the stock was bid up on the slim hope of some beneficial spillover if Florida gave the green light to gambling. The whole story was built on castles in the air, while the firm remained mired firmly in the red. Yet, during 1978, the market price of Allied Leisure stock enjoyed a 28-fold increase, from a low of ¼ to a high of 7. In 1980, after the speculative fever subsided, the stock sold as low as 1⅛ despite considerable improvement in the operating results of the company.

The Triumphant Return of New Issues

You can say one thing about speculators: they may be knocked down from time to time, but, by gum, they are never knocked out. During 1979 and the first two years of the eighties, these Street denizens tended to share the market's doldrums. That was a long time to remain depressed and inactive, and by late 1982, they were raring to go again. This time they resurrected an old favorite from the golden era of the sixties—new issues.

"When the market turned, you had a feeding frenzy," a managing director of First Boston Corporation recalled. "You threw anything on the table, and people gobbled it up."

The high technology new-issue boom of the first half of 1983 was an almost perfect replica of the 1960s episodes with the names altered slightly to include the new fields of biotechnology and microelectronics. The 1983 craze made the promoters of the sixties look like pikers. Fifteen billion dollars worth of new public offerings were floated, approximately four times the previous record established in 1981 and greater than the cumulative total of new issues for the entire preceding decade. For investors, initial public offerings were the hottest game in town. Just getting a piece of a new issue automatically made you a winner, or so it seemed, as prices often soared in the after-market.

Typical of the period was a promising new technology stock, Diasonics, Inc., a manufacturer of medical imaging equipment located in the heartland of technological America, Silicon Valley, south of San Francisco. Diasonics' shares were offered at $22 each. By the end of the first day of trading, Diasonics had spurted over 20 percent to 26$\frac{3}{4}$. Nothing to get excited about there. After all, the market value of Diasonics stock was "only" 10 times the company's total sales for the previous year and 100 times the previous year's earnings. In the feverish new-issue market of 1983, such multiples were commonplace. Arthur Rock, the chairman of Diasonics' executive committee, thought the price was so reasonable that he sold 50,000 of his shares for a total of $3.3 million.

Down the valley from Diasonics, another group was working hard to throw something on the table for investors. They thought a machine should do the dishing up—specifically a personal robot. Was the robot ready for the task? Well, not quite. The company, called Androbot, *planned* to manufacture a line of personal robots. The company's major product, B.O.B. (an acronym for Brains on Board), was *nearly* ready for manufacture; there were just a few small problems. Apparently, product development was not yet complete, and it was not clear that the "significant technological obstacles" mentioned in the prospectus could be overcome. Moreover, software applications had not been developed, and the prospectus suggested that early prototype models were not yet, in the computer vernacular, user friendly. Finally, it was not clear that any of Androbot's products could be mass-produced or that a market for the products existed at the prices that would have to be charged. But the proposed market capitalization of Androbot was less than $100 million (for a company with no sales, earnings, or net assets), and that didn't buy much in the heady new-issue market of 1983. Incidentally, the underwriter for this proposed floatation was not one of the small schlock houses on the fringe of respectability, but the thundering herd itself, Merrill Lynch.

The flood of new issues contained such names as Fortune Systems, Spectravideo, and Whirlyball International. As was true in the earlier new-issue booms, even companies in more mundane businesses were favored in the market. A chain of three restaurants in New Jersey called "Stuff Your Face, Inc." was registered with the SEC. Indeed, the enthusiasm extended to "quality" issues such as Fine Art Acquisitions Ltd. This was not some Philistine outfit peddling discount clothing or making computer hardware. This was a truly aesthetic enterprise. Fine Art Acquisitions, the prospectus tells us, was in the business of acquiring and distributing fine prints and art deco sculpture replicas. One of the company's major assets consisted of a group of nude photographs of Brooke Shields taken about midway between her time in the stroller and her entrance to Princeton. Apparently, there were some potential legal problems, such as a suit by Mom Shields, who had some objection to the exploitation of these pictures of the prepubescent eleven-year-old Brooke. But, after all, this was for "artistic" purposes and obviously this was a class company.

The bubble appears to have burst early in the second half of 1983. The market itself had peaked by mid-year and had declined slightly, but the carnage in the small company and new-issue markets was truly catastrophic. Frank Wisneski, the brilliant portfolio manager of the Explorer Fund, which has had an outstanding record in the small company field, suggests that it was the offering of Muhammed Ali Arcades International that started the debacle.

In a sense, the proposed Muhammed Ali Arcades offering was not particularly remarkable considering all the other garbage that was coming out at the time. But the offering was unique in that it showed that a penny could still buy a lot. The company proposed to offer units of one share and two warrants for the modest price of 1¢. Of course, this was 333 times what insiders had recently paid for their own shares. That wasn't unusual either, but when it was discovered that the champ himself had resisted the temptation to buy any stock in his namesake company, investors began to take a good look at where they were. Most did not like what they saw. The result was a dramatic decline in small company stocks in general and in the market prices of initial public offerings in particular. The following table describes how in the course of a year many investors lost as much as 80 or 90 percent of their money.

	Initial 1983 Offering Price	High Price	Price Mid-1984	Percentage Decline from High to Mid-1984
Activision	12	12¾	1⅜	89
Diasonics	22	27½	1⅞	93
Fine Arts Acquisitions	2	2⅛	1¼	41
Fortune Systems	22	22	3	86
Spectravideo	6¼	16¾	¼	99
Teleram Communications	7½	31	1½	95
Victor Technologies	17½	22⅛	⅜	98
Wilcat Systems	18	18¼	1⅞	89

Nor were these isolated examples or simply the worst of the new issues of the early 1980s. A study by the investment firm of Wertheim and Company looked at all initial public offerings from late 1982 through mid-1983 whose offering size was $5 million or more. They calculated that, by early March of 1984, the average price decline for these offerings was more than 50 percent from the most recent 52-week high. These stocks declined even further as the market weakened during the spring.

The cover of the prospectus of Muhammed Ali Arcades International featured a picture of the former champ standing over a fallen opponent. In his salad days, Ali used to claim that he could "float like a butterfly and sting like a bee." It turned out that the Ali Arcades offering (as well as the Androbot offering that was scheduled for July 1983) never did get floated. But many others did, particularly stocks of those companies on the bleeding edge of technology. As has been true time and time again, it was the investors who got stung.

The lessons of market history are clear. It is very hard to be neutral about things as difficult to forecast as the earnings prospects of corporations (or the hopes and fears of other investors). Styles and fashions in investors' evaluations of securities can and often do play a critical role in the pricing of securities. The stock market at times conforms well to the castle-in-the-air theory. For this reason, the game of investing can be extremely dangerous. When the market favors some particular characteristic in a stock, financial entrepreneurs usually find some way of manufacturing it—or at least a close substitute. The public inevitably pays dearly for such creativity.

CHAPTER FOUR

The Firm-Foundation Theory of Stock Prices

The greatest of all gifts is the power to estimate things at their true worth. — La Rochefoucauld, *Reflexions; ou sentences et maximes morales*

Investors can and should learn vicariously from the stock market. And I hope the historical review in Chapter Three has provided sufficient warning to save you from the traps that ensnare builders of castles in the air. Autopsies should be as useful in the practice of investment as in medicine. At the same time, to be forewarned is not to be forearmed in the investment world. Investors also need a sense of justification for market prices — a standard, even if only a very loose one, with which to compare current market prices. Is there such a thing? I happen to think so — though I believe it neither rests on a firm foundation nor floats like a castle in the air.

The firm-foundation theorists, who include many of Wall Street's most prosperous and highly paid security analysts, know full well that purely psychic support for market valuations has proved a most undependable pillar, and skyrocketing markets have invariably succumbed to the financial laws of gravity. Therefore, many security analysts devote their energies to estimating a stock's firm foundation of value. Let's see what lies behind such estimates.

The "Fundamental" Determinants of Stock Prices

What is it that determines the real or intrinsic value of a share? What are the so-called fundamentals that security analysts look at in estimating a security's firm foundation of value?

I said in the first chapter that firm-foundation theorists view the worth of any share as the present value of all dollar benefits the investor expects to receive from it. Remember that the word "present" indicates that a distinction must be made between dollars expected immediately and those anticipated later on, which must be "discounted." All future income is worth less than money in hand; for if you had the money now you could be earning interest on it. In a very real sense, time is money.

In arriving at their value estimates, firm-foundation theorists usually take the standpoint of a very long-term investor who buys his shares "for keeps." The only benefits such an investor receives will come to him if the company pays out some part of its earnings in cash dividends. Thus the worth of a share to a long-term investor will be the present or discounted value of all the future dividends the firm is expected to pay.

Of course, the price of a common stock is dependent on a number of factors. I will now describe four determinants affecting the value of shares and then give four broad rules for applying these to determine the present (or firm-foundation) value of the stocks you are considering. If you follow these rules consistently, firm-foundation theorists suggest you will find yourself safe from the speculative crazes I have just described.

Determinant 1: The expected growth rate   Most people don't realize the implications of compound growth on financial decisions. It is often said that the Indian who sold Manhattan Island in 1626 for $24 was rooked by the white man. In fact, he may have been an extremely sharp salesman. Had he put his $24 away at 6 percent interest, compounded semiannually, it would now be worth over $30 billion, and with it he could buy back much of the now-improved land. Such is the magic of compound growth!

Similarly, the implications of various growth rates on the size of future dividends may be surprising to many readers. As the table below shows, growth at a 15 percent rate means that dividends will double every five years.* Alternate rates are also presented.

Growth Rate of Dividends	Present Dividend	Dividend in Five Years	Dividend in Ten Years	Dividend in Twenty-Five Years
5 percent	$1.00	$1.28	$1.68	$ 3.39
15 percent	1.00	2.01	4.05	32.92
25 percent	1.00	3.05	9.31	264.70

The catch (and doesn't there always have to be at least one, if not twenty-two?) is that dividend growth does not go on forever. Corporations and industries have life cycles similar to most living things. There is, for corporations in particular, a high mortality rate at birth. Survivors can look forward to rapid growth, maturity, and then a period of stability. Later in the life cycle, companies eventually decline and either perish or undergo a substantial metamorphosis. Consider the leading corporations in the United States 100 years ago. Such names as Eastern Buggy Whip Company, La Crosse and Minnesota Steam Packet Company,

---

*A handy rule for calculating how many years it takes dividends to double is to divide 72 by the long-term growth rate. Thus, if dividends grow at 15 percent per year they will double in a bit less than five years (72 ÷ 15).

Lobdell Car Wheel Company, Savanna and St. Paul Steamboat Line, and Hazard Powder Company, the already mature enterprises of the time, would have ranked high in a *"Fortune* Top 500" list of that era. All are now deceased.

Look at the industry record. Railroads, the most dynamic growth industry a century ago, finally matured and enjoyed a long period of prosperity before entering their recent period of decline. The paper and aluminum industries provide more recent examples of the cessation of rapid growth and the start of a more stable, mature period in the life cycle. These industries were the most rapidly growing in the United States during the 1940s and early 1950s. By the 1960s they were no longer able to grow any faster than the economy as a whole. Similarly, the most rapidly growing industry of the late 1950s and 1960s, the electronics industry, had slowed to a crawl by the 1970s.

And even if the natural life cycle doesn't get a company, there's always the fact that it gets harder and harder to grow at the same percentage rate. A company earning $1 million need increase its earnings by only $100,000 to achieve a 10 percent growth rate, whereas a company starting from a base of $10 million in earnings needs $1 million in additional earnings to produce the same record.

The nonsense of relying on very high long-term growth rates is nicely illustrated by working with population projections for the United States. If the populations of the nation and of California continue to grow at their recent rates, 120 percent of the United States population will live in California by the year 2035! Using similar kinds of projections, it can be estimated that at the same time 240 percent of the people in the country with venereal disease will live in California. As one Californian puts it on hearing these forecasts, "Only the former projections make the latter one seem at all plausible."

As hazardous as projections may be, share prices must reflect differences in growth prospects if any sense is to be made of market valuations. Also, the probable length of the growth phase is very important. If one company expects to enjoy a rapid 20 percent growth rate for ten years, and another growth company expects to sustain the same rate for only five years, the former company is, other things being equal, more valuable to the investor than the latter. The point is that growth rates are general rather than gospel truths. And this brings us to the firm-foundation theorists' first rule for evaluating securities:

> *Rule 1: A rational investor should be willing to pay a higher price for a share, the larger the growth rate of dividends.*

To this is added an important corollary:

> *Corollary to Rule 1: A rational investor should be willing to pay a higher price for a share the longer the growth rate is expected to last.*

Determinant 2: The expected dividend payout The amount of dividends you receive at each payout — as contrasted to their growth rate — is readily understandable as being an important factor in determining a stock's price. The higher the dividend payout, other things being equal, the greater the value of the stock. The catch here is the phrase *other things being equal.* Stocks that pay out a high percentage of earnings in dividends may be poor investments if their growth prospects are unfavorable. Conversely, many companies in their most dynamic growth phase often pay out little or none of their earnings in dividends. But for two companies whose expected growth rates are the same, you are better off with the one whose dividend payout is higher.

Beware of the stock dividend. This provides no benefits whatever. The practice is employed on the pretext that the firm is preserving cash for expansion while providing dividends in the form of additional shares. Stockholders presumably like to receive new pieces of paper — it gives them a warm feeling that the firm's managers are interested in their welfare. Some even think that by some alchemy the stock dividend increases the worth of their holdings.

In actuality, only the printer profits from the stock dividend. To distribute a 100 percent stock dividend, a firm must print one additional share for each share outstanding. But with twice as many shares outstanding, each share represents only half the interest in the company that it formerly did. Earnings per share and all other relevant per-share statistics about the company are now halved. This unit change is the only result of a stock dividend. When Great Britain replaced one shilling with five new pence, the English, being a sensible people, did not celebrate. Neither should stockholders greet with any joy the declaration of stock splits or dividends — unless these are accompanied by higher cash dividends or news of higher earnings.

The only conceivable advantage of a stock split (or large stock dividend) is that lowering the price level of the shares might induce more public investors to purchase them. People like to buy in 100-share lots, and if a stock's price is very high many investors will feel excluded. But 2 and 3 percent stock dividends, which are so commonly declared, do no good at all.

The distribution of new certificates for stock dividends brings up the whole concept of actual certificates of ownership. This is an incredibly cumbersome and archaic system and should be eliminated. Records of ownership could easily be kept on the memory disks of large computers. If stockholders could rid themselves of their atavistic longing for pretty embossed certificates, Wall Street's current paperwork dilemma could be made manageable, commission rates might be reduced, and my wife and other environmentalists could congratulate themselves on another victory.

Now that I've got that off my chest, let's sum up by printing the second rule:

> *Rule 2: A rational investor should be willing to pay a higher price for a share, other things being equal, the larger the proportion of a company's earnings that is paid out in cash dividends.*

Determinant 3: The degree of risk   Risk plays an important role in the stock market, no matter what your overeager mutual fund salesman may tell you. There is always a risk — and that's what makes it so fascinating. Risk also affects the valuation of a stock. Some people think risk is the only aspect of a stock to be examined.

The more respectable a stock is — that is, the less risk it has — the higher its quality. Stocks of the so-called blue-chip companies, for example, are said to deserve a quality premium. (Why high-quality stocks are given an appellation derived from the poker tables is a fact known only to Wall Street.) Most investors prefer less risky stocks and, therefore, these stocks can command higher price-earnings multiples than their risky, low-quality counterparts.

While there is general agreement that the compensation for higher risk must be greater future rewards (and thus *lower* current prices), measuring risk is well-nigh impossible. This has not daunted the economist, however. A great deal of attention has been devoted to risk measurement by both academic economists and practitioners. Indeed, risk measurement is so important that an entire part of this book (Part Three) is devoted to this subject.

According to one well-known theory, the bigger the swings — relative to the market as a whole — in an individual company's stock prices (or in its total yearly returns, including dividends), the greater the risk. For example, a nonswinger such as AT&T gets the *Good Housekeeping* seal of approval for "widows and orphans." That's because its earnings do not decline much if at all during recessions, and its dividend has never been cut. Therefore, when the market goes down 20 percent, AT&T usually trails with perhaps only a 10 percent decline. AT&T is probably not as safe as it was before the 1983 divestiture and deregulation, which led to increased competition in the telecommunications industry. Nevertheless, the stock still qualifies as one with less than average risk. Amdahl, on the other hand, has a very volatile past record and it characteristically falls by 40 percent or more when the market declines by 20 percent. It is called a "flyer," or an investment that is a "businessman's risk." The investor gambles in owning stock in such a company, particularly if he may be forced to sell out during a time of unfavorable market conditions.

When business is good and the market mounts a sustained upward drive, however, Amdahl can be expected to outdistance AT&T. But if you are like most investors, you value stable returns over speculative hopes, freedom from worry about your portfolio over sleepless nights, and limited loss exposure over the possibility of a downhill roller-coaster ride. You will prefer the more stable security, other things being the same. This leads to a third basic rule of security valuation.

Rule 3: A rational (and risk-averse) investor should be willing to pay a higher price for a share, other things being equal, the less risky the company's stock.

I should warn the reader that a "relative volatility" measure may not fully capture the relevant risk of a company. Part Three will present a thorough discussion of this important risk element in stock valuation.

Determinant 4: The level of market interest rates   The stock market, no matter how much it may think so, does not exist as a world unto itself. Investors should consider how much profit they can obtain elsewhere. Interest rates, if they are high enough, can offer a stable, profitable alternative to the stock market. Consider periods such as the early 1980s when yields on *prime* quality corporate bonds soared to over 15 percent. Long-term bonds of somewhat lower quality were being offered at even higher interest rates. The expected returns from stock prices had trouble matching these bond rates; money flowed into bonds while stock prices fell sharply. Finally, stock prices reached such a low level that a sufficient number of investors were attracted to stem the decline. To put it another way, in order to attract investors from high-yielding bonds, stock must offer bargain-basement prices.* Thus, the last rule for the firm-foundation theory is:

> *Rule 4: A rational investor should be willing to pay a higher price for a share, other things being equal, the lower are interest rates.*

Two Important Caveats

The four valuation rules imply that a security's firm-foundation value (and its price-earnings multiple) will be higher the larger the company's growth rate and the longer its duration; the larger the dividend payout for the firm; the less risky the company's stock; and the lower the general level of interest rates.

As I indicated earlier, economists have taken rules such as these and expressed in a mathematical formula the exact price (present value) at which shares should sell. In principle, such theories are very useful in suggesting a rational basis for stock prices and in giving investors some standard of value. Of course, the rules must be compared with the facts to see if they conform at all to reality, and I will get to that in a moment. But before we

---

*The point can be made another way by noting that since higher interest rates enable us to earn more now, any deferred income should be "discounted" more heavily. Thus the present value of any flow of future dividend returns will be lower when current interest rates are relatively high. The relationship between interest rates and stock prices is somewhat more complicated, however, than this discussion may suggest. Suppose investors expect that the rate of inflation will increase from 5 to 10 percent. Such an expectation is likely to drive interest rates up by about 5 percentage points to compensate investors for holding fixed-dollar-obligation bonds whose purchasing power will be adversely affected by greater inflation. Other things being the same, this should make stock prices fall. But with higher expected inflation, investors may reasonably project that corporate earnings and dividends will also increase at a faster rate, causing stock prices to rise. A full discussion of inflation, interest rates, and stock prices is contained in Chapter Eleven, where it is shown that corporate earnings and dividends do tend to grow with inflation.

even think of using and testing these rules in a very precise way, there are two important caveats to bear in mind.

Caveat 1: Expectations about the future cannot be proven in the present.   Remember, not even Jeane Dixon can accurately predict all of the future. Yet some people have absolute faith in security analysts' estimates of the long-term growth prospects of a company and the duration of that growth.

Predicting future earnings and dividends is a most hazardous occupation. It requires not only the knowledge and skill of an economist, but also the acumen of a psychologist. On top of that, it is extremely difficult to be objective; wild optimism and extreme pessimism constantly battle for top place. During the early 1960s, when the economy and the world situation were relatively stable, investors had no trouble convincing themselves that the coming decade would be soaring and prosperous. As a result, very high growth rates were projected for a large number of corporations. Years later, in 1980, the economy was suffering from severe "stagflation" and an unstable international situation. The best that investors could do that year was to project modest growth rates for most corporations.

The point to remember is that no matter what formula you use for predicting the future, it always rests in part on the indeterminate premise. Although many Wall Streeters claim to see into the future, they are just as fallible as the rest of us.

Caveat 2: Precise figures cannot be calculated from undetermined data.   It stands to reason that you can't obtain precise figures by using indefinite factors. Yet to achieve desired ends, investors and security analysts do this all the time. Here's how it's done.

Take a company that you've heard lots of good things about. You study the company's prospects, and suppose you conclude that it can maintain a high growth rate for a long period. How long? Well, why not ten years?

You then calculate what the stock should be "worth" on the

basis of the current dividend payout, the expected future growth rate of dividends, and the general level of interest rates, perhaps making an allowance for the riskiness of the shares.* It turns out to your chagrin that the price the stock is worth is just slightly less than its present market price.

You now have two alternatives. You could regard the stock as overpriced and refuse to buy it, or you could say, "Perhaps this stock could maintain a high growth rate for eleven years rather than ten. After all, the ten was only a guess in the first place, so why not eleven years?" And so you go back to your calculator and lo and behold you now come up with a worth for the shares that is larger than the current market price. Armed with this "precise" knowledge, you make your sound purchase.

The reason the game worked is that the longer one projects growth, the greater is the stream of future dividends. Thus, the present value of a share is at the discretion of the calculator. If eleven years was not enough to do the trick, twelve or thirteen might well have sufficed. There is always some combination of growth rate and growth period that will produce any specific price. In this sense it is intrinsically impossible, given human nature, to calculate the intrinsic value of a share.

J. Peter Williamson, author of an excellent textbook for financial analysts entitled *Investments*, provides another example. In the book, Williamson estimated the present (or firm-foundation) value of IBM shares by using the same general principle of valuation I have described above; that is, by estimating how fast IBM's dividends would grow and for how long. Williamson first made the sensible assumption that IBM would grow at a fairly high rate for some number of years before falling into a much smaller mature growth rate. In 1968, when he made his estimate, IBM was selling at $320 per share.

---

*If you actually want to do the calculation, just write out your estimates for the future flow of dividends expected, get hold of a vest-pocket calculator, and perform the whole operation while riding into work on the train.

> I began by forecasting growth in earnings per share at 16%. This
> was a little under the average for the previous ten years . . . I fore-
> cast at 16% growth rate for 10 years, followed by indefinite growth
> at . . . 2% . . . When I put all these numbers into the formula I
> got an intrinsic value of $172.94, about half of the current market
> value.

Since the intrinsic value and market value of IBM stock were
so far apart, Williamson decided that perhaps his estimates of the
future might not be accurate. He experimented further:

> It doesn't really seem sensible to predict only 10 years of above
> average growth for IBM, so I extended my 16% growth forecast to
> 20 years. Now the intrinsic value came to $432.66, well above the
> market.

Had Williamson opted for thirty years of above-average
growth, he would be projecting IBM to generate a future sales
volume about one half the then current U.S. national income.
With all due respect to IBM, such a growth rate does not seem
possible.

The point to remember from such examples is that the mathematical precision of the firm-foundation value formulas is based
on treacherous ground: forecasting the future. The major fundamentals for these calculations are never known with certainty;
they are only relatively crude estimates—perhaps one should say
guesses—about what might happen in the future. And depending on what guesses you make, you can convince yourself to pay
any price you want to for a stock.

There is, I believe, a fundamental indeterminateness about
the value of common shares even in principle. God Almighty does
not know the proper price-earnings multiple for a common stock.

Testing the Rules

With the rules and caveats in mind, let us take a closer look at
stock prices and examine whether the rules seem to conform to
actual practices. Let's start with Rule 1—the larger the anticipated growth rate, the higher the price of a share.

To begin, we'll reformulate the question in terms of price-earnings (P/E) multiples rather than the market price themselves. This provides a good yardstick for comparing stocks—which have different prices and earnings—against one another. A stock selling at $100 per share with earnings of $10 per share would have the same P/E multiple (10) as a stock selling at $40 with earnings of $4 per share. It is the P/E multiple, not the dollar price, that really tells you how a stock is valued in the market.

Our reformulated question now reads: Are actual price-earnings multiples higher for stocks where a high growth rate is anticipated? A major study by John Cragg and myself strongly indicates the answer is yes.

It was easy to collect the first half of the data required. P/E multiples are printed daily in papers such as the *New York Times* and the *Wall Street Journal*. To obtain information on expected long-term growth rates, we surveyed eighteen leading investment firms whose business it is to produce the forecasts upon which buy and sell recommendations are made. (I'll describe later how they make these forecasts.) Estimates were obtained from each firm of the five-year growth rates anticipated for a large sample of stocks.

I will not bore you with the details of the actual statistical study that was perfomed.* The results are illustrated, however, for a few representative securities in the chart below. It is clear that, just as Rule 1 asserts, high P/E ratios are associated with high expected growth rates. This general pattern has held up in every year since 1961, when we began the study.

In addition to demonstrating how the market values different growth rates, the chart can also be used as a practical investment guide. Suppose you were considering the purchase of a stock with an anticipated 13 percent growth rate and you knew that, on average, stocks with 13 percent growth sold, like IBM, at 11 times earnings. If the stock you were considering sold at a price-earnings multiple of 20, you might reject the idea of buying the stock in favor of one more reasonably priced in terms of current

---

*It is listed among the references for this chapter.

Effect of High Expected Long-Term Growth Rates — Price-Earnings Multiples Pushed Up*

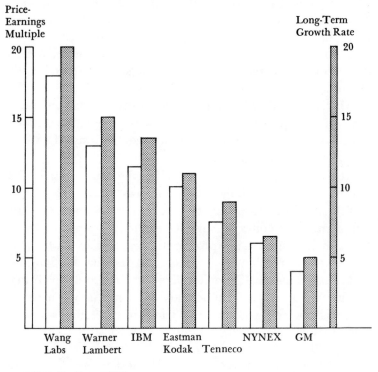

* Data for August 1984

market norms. If, on the other hand, your stock sold at a multiple below the average in the market for that growth rate, the security is said to represent good value for your money. I'll return to the practical use of such techniques, as well as the pitfalls, at several later points.

How about Rule 2, 3, and 4? Just as we were able to test for a relationship between earnings multiples and anticipated growth rates, it was also possible to collect the necessary data and find the way in which not only growth, but dividend payout, risk, and interest rates influence price-earnings multiples in the market.

The particular techniques used need not concern us. What is important to realize is that there does seem to be a logic to market valuations. Market prices seem to behave just as the four rules developed by the firm-foundation theorists would lead us to expect. It is comforting to know that at least to this extent there is an underlying rationality to the stock market.

One More Caveat

So market prices do seem to have an inherent logic. In each of many recent years, stock prices have been closely related to differential patterns of expected growth as well as to the other "fundamental" valuation influences so important to proponents of the firm-foundation theory. Yes, Virginia, it looks like there may be a firm foundaton of value after all, and some jokers in Wall Street actually think you can make money knowing what it is.

Caveat 3: What's growth for the goose is not always growth for the gander.   The difficulty comes with the value the market puts on specific fundamentals. It is always true that the market values growth, and that higher growth rates and larger multiples go hand in hand. But the crucial question is: How much more should you pay for higher growth?

There is no consistent answer. In some periods, as in the early 1960s and 1970s, when growth was thought to be especially desirable, the market has been willing to pay an enormous price for stocks exhibiting high growth rates. At other times, such as the early 1980s, high-growth stocks commanded only a modest premium over the multiples of common stocks in general.

The point is illustrated in the following table. IBM has consistently sold at a much higher multiple than the market. But the differential in multiples has been quite volatile. IBM's multiple was over three times that of the market in December 1961. Five months later it was not even two times as great. At the low points in the market in 1970 and especially in 1980, IBM sold at only very small premiums over the general market.

Price-Earnings Multiples for IBM and for
the Market in General[a]

| | P/E Multiples | | Premium: IBM P/E |
	IBM	S&P Index	as a % of S&P P/E
Market Peak 1961	64	20	320%
Market Low 1962	29	16	181
Market Peak 1968	50	18	278
Market Low 1970	25	16	156
Market Peak 1972	44	17	259
Market Low 1980	9	7	129

[a]As measured by Standard & Poor's Industrial Index (425-Stock Index
through 1972, 400-Stock Index for 1980 figures).

A similar way of looking at the changing premiums paid for
growth stocks since 1959 is shown in the following chart, which
graphs the premiums for the Babson 28 Growth Stocks compared
with the stocks of Standard & Poor's 500-Stock Index. The chart
tells a disappointing story for anyone looking for a consistent
long-term valuation relationship. Growth can be as fashionable
as tulip bulbs, as investors in growth stocks painfully learned in
the 1970s. During the Nifty Fifty craze, growth stocks reached
their highest valuations relative to the market as a whole. During
the first half of the 1980s, the premium for growth was lower than
at any time during the preceding twenty years.

From a practical standpoint, the rapid changes in market
valuations that have occurred suggest that it would be very
dangerous to use any one year's valuation relationships as an indication of market norms. However, by comparing how growth
stocks are currently valued with historical precedent, investors
should at least be able to isolate those periods when a touch of the
tulip bug has smitten investors. When the first edition of this
book was published in 1973, I warned that growth stocks were
extremely richly priced and that investors should approach these
stocks with extraordinary care. In my *Inflation Beater's Invest-*

The Premium for Growth Stocks (P/E of Babson 28 Growth Stocks Relative to S&P 500-Stock Index)

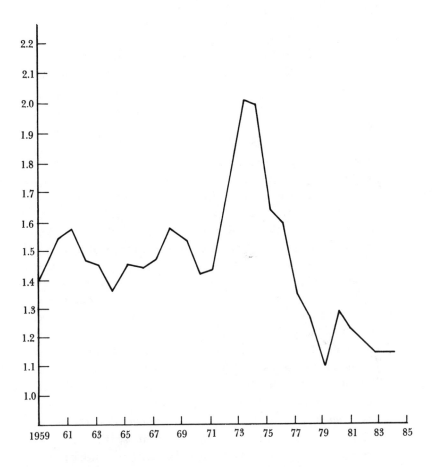

ment Guide, published in 1980, I suggested that growth stocks appeared to offer attractive value relative to the market. Although the quality growth stocks such as IBM performed very well during the first half of the 1980s, their earnings multiples are still modest and thus they continue to represent good value in the market as of early 1985.

What's Left of the Firm Foundation?

A renowned rabbi, whose fame for adjudicating disputes had earned him the reputation of a modern-day Solomon, was asked to settle a long-standing argument between two philosophers. The rabbi listened intently as the first disputant vigorously presented his case. The rabbi reflected on the argument and finally pronounced, "Yes, you are correct." Then the second philosopher presented his case with equal vigor and persuasion and argued eloquently that the first philosopher could not be correct. The rabbi nodded his approval and indicated, "You are correct." A bystander, somewhat confused by this performance, accosted the rabbi to complain, "You told both philosophers they were right, but their arguments were totally contradictory. They both can't be correct." The rabbi needed only a moment to formulate his response: "Yes, you are indeed correct."

In adjudicating the dispute between the firm-foundation theorists and those who take a castle-in-the-air view of the stock market, I feel a little like the accommodating rabbi. It seems clear that so-called "fundamental" considerations do have a profound influence on market prices. We have seen that price-earnings multiples in the market are influenced by expected growth, dividend payouts, risk, and the rate of interest. Higher anticipations of earnings growth and higher dividend payouts tend to increase price-earnings multiples. Higher risk and higher interest rates tend to pull them down. There is a logic to the stock market, just as the firm foundationists assert.

Thus, when all is said and done, it appears that there is a yardstick for value, but one that is a most flexible and undependable instrument. To change the metaphor, stock prices are in a sense anchored to certain "fundamentals" but the anchor is easily pulled up and then dropped in another place. For the standards of value, we have found, are not the fixed and immutable standards that characterize the laws of physics, but rather the more flexible and fickle relationships that are consistent with a marketplace heavily influenced by mass psychology.

Not only does the market change the values it puts on the various fundamental determinants of stock prices, but the most important of these fundamentals are themselves liable to change depending on the state of market psychology. Stocks are bought on expectations — not on facts.

The most important fundamental influence on stock prices is the level and duration of the future growth of corporate earnings and dividends. But, as I pointed out earlier, future earnings growth is not easily estimated, even by market professionals. In times of great optimism it is very easy for investors to convince themselves that their favorite corporations can enjoy substantial and persistent growth over an extended period of time. By raising his estimates of growth, even the most sober firm-foundation theorist can convince himself to pay any price whatever for a share.

During periods of extreme pessimism, many security analysts will not project any growth that is not "visible" to them over the very short run and hence will estimate only the most modest of growth rates for the corporations they follow. But if expected growth rates themselves and the price the market is willing to pay for this growth can both change rapidly on the basis of market psychology, then it is clear that the concept of a *firm* intrinsic value for shares must be an elusive will-o'-the-wisp. As an old Wall Street proverb runs: No price is too high for a bull or too low for a bear.

Dreams of castles in the air, of getting rich quick, may therefore play an important role in determining actual stock prices. And even investors who believe in the firm-foundation theory might buy a security on the anticipation that eventually the average opinion would expect a larger growth rate for the stock in the future. After all, investors who want to reap extraordinary profits may find that the most profitable course of action is to beat the gun and anticipate future changes in the intrinsic value of shares.

Still, this analysis suggests that the stock market will not be a perpetual tulip-bulb craze. The existence of some generally accepted principles of valuation does serve as a kind of balance wheel. For the castle-in-the-air investor might well consider that if prices get too far out of line with normal valuation standards, the average opinion may soon expect that others will anticipate a reaction. To be sure, these standards of value are extremely loose ones and difficult to estimate. But sooner or later in a skyrocketing market, some investors may begin to compare the growth rates that are implicit in current prices with more reasonable and dispassionate estimates of the growth likely to be achieved.

It seems eminently sensible to me that both views of security pricing tell us something about actual market behavior. But the important investment question is how you can use the theories to develop practically useful investment strategies. More about this in Part Two, where we take a close look at how the professionals use the two theories in their own investing, and in Part Three, where we examine the academic approach to investing.

How the Pros Play the Biggest Game in Town

CHAPTER FIVE

Technical and Fundamental Analysis

A picture is worth ten thousand words — Old Chinese proverb.

On one hot August day in 1984, 236 million shares, with a value of about $10 billion, were traded on the New York Stock Exchange. Exchanges of shares valued at $4 billion are now considered routine for a day's trading on the big board. And this is only part of the story. A large volume of trading is also carried out on the American Stock Exchange, on the over-the-counter markets, and on a variety of regional exchanges across the country. Professional investment analysts and counselors are involved in what has been called the biggest game in town.

If the stakes are high, so are the rewards. New trainees from the Harvard Business School and the Yale School of Management routinely draw salaries of well over $50,000 per year. Experienced security analysts and successful salesmen, euphemistically called "account executives," make considerably more. At the top of the salary scale are the money managers themselves — the men who run the large mutual, pension, and trust funds. "Adam Smith," after writing *The Money Game*, the number-one best-seller of 1968, boasted that he would make a quarter of a million dollars from his book. His Wall Street friends retorted, "You're only going to make as much as a second-rate institutional sales-man." Admittedly, the depression that hit Wall Street during the 1970s and the change from fixed to negotiated brokerage com-missions have made such talk appear somewhat overstated. Still, it is fair to conclude that while not the oldest, the profession of high finance is certainly one of the most generously compensated.

Part Two of this book concentrates on the methods and results of the professionals of Wall Street, State Street, Mont-gomery Street, and the various road-town financial centers. It then shows how academics in sleepy towns like Princeton and hazy towns like Berkeley analyze these professional results and conclude that they are not worth the money you pay for them.

Academicians are a notoriously picayune lot. With their ringing motto, "Publish or perish," they keep themselves busy by preparing papers demolishing other people's theories, defending their own work, or constructing elaborate embellishments to generally accepted ideas.

The random-walk, or efficient-market, theory is a case in point. We now have three versions—the "weak," the "semi-strong," and the "strong." All three espouse the general idea that except for long-run trends, future stock prices are difficult, if not impossible, to predict. The weak says you cannot predict future stock prices on the basis of past stock prices. The semi-strong says you cannot even utilize published information to predict future prices. The strong goes flat out and says that nothing—not even unpublished developments—can be of use in predicting future prices; everything that is known, or even knowable, has already been reflected in present prices. The weak form attacks the underpinnings of technical analysis, and the semi-strong and strong forms argue against many of the beliefs held by those using fundamental analysis.

Technical versus Fundamental Analysis

The attempt to predict accurately the future course of stock prices and thus the appropriate time to buy or sell a stock must rank as one of man's most persistent endeavors. This search for the golden egg has spawned a variety of methods ranging from the scientific to the occult. There are people today who forecast future stock prices by measuring sunspots, looking at the phases of the moon, or measuring the vibrations along the San Andreas Fault. Most, however, opt for one of two methods: technical or fundamental analysis.

The alternative techniques used by the investment pros are related to the two theories of the stock market I covered in Part One. Technical analysis is the method of predicting the appropriate time to buy or sell a stock used by those believing in the castle-in-the-air view of stock pricing. Fundamental analysis is the technique of applying the tenets of the firm-foundation theory to the selection of individual stocks.

Technical analysis is essentially the making and interpreting of stock charts. Thus its practitioners, a small but abnormally dedicated cult, are called chartists. They study the past — both the movements of common stock prices and the volume of trading — for a clue to the direction of future change. Most chartists believe that the market is only 10 percent logical and 90 percent psychological. They generally subscribe to the castle-in-the-air school and view the investment game as one of anticipating how the other players will behave. Charts, of course, tell only what the other players have been doing in the past. The chartist's hope, however, is that a careful study of what the other players are doing will shed light on what the crowd is likely to do in the future.

Fundamental analysts take the opposite tack, believing the market to be 90 percent logical and only 10 percent psychological. Caring little about the particular pattern of past price movement, fundamentalists seek to determine an issue's proper value. Value in this case is related to growth, dividend payout, and risk, according to the rules of the firm-foundation theory outlined in the last chapter. By estimating such factors as growth for each company, the fundamentalist arrives at an estimate of a security's intrinsic value. If this is above the market price, then the investor is advised to buy. Fundamentalists believe that eventually the market will reflect accurately the security's real worth. Perhaps 90 percent of the Wall Street security analysts consider themselves fundamentalists. Many would argue that chartists are lacking in dignity and professionalism.

What Can Charts Tell You?

The first principle of technical analysis is that all information about earnings, dividends, and the future performance of a company is automatically reflected in the company's past market prices. A chart showing these prices and the volume of trading already comprises all the fundamental information, good or bad, that the security analyst can hope to know. The second principle is that prices tend to move in trends: a stock that is rising tends to keep on rising, whereas a stock at rest tends to remain at rest.

A true chartist doesn't even care to know what business or industry a company is in, as long as he can study its stock chart. A chart shaped in the form of an "inverted bowl" or "pennant" means the same for Digital Equipment as it does for IBM. Fundamental information on earnings and dividends is considered at best to be useless — and at worst a positive distraction. It is either of inconsequential importance for the pricing of the stock or, if it is important, it has already been reflected in the market days, weeks, or even months before the news has become public. For this reason, many chartists will not even read the newspaper except to follow the daily price quotations.

One of the most prominent chartists, John Magee, operated from a small office in Springfield, Massachusetts, where even the windows were boarded up to prevent any outside influences from distracting his analysis. Magee was once quoted as saying, "When

I come into this office I leave the rest of the world outside to concentrate entirely on my charts. This room is exactly the same in a blizzard as on a moonlit June evening. In here I can't possibly do myself and my clients the disservice of saying 'buy' simply because the sun is out or 'sell' because it is raining."

As shown in the figure below, you can easily construct a

chart. You simply draw a vertical line whose bottom is the stock's low for the day and whose top is the high. This line is crossed to indicate the closing price for the day. In the figure, the stock had a range of quotations that day between 20 and 21 and closed at $20\frac{1}{2}$. The process can be repeated for each trading day. It can be used for individual stocks or for one of the stock averages that you see in the financial pages of most newspapers. Often the chartist will also indicate the volume of shares of stock traded during the day by another vertical line at the bottom of the chart. Gradually, the highs and lows on the chart of the stock in question jiggle up and down sufficiently to produce patterns. To the chartist, these patterns have the same significance as X-ray plates to a surgeon.

One of the first things the chartist looks for is a trend. The figure below shows one in the making. It is the record of price changes for a stock over a number of days—and the prices are obviously on the way up. The chartist draws two lines connecting the tops and bottoms, creating a "channel" to delineate the

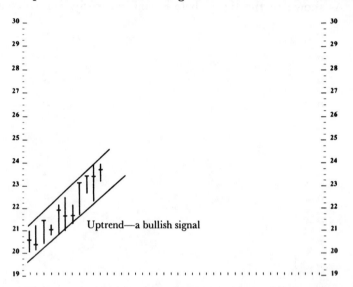

uptrend. Since the presumption is that momentum in the market will tend to perpetuate itself, the chartist interprets such a pattern as a bullish augury—the stock can be expected to continue to rise. As Magee has written in the bible of charting, *Technical Analysis of Stock Trends*, "Prices move in trends, and trends tend to continue until something happens to change the supply-demand balance."

Suppose, however, that at about 24, the stock finally runs into trouble and is unable to gain any further ground. This is called a resistance level. The stock may wiggle around a bit and then turn downward. One pattern, which chartists claim reveals a clear signal that the market has topped out, is a head and shoulders formation. This is shown in the figure below.

The stock first rises and then falls slightly, forming a rounded shoulder. It rises again, going slightly higher, before once more

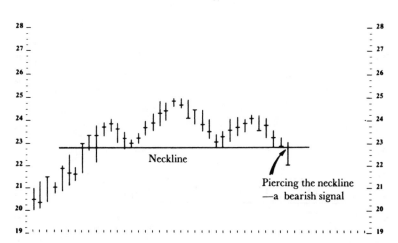

Neckline

Piercing the neckline
—a bearish signal

receding, forming a head. Finally the right shoulder is formed, and chartists wait with bated breath for the sell signal, which sounds loud and clear when the stock "pierces the neckline." With the glee of Count Dracula surveying one of his victims, the chartists are off and selling, anticipating that a prolonged downtrend will follow as it allegedly has in the past. Of course, sometimes the market surprises the chartist. For example, the stock may make an end run up to 30 right after giving a bear signal. This is called a bear trap or, to the chartist, the exception that proves the rule.

It follows from the technique that the chartist is a trader, not a long-term investor. The chartist buys when the auguries look favorable and sells on bad omens. He flirts with stocks just as some flirt with women, and his scores are successful in-and-out trades, not rewarding long-term commitments. Indeed, the psychiatrist Dr. Don D. Jackson, author with Albert Haas, Jr. of *Bulls, Bears and Dr. Freud*, has suggested that such an individual may be playing a game with overt sexual overtones.

When the chartist chooses a stock for potential investment there is typically a period of observation and flirtation before he commits himself, since for the chartist—as in romance and sexual conquest—timing is essential. There is mounting excitement as the stock penetrates the base formation and rises higher.

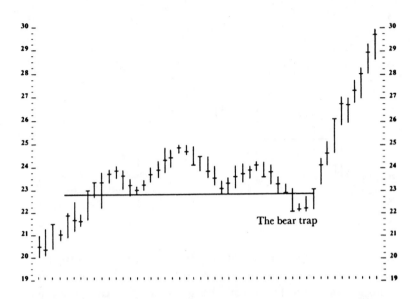

The bear trap

Finally, if the affair has gone well, there is the moment of fulfill-ment—profit-taking, and the release and afterglow that follow. The chartist's vocabularly features such terms as double bottoms, breakthrough, violating the lows, firmed up, big play, ascending peaks, and buying climax. And all this takes place under the pennant of that great symbol of sexuality: the bull.

The Rationale for the Charting Method

Probably the hardest question to answer is: Why is charting supposed to work? Some of my best friends are chartists and I have listened very carefully to their explanations, but I have yet really to understand them. Indeed, many chartists freely admit *they* don't know why charting should work—history just has a habit of repeating itself. Even Magee, the chartist seer, goes so far as to say that we can never hope to know "why" the market behaves as it does, we can only aspire to understand "how."

According to Magee, the situation in the stock market is

analogous to that of a pig in a barn. The barn is all closed up on the ground floor, but it has a hayloft above with a large open door. The pig has a harness around his body to which is attached a long pole, the top of which is visible through the hayloft door. Of course, when the pig moves about, so will the pole. Magee supposes that we are perched in a nearby tree observing the motions of the top of the pole, which is all we can see. We must deduce from the pole's movement what is happening below, just as market participants must deduce what is happening in the market from the price movements they can observe. Magee goes on to say that it is not important to know the color or size of the pig . . . or even whether it is a pig at all; it is only important to be able to make predictions about the next movement of the pole.

> Some of the watchers who are not comfortable with highly abstract symbols will assign "meanings" to the pole's movements. They will try to "interpret" these movements as corresponding to various assimilative, combative, copulative, etc., actions of the pig. Others, [like Magee, the author] who might consider themselves "pure technicians," will watch the pole, and work entirely on the basis of what the pole has done, is doing, or might be expected to do according to trends, repetitive motions, extrapolations, etc.

Yet it is in our nature to ask why. To me, the following explanations of technical analysis appear to be the most plausible. Trends might tend to perpetuate themselves for either of two reasons. First, it has been argued that the crowd instinct of mass psychology makes it so. When investors see the price of a speculative favorite going higher and higher, they want to jump on the bandwagon and join the rise. Indeed, the price rise itself helps fuel the enthusiasm in a self-fulfilling prophecy. Each rise in price just whets the appetite and makes investors expect a further rise.

Second, there may be unequal access to fundamental information about a company. When some favorable piece of news occurs, such as the discovery of a rich mineral deposit, it is alleged that the insiders are the first to know and they act, buying the stock and causing its price to rise. The insiders then tell their friends, who act next. Then the professionals find out the news and the big institutions put blocks of the shares in their portfolios. Finally, the poor slobs like you and me get the information and buy, pushing the price still higher. This process is supposed to result in a rather gradual increase in the price of the stock when the news is good and a decrease when the news is bad. Chartists claim that this scenario is somewhat close to what actually happened in the notorious Texas Gulf Sulphur case, and that even if they do not have access to this inside information, observation of price movements alone enables them to pick up the scent of the "smart money" and permits them to get in long before the general public.

Chartists believe that another reason their techniques have validity is that people have a nasty habit of remembering what they paid for a stock, or the price they *wish* they had paid. For example, suppose a stock sold for about $50 a share for a long period of time, during which a number of investors bought in. Suppose then that the price drops to $40.

The chartists claim that the public will be anxious to sell out the shares when they rise back to the price at which they were bought, and thus break even on the trade. Consequently, the price of $50 at which the stock sold initially becomes a "resistance area." Each time the resistance area is reached and the stock turns down again, the theory holds that the resistance level becomes even harder to cross, because more and more investors get the idea that the market or the individual stock in question cannot go any higher.

A similar argument lies behind the notion of "support levels." Chartists say that many investors who failed to buy when the market fluctuated around a relatively low price level will feel they have missed the boat when prices rise. Presumably such investors will jump at the chance to buy when prices drop back to the original low level.

Chartists also believe that investors who sold shares when the market was low and then saw prices rise will be anxious to buy those shares back if they can get them again at the price for which they sold. The argument then is that the original low price level becomes a "support area," since investors will believe that prices will again rise above that level. In chart theory, a "support area" that holds on successive declines becomes stronger and stronger. So if a stock declines to a support area and then begins to rise, the traders will jump in believing the stock is just "coming off the pad." Another bullish signal is flashed when a stock finally breaks through a resistance area. In the lexicon of the chartists, the former resistance area becomes a support area, and the stock should have no trouble gaining further ground.

Why Might Charting Fail to Work?

It is easier for me to present the *logical* arguments against charting. First, it should be noted that the chartist buys in only after price trends have been established, and sells only after they have been broken. Since sharp reversals in the market may occur quite suddenly, the chartist will often miss the boat. By the time an uptrend is signaled it may already have taken place. Second, such techniques must ultimately be self-defeating. As more and more people use it, the value of any technique depreciates. No buy or sell signal can be worthwhile if everyone tries to act on it simultaneously.

Moreover, traders will tend to anticipate technical signals. If they see a price about to break through a resistance area, they will tend to buy before, not after, it breaks through. If it ever was profitable to use such charting techniques, it will now be possible only for those who anticipate the signals. This suggests that others will try to anticipate the signal still earlier. Of course, the earlier they anticipate, the less certain they are that the signal will occur, and in the scrambling to anticipate signals it is doubtful that any profitable technical trading rules can be developed.

Perhaps the most telling argument against technical methods comes from the logical implications of profit-maximizing behavior on the part of investors. Suppose, for example, that

Universal Polymers is selling at around 20 when Sam, the chief research chemist, discovers a new production technique that promises to double the company's earnings and stock price. Now Sam is convinced that the price of Universal will hit 40 when the news of his discovery comes out. Since any purchases below 40 will provide a swift profit, he may well buy up all the stock he can until the price hits 40, a process that could take no longer than a few minutes.

Even if Sam doesn't have enough money to drive up the price himself, surely his friends and the financial institutions do have the funds to move the price so rapidly that no chartist could get into the act before the whole play is gone. The point is that the market may well be a most efficient mechanism. If some people know that the price will go to 40 tomorrow, it will go to 40 today. Of course if Sam makes a public announcement of his discovery as the law requires, the argument holds with even greater force. Prices may adjust so quickly to new information as to make the whole process of technical analysis a futile exercise. In the next chapter, I'll examine whether the evidence supports such a pessimistic view of charting.

From Chartist to Technician

Though chartists are not held in high repute in Wall Street their colorful methods, suggesting an easy way to get rich quick, have attracted a wide following. The companies that manufacture and distribute stock charts and charting paper have enjoyed a boom in their sales; and chartists themselves, still find excellent employment opportunities with mutual funds and brokerage firms.

In the days before the computer, the laborious task of charting a course through the market was done by hand. Chartists were often viewed as peculiar men, with green eyeshades and carbon on their fingers, who were tucked away in a small closet at the back of the office. Now chartists have the services of a marvelous electronic computer, replete with a large display terminal which, at the tap of a finger, can produce any conceivable chart one might want to see. The chartist (now always called a technican) can, with the glee of a little child playing with a new electric train, produce a complete chart of a stock's past performance, including measures of volume, the 200-day moving average (an average of prices over the previous 200 days recalculated each day), the strength of the stock relative to the market and relative to its industry, and literally hundreds of other averages, ratios, oscillators, and indicators.

Once the chart has been thus displayed, another press of the button will make a Xerox copy of the entire picture, which may be studied further on the train back to Larchmont and later tacked on one of the bulletin boards around the room. The result is akin to the Pentagon war room. One mutual fund was known to concentrate its technical information in what it called "information central." The computer also adds an aura of mystery and wonder to charting. Even if the chartist's techniques are unscientific, it is difficult to make fun of the computer, and some of the public's awe and admiration for computers has rubbed off on the technical analysts. While there is not, to my knowledge, a "Chartists' Liberation Movement," technicians have now come out of their closets and have received newfound recognition and approval.

The Technique of Fundamental Analysis

Fred Schwed, Jr., in his charming and witty exposé of the financial community in the 1930s, *Where Are the Customers' Yachts?*, tells of a Texas broker who sold some stock to a customer at $760 a share at the moment when it could have been purchased anywhere else at $730. When the outraged customer found out what had happened, he complained bitterly to the broker. The Texan cut him short, "Suh," he boomed, "you-all don't appreciate the policy of this firm. This heah firm selects investments foh its clients not on the basis of Price, but of Value."

In a sense, this story illustrates the difference between the technician and the fundamentalist. The technician is interested only in the record of the stock's price, whereas the fundamentalist's primary concern is with what a stock is really worth. The fundamentalist strives to be relatively immune to the optimism and pessimism of the crowd and makes a sharp distinction between a stock's current price and its true value.

In estimating the firm-foundation value of a security, the fundamentalist's most important job is to estimate the firm's future stream of earnings and dividends. To do this, he or she must estimate the firm's sales level, operating costs, corporate tax rates, depreciation policies, and the sources and costs of its capital requirements.

Basically, the security analyst must be a prophet without the benefit of divine inspiration. As a poor substitute, the analyst turns to a study of the past record of the company, a review of the company's investment plans, and a firsthand visit to and appraisal of the company's management team. This yields a wealth of data. The analyst must then separate the important from the unimportant facts. As Benjamin Graham put it in *The Intelligent Investor*, "Sometimes he reminds us a bit of the erudite major general in 'The Pirates of Penzance,' with his 'many cheerful facts about the square of the hypotenuse.'"

Since the general prospects of a company are strongly influenced by the economic position of its industry, the obvious starting point for the security analyst is a study of industry prospects. Indeed, in almost all professional investment firms, security analysts specialize in particular industry groups. The fundamentalist hopes that a thorough study of industry conditions will produce valuable insights into factors that may be operative in the future but are not yet reflected in market prices.

A brief, but deadly, example will help illustrate the process. It involves a research study undertaken late in 1980 by the investment firm of Smith, Barney & Co. The analysis covered the funeral service industry and the prospects for Service Corporation International, a small company in the industry.

The report first gave a broad picture of the funeral service industry. Demand for the industry's services is governed by an indisputable fact: we all die. Thanks to the abundance of data gathered by the U.S. Census, it is easy to estimate the industry's potential market. You just look at the number of people in various age categories and then multiply by the mortality rate for each age group. The Smith, Barney report presented two tables, based on Census data, that showed the mortality rate rising until the year 2000. The grim fact is that funeral services is a growth industry. The Smith, Barney report also pointed out that the industry was highly fragmented, consisting of small, family-owned and -operated companies averaging about $150,000 in annual revenues. Because of their small size, most operations could not take advantage of economies of sale and were not well suited to professional management techniques.

The report then turned to an analysis of Service Corporation International, which at the time operated 189 funeral homes. Not only was this the largest organization in the industry, its revenues of $550,000 per unit were more than three times the national average. Management, of course, is key to any firm's profitability, and in this case the executives had decided to make the company an industry leader through selective acquisitions and the introduction of professional management practices. This decision was not being executed with a sledge hammer. Rather, generous financial incentives were used to encourage the principals of all acquired firms to remain, and a decentralized management system was put in effect. Service Corporation International believed its advanced managerial approach was unique within the industry and the Smith, Barney report did not contradict this assumption.

The report went on to note the particular innovations made by Service Corporation's management. Its relatively large size permitted it to take advantage of centralized purchasing power for all its supplies from caskets to floral arrangements. The latter aspect of the business was particularly profitable. Service

Corp. opened floral shops in all of its larger funeral homes. Since almost half of all floral sales are funeral related, these shops gave the company a substantial captive market. In addition, the company pioneered in marketing prearranged funeral services where customers make downpayments in advance for future funeral services. These "pre-need" sales had two important advantages for Service Corp.:(1) they assured continuing volume stability and future revenue growth and (2) they produced interest earnings on the prearranged payments, which became a major source of the company's earnings.

For the preceding decade, Service Corp.'s sales and earnings per share had grown at better than a 15 percent rate. The Smith, Barney report projected that future growth would be at least as large, particularly since Service Corp.'s management had positioned the company to increase its share of the market. This, plus the fact that the company's stock was selling at a P/E multiple 40 percent below that of the S&P 500, indicated that the stock's price was below reasonable estimates of its firm foundation of value.

Recall that the first principle of valuation of the firm-foundation theory is that a stock is worth more—should sell at a higher price-earnings multiple—the larger its anticipated rate of growth. In late 1980, Service Corporation International sold at a price-earnings ratio of 5, while the price-earnings multiple for the market as a whole was approximately 9. The expected growth rate of earnings and dividends for the market as a whole in 1980 was less than 10 percent, but Service Corp. was expected to grow at a rate of better than 15 percent; hence, by our first valuation principle, it deserved to sell at a *higher* multiple than that of the market as a whole. Since the stock actually sold at a lower multiple than that of the market (5 versus 9), it could be considered undervalued.

Of course, other principles of valuation mentioned in Chapter Four were also relevant. By the second principle, stocks are worth more to investors, other things being the same, if the company can finance its growth and still pay out a reasonable share of its earnings in dividends. On this score, one could probably justify a bit of a discount for Service Corp., since its dividend yield (based on the estimated dividend for 1980) was only about half of that for the market as a whole. Still, on balance, the extraordinary growth potential of the company had to be the dominant factor for valuation.

The firm-foundation theory also suggests that the riskier a stock, the lower the multiple it should sell at. While it is true that Service Corp. was a small company and thus riskier than some of the more established blue-chip companies, other aspects of its business actually made it less risky than the general market. Service Corp. had a great deal of resistance to economic downturns, since people do not stop dying during recessions. Moreover, it dealt in those markets where the parameters of growth could be relatively precisely defined. Hence, on this score, Service Corp. would deserve a premium multiple to the market.

It is also possible to use the empirical relationships discussed in Chapter Four to argue that Service Corp. represented a good value. In 1980, when the analysis was made, stocks for which a 15 percent rate of growth was expected sold, on average, at over 15 times earnings, and Service Corp.'s multiple was only one-third of that. This further enhanced its appeal and made it an excellent candidate for multiple improvement. For all these reasons, Smith, Barney recommended purchase of Service Corporation International.

The Smith, Barney report represents the technique of fundamental analysis at its finest. People who followed its "buy" advice found that Service Corp. enjoyed much better performance than the market, at least into the mid-1980s. Here was an example of research that would have made even John Houseman proud.

Why Might Fundamental Analysis Fail to Work?

Despite its plausibility and scientific appearance, there are three potential flaws in this type of analysis. First, the information and analysis may be incorrect. Second, the security analyst's estimate of "value" may be faulty. Third, the market may not correct its "mistake" and the stock price might not converge to its value estimate.

The security analyst traveling from company to company and consulting with industry specialists will receive a great deal of fundamental information. Some critics have suggested that, taken as a whole, this information will be worthless. What investors make on the valid news (assuming it is not yet recognized by the market) they lose on the bad information. Moreover, the analyst wastes considerable effort in collecting the information and investors pay heavy brokerage fees in trying to act on it. To make matters even worse, the security analyst may be unable to translate correct facts into accurate estimates of earnings for several years into the future. A faulty analysis of valid information could throw estimates of the rate of growth of earnings and dividends far wide of the mark.

The second problem is that even if the information is correct and its implications for future growth are properly assessed, the analyst might make a faulty value estimate. We have already seen how difficult it is to translate specific estimates of growth and other valuation factors into a single estimate of intrinsic value. Recall the widely different estimates of the value for IBM shown in Chapter Four. I have suggested earlier that the attempt to obtain a precise measure of intrinsic value may be an unrewarding search for a will-o'-the-wisp. Thus, even if the security analyst's estimates of growth are correct, this information may already be reflected accurately by the market, and any difference between a security's price and value may result simply from an incorrect estimate of value.

The final problem is that even with correct information and value estimates, the stock you buy might still go down. For example, suppose that Biodegradable Bottling Company is selling at 20 times earnings, and the analyst estimates that it can sustain a long-term growth rate of 25 percent. If, on average, stocks with 25 percent anticipated growth rate are selling at 30 times earnings, the fundamentalist might conclude that Biodegradable was a "cheap stock" and recommend purchase.

But suppose, a few months later, stocks with 25 percent growth rates are selling in the market at only 20 times earnings. Even if the analyst was absolutely correct in his growth rate estimate, his customers might suffer badly because the market revalued its estimates of what growth stocks in general were worth. The market might correct its "mistake" by revaluing all stocks downward, rather than raising the price for Biodegradable Bottling.

And as the chart in Chapter Four indicated, such changes in valuation are not extraordinary—these are the routine fluctuations in market sentiment that have been experienced in the past. Not only can the average multiple change rapidly for stocks in general but the market can also dramatically change the premium assigned to growth. Both these phenomena were important during the early 1970s. It became apparent that accurately forecasting future earnings and dividend growth provided no guarantees: even the most successful growth companies of the early 1970s turned in miserable price performances from 1972 on because of the devastating fall in earnings multiples, especially for rapidly growing companies. Clearly, then, one should not take the success of fundamental analysis for granted.

Using Fundamental and Technical Analysis Together

Many analysts use a combination of techniques to judge whether individual stocks are attractive for purchase. One of the most sensible procedures can easily be summarized by the following three rules. The persistent, patient reader will recognize that the rules are based on principles of stock pricing I have developed in the previous chapters.

Rule 1: Buy only companies that are expected to have above-average earnings growth for five or more years. An extraordinary long-run earnings growth rate is the single most important element contributing to the success of most stock investments. IBM, Xerox, American Home Products, Service Corporation International, and practically all the other really outstanding common stocks of the past were growth stocks. As difficult as the job may be, picking stocks whose earnings grow is the name of the game. Consistent growth not only increases the earnings and dividends of the company but may also increase the multiple that the market is willing to pay for those earnings. Thus the purchaser of a stock whose earnings begin to grow rapidly has a chance at a *potential* double benefit—both the earnings *and* the multiple may increase.

Rule 2: Never pay more for a stock than its firm foundation of value. While I have argued, and I hope persuasively, that you can never judge the exact intrinsic value of a stock, many analysts feel that you can roughly gauge when a stock seems to be reasonably priced. Generally, the earnings multiple for the market as a whole is a helpful benchmark. Growth stocks selling at multiples in line with or not very much above this multiple often represent good value. Service Corp. in the study just described is a good example. Its multiple was actually below the market's.

There are important advantages to buying growth stocks at very reasonable earnings multiples. If your growth estimate turns out to be correct you may get the double bonus I mentioned in connection with Rule 1: The price will tend to go up simply because the earnings went up, but also the multiple is likely to expand in recognition of the growth rate that is established. Hence the double bonus. Suppose, for example, you buy a stock earning $1 per share and selling at $7.50. If the earnings grow to $2 per share and if the price-earnings multiple increases from $7\frac{1}{2}$ to 15 (in recognition that the company now can be considered a growth stock) you don't just double your money—you quadruple it. That's because your $7.50 stock will be worth $30 (15, the multiple, times $2, the earnings).

Now consider the other side of the coin. There are special risks involved in buying "growth stocks" where the market has already recognized the growth and has bid up the price-earnings multiple to a hefty premium over that accorded more run-of-the-mill stocks. Stocks like International Flavors and Fragrances,

Avon Products, and other recognized growth companies had earnings multiples well above 50 when the first edition of *Random Walk* came out. The warning was made very clear that the risks with very-high-multiple stocks were enormously high.

The problem is that the very high multiples may already fully reflect the growth that is anticipated, and if the growth does not materialize and earnings in fact go down (or even grow more slowly than expected), you will take a very unpleasant bath. The double benefits that are possible if the earnings of low-multiple stocks grow can become double damages if the earnings of high-multiple stocks decline. When earnings fall the multiple is likely to crash as well. But the crash won't be so loud if the multiple wasn't that high in the first place. Reread the grim stories of National Student Marketing and Four Seasons Nursing or of the Nifty Fifty growth stocks in Chapter Three if you want more evidence of the enormous risks involved with very-high-multiple stocks.

What is proposed, then, is a strategy of buying unrecognized growth stocks whose earnings multiples are not at any substantial premium over the market. Of course, it is very hard to predict growth. But even if the growth does not materialize and earnings decline, the damage is likely to be only single if the multiple is low to begin with, while the benefits may double if things do turn out as you expected. This is an extra way to put the odds in your favor.

We can summarize the discussion thus far by restating the first two rules: *Look for growth situations with low-price earnings multiples. If the growth takes place there's often a double bonus—both the earnings and the multiple rise, producing large gains. Beware of very-high-multiple stocks where future growth is already discounted. If growth doesn't materialize, losses are doubly heavy—both the earnings and the multiple drop.*

Rule 3: Look for stocks whose stories of anticipated growth are of the kind on which investors can build castles in the air. I have stressed the importance of psychological elements in stock price determination. Individual and institutional investors are not computers that calculate warranted price-earnings multiples and print out buy and sell decisions. They are emotional human beings—driven by greed, gambling instincts, hope, and fear in their stock-market decisions. This is why successful investing demands both intellectual and psychological acuteness.

Stocks that produce "good vibes" in the minds of investors can sell at premium multiples for long periods even if the growth rate is only average. Those not so blessed may sell at low multiples for long periods even if their growth rate is above average. To be sure, if a growth rate appears to be established, the stock is almost certain to attract some type of following. The market is not irrational. But stocks are like people—what stimulates one may leave another cold, and the multiple improvement may be smaller and slower to be realized if the story never catches on.

So Rule 3 says to ask yourself whether the story about your stock is one that is likely to catch the fancy of the crowd. Is it a story from which contagious dreams can be generated? Is it a story on which investors can build castles in the air—but castles in the air that really rest on a firm foundation?

You don't have to be a technician to follow Rule 3. You might simply use your intuition or speculative sense to judge whether the "story" on your stock is likely to catch the fancy of the crowd—particularly the notice of institutional investors. Technical analysts, however, would look for some tangible evidence before they could be convinced that the investment idea was, in fact, catching on. This tangible evidence is, of course, the beginning of an uptrend or a technical signal that could "reliably" predict that an uptrend would develop.

While the rules I have outlined seem sensible, the important question is whether they really work. After all, lots of other people are playing the game and it is by no means obvious that anyone can win consistently.

In the next two chapters I shall look at the actual record. Chapter Six asks the question: Does technical analysis work? Chapter Seven looks at the performance record of fundamentalists. Together they should help us evaluate how well professional investment people do their job and what value we should put on their advice.

CHAPTER SIX

Technical Analysis and the Random-Walk Theory

> Things are seldom what they seem. Skim milk masquerades as cream. — Gilbert and Sullivan, *H.M.S. Pinafore*

Not earnings, nor dividends, nor risk, nor gloom of high interest rates stay the chartists from their assigned task: studying the price movements of stocks. Such singleminded devotion to numbers has somehow yielded the most colorful theories and has produced much of the folk language of Wall Street:

"Hold the winners, sell the losers."

"Switch into the strong stocks."

"Sell this issue, it's acting poorly."

"Don't fight the tape."

All are popular prescriptions of technical analysts as they cheerfully collect their brokerage fees for churning your account.

Technical analysts build their strategies upon dreams of castles in the air and expect their tools to tell them which castle is being built and how to get in on the ground floor. The question is: Do they work?

Holes in Their Shoes and
Ambiguity in Their Forecasts

University professors are sometimes asked by their students, "If you're so smart, why aren't you rich?" The question usually rankles professors, who think of themselves as passing up worldly riches to engage in such an obviously socially useful occupation as teaching. The same question might more appropriately be addressed to technicians. For, after all, the whole point of technical analysis is to make money, and one would reasonably expect that those who preach it should practice it successfully in their own investments.

On close examination, technicians are often seen with holes in their shoes and frayed shirt collars. I, personally, have never known a successful technician, but I have seen the wrecks of several unsuccessful ones. (This is, of course, in terms of following their own technical advice. Commissions from urging customers to act on their recommendations are very lucrative.) Curiously, however, the broke technician is never apologetic about his method. If anything, he is more enthusiastic than ever. If you commit the social error of asking him why he is broke, he will tell you quite ingenuously that he made the all-too-human error of not believing his own charts. To my great embarrassment, I once choked conspicuously at the dinner table of a chartist friend of mine when he made such a comment. I have since made it a rule never to eat with a chartist. It's bad for digestion.

When Joseph Granville, probably the best known and most followed chartist of the early 1980s, was asked how his "foolproof" system had led him to make some egregious errors during the 1970s, he answered calmly that he was "on drugs" during that period and simply had not paid proper attention to his charts. The "drug" in his case was golf and Granville was convinced that his joining "golfers anonymous" had made him a born-again savior. He believed that he would never again, for the rest of his life, "make a serious mistake on the stock market."

When asked why he didn't simply use his system to play the market himself and thereby make a fortune, he exclaimed that his mission in life was to enrich others, not himself: "Everyone I touch I make rich."*

While technicians might not get rich following their own advice, their store of words is precious indeed. Consider this advice offered by one technical service:

> The market's rise after a period of reaccumulation is a bullish sign. Nevertheless, fulcrum characteristics are not yet clearly present and a resistance area exists 40 points higher in the Dow, so it is clearly premature to say the next leg of the bull market is up. If, in the coming weeks, a test of the lows holds and the market breaks out of its flag, a further rise would be indicated. Should the lows be violated, a continuation of the intermediate term downtrend is called for. In view of the current situation, it is a distinct possibility that traders will sit in the wings awaiting a clearer delineation of the trend and the market will move in a narrow trading range.

If you ask me exactly what all this means, I'm afraid I cannot tell you, but I think the technician probably had the following in mind: "If the market does not go up or go down, it will remain unchanged." Even the weather forecaster can do better than that.

Obviously, I'm biased against the chartist. This is not only a personal predilection but a professional one as well. Technical analysis is anathema to the academic world. We love to pick on it. Our bullying tactics are prompted by two considerations: (1) the method is patently false and (2) it's easy to pick on. And while it may seem a bit unfair to pick on such a sorry target, just remember: it's your money we are trying to save.

While the advent of the large-scale electronic computer

---

*Granville predicted not only stock tremors, but earth tremors as well. In 1980, he predicted that Los Angeles would be destroyed in May 1981 by an earthquake measuring 8.3 or more on the Richter scale.

may have enhanced the standing of the technician for the time being, it will ultimately prove to be his undoing. Just as fast as the technician creates charts to show where the market is going, the academic gets busy constructing charts showing where the technician has been. Since it's so easy to test all the technical trading rules on the computer, it has become a favorite pastime for academics to see if they really work.

Is There Momentum in the Stock Market?

The technician believes that knowledge of a stock's past behavior can help predict its probable future behavior. In other words, the sequence of price changes prior to any given day is important in predicting the price change for that day. This might be called the wallpaper principle. The technical analyst tries to predict future stock prices just as we might predict that the pattern of wallpaper behind the mirror is the same as the pattern above the mirror. The basic premise is that there are repeatable patterns in space and time.

Chartists believe there is momentum in the market. Supposedly, stocks that have been rising will continue to do so, and those that begin falling will go on sinking. Investors should, therefore, buy stocks that start rising and continue to hold their strong stocks. Should the stock begin to fall or "act poorly," investors are advised to sell.

These technical rules have been tested exhaustively by using stock price data on both major exchanges going back as far as the beginning of the twentieth century. The results reveal conclusively that past movements in stock prices cannot be used to foretell future movements. The stock market has no memory. The central proposition of charting is absolutely false, and investors who follow its precepts will accomplish nothing but increasing substantially the brokerage charges they pay.*

---

*References to all the studies cited may be found in the bibliography.

One set of tests, perhaps the simplest of all, simply compares the price change for a stock in a given period with the price change in a subsequent period. For example, technical lore has it that if the price of a stock rose yesterday it is more likely to rise today. It turns out that the correlation of past price movements with present and future price movements is essentially zero. Last week's price change bears no relationship to the price change this week, and so forth.

Economists have also examined the technician's thesis that there are often sequences of price changes in the same direction over several days (or several weeks or months). Stocks are likened to fullbacks who, once having gained some momentum, can be expected to carry on for a long gain. It turns out that this is simply not the case. Sometimes one gets positive price changes (rising prices) for several days in a row; but sometimes when you are flipping a fair coin you also get a long string of "heads" in a row, and you get sequences of positive (or negative) price changes no more frequently than you can expect random sequences of heads or tails in a row. What are often called "persistent patterns" in the stock market occur no more frequently than the runs of luck in the fortunes of any gambler playing a game of chance. This is what the economist means when he says that stock prices behave as a random walk.

Just What Exactly Is a Random Walk?

To many people this appears to be arrant nonsense. Even the most casual reader of the financial pages can easily spot patterns in the market. For example, look at the stock chart on the following page.

The chart seems to display some obvious patterns. After an initial rise the stock turned down, and once the decline got under way the stock headed persistently downhill. Happily for the bulls, the decline was arrested and the stock had another sustained upward move. One cannot look at a stock chart like

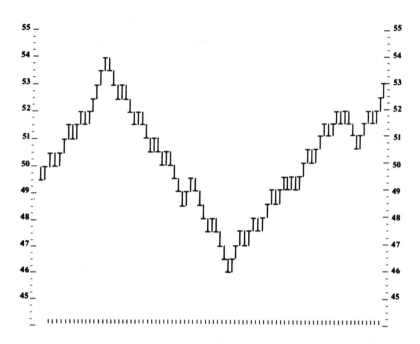

this without realizing the self-evidence of these statements. How can the economist be so myopic that he cannot see what is so plainly visible to the naked eye?

The persistence of this belief in repetitive patterns in the stock market is due to statistical illusion. To illustrate, let me describe an experiment in which I recently asked my students to participate. The students were asked to construct a normal stock chart showing the movements of a hypothetical stock initially selling at $50 per share. For each successive trading day, the closing stock price would be determined by the flip of a fair coin. If the toss was a head, the students assumed that the stock closed ½ point higher than the preceding close. If the flip was a tail, the price was assumed to be down by ½. The chart displayed above was actually the hypothetical stock chart derived from one of these experiments.

The chart derived from random coin tossings looks remarkably like a normal stock price chart and even appears to display cycles. Of course, the pronounced "cycles" that we seem to observe in coin tossings do not occur at regular intervals as true cycles do, but neither do the ups and downs in the stock market.

It is this lack of regularity that is crucial. The "cycles" in the stock charts are no more true cycles than the runs of luck or misfortune of the ordinary gambler. And the fact that stocks seem to be in an uptrend, which looks just like the upward move in some earlier period, provides no useful information on the dependability or duration of the current uptrend. Yes history does tend to repeat itself in the stock market, but in an infinitely surprising variety of ways that confound any attempts to profit from a knowledge of past price patterns.

In other simulated stock charts derived through student coin tossings, there were head-and-shoulders formations, triple tops and bottoms, and other more esoteric chart patterns. One of the charts showed a beautiful upward breakout from an in-verted head and shoulders (a very bullish formation). I showed it to a chartist friend of mine who practically jumped out of his skin. "What is this company?" he exclaimed. "We've got to buy immediately. This pattern's a classic. There's no question the stock will be up 15 points next week." He did not respond kindly to me when I told him the chart had been produced by flipping a coin. Chartists have no sense of humor. I got my comeup-pance when *Business Week* hired a technician, who was adept at hatchet work, to review the first edition of this book.

My students used a completely random process to produce their stock charts. With each toss, as long as the coins used were fair, there was a 50 percent chance of heads, implying an upward move in the price of the stock, and a 50 percent chance of tails and a downward move. Even if they flip ten heads in a row, the chance of getting a head on the next toss is still 50 per-cent. Mathematicians call a sequence of numbers produced by a random process (such as those on our simulated stock chart) a random walk. The next move on the chart is completely unpre-dictable on the basis of what has happened before.

To a mathematician, the sequence of numbers recorded on

a stock chart behaves no differently from those in the simulated stock charts—with one exception. There is a long-run uptrend in most averages of stock prices in line with the long-run growth of earnings and dividends. After adjusting for this trend, there is essentially no difference. The next move in a series of stock prices is unpredictable on the basis of past price behavior. No matter what wiggle or wobble the prices have made in the past, tomorrow starts out fifty-fifty. The next price change is no more predictable than the flip of a coin.

Now, in fact, the stock market does not quite measure up to the mathematician's ideal of the complete independence of present price movements from those in the past. There have been some *very slight* dependencies found. But any systematic relationships that exist are so small that they are not useful for an investor. The brokerage charges involved in trying to take advantage of these dependencies are far greater than any advantage that might be obtained. This is the consistent finding of the academic research on stock prices. Thus, an accurate statement of the "weak" form of the random-walk hypothesis goes as follows:

> The history of stock-price movements contains no useful information that will enable an investor consistently to outperform a buy-and-hold strategy in managing a portfolio.

If the weak form of the random-walk hypothesis is a valid description of the stock market, then, as my colleague Richard Quandt says, "Technical analysis is akin to astrology and every bit as scientific."

I am *not* saying that technical strategies never make money. They very often do make profits. The point is rather that a simple "buy-and-hold" strategy (that is, buying a stock or group of stocks and holding on for a long period of time) typically makes as much or more money.

When scientists want to test the efficacy of some new drug they usually run an experiment where two groups of patients are administered pills—one containing the drug in question, the other a worthless placebo (a sugar pill). The results of the administration to the two groups are compared and the drug is deemed effective only if the group receiving the drug did better than the group getting the placebo. Obviously, if both groups got better in the same period of time the drug should not be given the credit, even if the patients did recover.

In the stock-market experiments, the placebo with which the technical strategies are compared is the buy-and-hold strategy. Technical schemes often do make profits for their users, but so does a buy-and-hold strategy. Indeed, as we shall see later, a naïve buy-and-hold strategy using a dart-board-selected portfolio has provided investors with an average annual rate of return of approximately $9\frac{1}{2}$ percent over the past half-century. I believe that return will be 15 percent for the remainder of the 1980s. Only if technical schemes produce better returns than the market can they be judged effective. To date, none has consistently passed the test.

Some More Elaborate Technical Systems

Devotees of technical analysis may argue with some justification that I have been unfair. The simple tests I have just described do not do justice to the "richness" of technical analysis. Unfortunately for the technician, even some of his more elaborate trading rules have been subjected to scientific testing. Since many of the systems tested are very popular, let's briefly examine a few in detail.

THE FILTER SYSTEM

Under the popular "filter" system a stock that has reached a low point and has moved up, say 5 percent (or any other percent you wish to name here and throughout this discussion), is said to be in an uptrend. A stock that has reached a peak and has moved down 5 percent is said to be in a downtrend. You're supposed to buy any stock that has moved up 5 percent from its low and hold it until the price moves down 5 percent from a subsequent high, at which time you sell the stock and, perhaps, even sell short. The short position is maintained until the price rises at least 5 percent from a subsequent low.

This scheme is very popular with brokers, and forms of it have been recommended in investment books such as Ira Cobleigh's *Happiness Is a Stock that Doubles in a Year* and Nicholas Darvas' *How I Made Two Million Dollars in the Stock Market*. Indeed, the filter method is what lies behind the popular "stoploss" order favored by brokers, where the client is advised to sell his stock if it falls 5 percent below his purchase price to "limit his potential losses." The argument is that presumably a stock that falls by 5 percent will be going into a downtrend anyway.

Exhaustive testing of various filter rules based on past price changes has been undertaken. The percentage drop or rise that filters out buy and sell candidates has been allowed to vary from 1 percent to 50 percent. The tests covered different time periods from 1897 to the present, and involved individual stocks as well as assorted stock averages. Again, the results are remarkably consistent. When the higher brokerage commissions incurred under the filter rules are taken into consideration, these techniques cannot consistently beat a policy of simply buying the individual stock (or the stock average in question) and holding it over the period during which the test is performed. The individual investor would do well to avoid employing any filter rule and, I might add, any broker who recommends it.

THE DOW THEORY

The Dow theory is a great tug-of-war between resistance and support. When the market tops out and moves down, that previous peak defines a resistance area, since people who missed selling at the top will be anxious to do so if given another opportunity. If the market then rises again and nears the previous peak, it is said to be "testing" the resistance area. Now comes the moment of truth. If the market breaks through the resistance area, it is likely to keep going up for a while and the previous resistance area becomes a support area. If, on the other hand, the market "fails to penetrate the resistance area" and instead falls through the preceding low where there was previous support, a bear-market signal is given and the investor is advised to sell.

The basic Dow principle implies a strategy of buying when the market goes higher than the last peak and selling when it sinks through the preceding valley. There are various wrinkles to the theory, such as penetration of a double or triple top being especially bullish, but the basic idea is followed by many chartists and is part of the gospel of charting.

Unhappily, the signals generated by the Dow mechanism have no significance for predicting future price movements. The market's performance after *sell* signals is no different from its performance after *buy* signals. Relative to simply buying and holding the representative list of stocks in the market averages, the Dow follower actually comes out a little behind, since the strategy entails a number of extra brokerage costs as the investor buys and sells when the strategy decrees.

THE RELATIVE STRENGTH SYSTEM

Here an investor buys and holds those stocks that are acting well, that is, outperforming the general market indices in the recent past. Conversely, the stocks that are acting poorly relative to the market should be avoided or, perhaps, even sold short. While there do seem to be some time periods when a relative-strength strategy would have outperformed a buy-and-hold strategy, there is no evidence that it can do so consistently. A computer test of relative-strength rules over a twenty-five-year period suggests that such rules do not, after accounting for brokerage charges, outperform the placebo of a buy-and-hold investment strategy.

PRICE-VOLUME SYSTEMS

These strategies suggest that when a stock (or the general market) rises on large or increasing volume, there is an unsatisfied excess of buying interest and the stock can be expected to continue its rise. Conversely, when a stock drops on large volume, selling pressure is indicated and a sell signal is given.

Again, the investor following such a system is likely to be disappointed in the results. The buy and sell signals generated by the strategy contain no information useful for predicting future price movements. As with all technical strategies, however, the investor is obliged to do a great deal of in-and-out trading, and thus his brokerage costs are far in excess of those necessitated in a buy-and-hold strategy. After accounting for these brokerage charges, the investor does worse than he would by simply buying and holding a diversified group of stocks.

READING CHART PATTERNS

Perhaps some of the more complicated chart patterns, such as were described in the preceding chapter, are able to reveal the future course of stock prices. For example, is the downward penetration of a head-and-shoulders formation a reliable bearish omen? As one of the gospels of charting, *Technical Analysis*, puts it, "One does not bring instantly to a stop a heavy car moving at seventy miles per hour and, all within the same split second, turn it around and get it moving back down the road in the opposite direction." Before the stock turns around, its price movements are supposed to form one of a number of extensive reversal patterns as the smart-money traders slowly "distribute" their shares to the "public." Of course, we know some stocks do reverse directions in quite a hurry (this is called an unfortunate V formation), but perhaps these reversal patterns and other chart configurations can, like the Roman soothsayers, accurately foretell the future. Alas, the computer has even tested these more arcane charting techniques, and the technician's tool (magician's wand) has again betrayed him.

In one elaborate study, the computer was programmed to draw charts for 548 stocks traded on the New York Stock Exchange over a five-year period. It was instructed to scan all the charts and identify any one of thirty-two of the most popularly followed chart patterns. The computer was told to be on the lookout for heads and shoulders, triple tops and bottoms, channels, wedges, diamonds, and so forth. Since the machine is a very thorough (though rather dull) worker, we can be sure it did not miss any significant chart patterns.

Whenever the machine found that one of the bearish chart patterns such as a head and shoulders was followed by a downward move through the neckline toward décolletage (a most bearish omen), it recorded a sell signal. If, on the other hand, a triple bottom was followed by an upside breakout (a most favorable augury), a buy signal was recorded. The computer then followed the performance of the stocks for which buy and sell signals were given and compared them with the performance record of the general market.

Again, there seemed to be no relationship between the technical signal and subsequent performance. If you had bought only those stocks with buy signals, and sold on a sell signal, your performance after brokerage costs would have been no better than that achieved with a buy-and-hold strategy. Indeed, the strategy that came closest to producing above-average returns (not accounting for brokerage costs) was to buy right after one of the bear signals.

A Gaggle of Other Technical Theories to Help You Lose Money

Once the academic world polished off most of the standard technical trading rules, it turned its august attention toward some of the more fanciful schemes. The world of financial analysis would be much quieter and duller without the chartists, as the following techniques amply demonstrate.

"BULL MARKETS AND BARE KNEES"

Not content with price movements, some technical analysts have broadened their investigations to include other movements as well. One of the most charming of these schemes has been called by Ira Cobleigh the "bull markets and bare knees" theory. Check the hemline of women's dresses in any given year and you'll have an idea of the level of stock prices. There does seem to be a loose tendency for bull markets in stocks to be associated with bare knees, and bear markets in stocks to be associated with bear markets for girl watchers.

For example, in the late nineteenth and early twentieth centuries, the stock market was rather dull, and so were hemlines. But then came rising hemlines and the great bull market of the twenties, to be followed by long skirts and the crash of the thirties. (Actually, the system cheats a bit; hemlines fell in 1927, prior to the most dynamic phase of the bull market.)

Unfortunately, things do not work out as well in the post-World War II period. The market declined sharply during the summer of 1946, well in advance of the introduction of the "New Look" featuring longer skirt lengths in 1947. Similarly, the sharp stock-market decline that began at the end of 1968 preceded the introduction of the midi skirt, which was high fashion in 1969 and especially in 1970. Nevertheless, the theory held up well in the early 1970s, when the market peaked at over 1000 for the Dow Jones Industrials just at the peak of popularity of the fanny-high micro-mini-skirt and hot pants. Hemlines then declined with the market in the mid-1970s. At the start of the 1980s, hemlines began to rise again and so did the stock market.

There is a problem, however, for those who would seriously try to project these relationships into the future. While there is no theoretical ceiling on the level of stock prices, there obviously is a ceiling on dress heights. Fanny-high micro-mini-skirts and hot pants seem to put a ceiling on stock prices. After all, hemlines cannot possibly go any higher. Can they?

THE ODD-LOT THEORY

This theory holds that except for the man who is always right, no person can contribute more to successful investment strategy than a man who is known to be invariably wrong. The "odd-lotter," according to popular superstition, is precisely that kind of person. Thus success is assured by buying when the odd-lotter sells and selling when the odd-lotter buys.

Odd-lotters are the people who trade stocks in less than 100-share lots (called round lots). Most amateurs in the stock market cannot afford the $5,000 investment to buy a round lot (100 shares) of stock selling at $50 a share. They are more likely to buy, say, ten shares for a more modest investment of $500.

By examining the ratio of odd-lot purchases (the number of shares these amateurs bought during a particular day) to odd-lot sales (the number of shares they sold) and by looking at what particular stocks odd-lotters buy and sell, one can supposedly make money. These uninformed amateurs presumably acting solely out of emotion and not with professional insight, are lambs in the street being led to slaughter. They are, according to legend, invariably wrong.

It turns out that the odd-lotter isn't such a stupendous dodo after all. A little stupid? Maybe. There is some indication that the performance of odd-lotters might be slightly worse than the stock averages. However, the available evidence (which admittedly does not match what has been accumulated in testing many of the other technical strategies) indicates that knowledge of his actions is not useful for the formulation of investment strategies.

One of the available studies examines the theory that an investor can make use of data on odd-lot sales and odd-lot purchases in selecting stocks. Supposedly, a switch from net odd-lot buying (where odd-lot shares purchased exceed odd-lot shares sold) to net odd-lot selling (odd-lot sales greater than odd-lot purchases) should be taken as a "buy" signal, since the boobs who sell odd-lots obviously don't know what they're doing. The data did not support this contention. Indeed, the rule failed to indicate the major turning points for individual stocks or for the market as a whole. Moreover, the odd-lot index was a very volatile one, switching back and forth from net sales to net purchases quite frequently. This suggests that an investor who followed the strategy would incur very heavy brokerage charges, which would eat substantially into his capital.

With the exception of a few technicians who sell their services to the public, few professional investment people believe in the odd-lot theory anymore. Indeed, some professional investors have seriously suggested that a new odd-lot theory is applicable to today's institutionally dominated market. Instead of looking at the behavior of the little guy in the market, it is suggested that the yo-yos who run the big mutual funds are the odd-lotters of today, and that investors should look at what they are doing and then do the opposite.

A FEW MORE SYSTEMS

To continue this review of technical schemes would soon generate rapidly diminishing returns. Probably few people seriously believe that the sunspot theory of stock-market movements can make money for them. But do you believe that by following the ratio of advancing to declining stocks on the New York Stock Exchange you can find a reliable leading indicator of general stock-market peaks? A careful computer study says no. Do you think that a rise in short interest (the number of shares of a stock sold short) is a bullish signal (since eventually the stock will be repurchased by the short seller to cover his position)? Exhaustive testing indicates no relationship either for the stock market as a whole or for individual issues. Do you think a moving-average system (for example, buy a stock if its price goes higher than its average price over the past 200 days and sell it if it goes below the average) can lead you to extraordinary stock-market profits? Not if you have to pay commissions to buy and sell!

I mentioned earlier that Joseph Granville was one of the most widely followed forecasters of the early 1980s. His record had been good for a time in the late 1970s, and at his heyday he had the power to move markets. At 6:30 PM on January 6, 1981, Granville sent word to his 3,000 investor-subscribers around the world, "Sell the market—sell everything." The next morning brokerage houses were deluged with sell orders, and the Dow Jones Industrial average dropped 24 points, representing some 40 billion dollars in paper losses, three times the dollar amount lost on Black Thursday in 1929. Granville's buy recommendation the previous April had sent the Dow up 30 points in one day and his sell signal in September 1981 touched off near panic on world financial markets. Think of the ego satisfaction. Public adulation for Granville resembled that accorded rock stars. His traveling seminars were always oversubscribed. Asked at one seminar how he stayed close to the market when traveling, he dropped his pants to reveal various stock quotes printed on his shorts. When Joseph Granville talked, investors really did listen—at least for a while.

Unfortunately for Granville, his forecast accuracy during the 1980s left much to be desired. The Granville market letter warned of stock-market disaster throughout the early 1980s. Indeed, with the Dow Jones Industrial average at 800, Granville told subscribers we were in a stock-market crash. He opined that investors should not only sell all their stock, but sell short as well, to take advantage of the coming financial Armageddon. The market responded by rising to the 1200 level. "The bull market has been just a bubble," Granville remarked in 1984, continuing to warn a somewhat smaller number of listeners that the crash was near at hand. Granville's reputation as a seer and a mover of markets had been severely tarnished. When the coast of California failed to fall into the Pacific in May 1981 as he had predicted, Granville also lost his reputation as a predictor of earthquakes.

Why Are Technicians Still Hired?

It seems very clear that under scientific scrutiny chart-reading must share a pedestal with alchemy. There has been a remarkable uniformity in the conclusions of all studies done on all forms of technical analysis. Not one has consistently outperformed the placebo of a buy-and-hold strategy. Technical methods cannot be used to make useful investment strategies. This is the fundamental conclusion of the random walk theory.

A former colleague of mine who believed that the capitalist system would be sure to weed out all useless growths such as the flourishing technicians, was convinced that the technical cult was just a passing fad. "The days of these modern-day soothsayers on Wall Street are numbered," he would say. "Brokers will soon learn they can easily do without the technicians' services."

The chartist's durability, and the fact that over the years he has been hired in increasing numbers, suggests that the capitalist system may garden like most of the rest of us. We like to see our best plants grow, but as summer wears on somehow the weeds often manage to get the best of us. And as I often tell my wife when she remarks about the abundance of weeds in our lawn, "At least they're green."

The point is, the technicians often play an important role in the greening of the brokers. Chartists recommend trades — almost every technical system involves some degree of in-and-out trading. Trading generates commissions, and commissions are the lifeblood of the brokerage business. The technicians do not help produce yachts for the customers, but they do help generate the trading that provides yachts for the brokers. Until the public catches on to this bit of trickery, technicians will continue to flourish.

Appraising the Counterattack

As you might imagine, the random-walk theory's dismissal of charting is not altogether popular among technicians. Academic proponents of the theory are greeted in some Wall Street quarters with as much enthusiasm as James Watt addressing a meeting of the Sierra Club. Technical analysts consider the theory and its implications to be, in the words of one veteran professional, "just plain academic drivel." Let us pause, then, and appraise the counterattack by beleaguered technicians.

Perhaps the most common complaint about the weakness of the random-walk theory is based on a distrust of mathematics and a misconception of what the theory means. "The market isn't random" the complaint goes, "and no mathematician is going to convince me it is." Even so astute a commentator on the Wall Street scene as "Adam Smith" displays this misconception when he writes:

> I suspect that even if the random walkers announced a perfect mathematic proof of randomness I would go on believing that in the long run future earnings influence present value, and that in the short run the dominant factor is the elusive *Australopithecus,* the temper of the crowd.

Of course earnings and dividends influence market prices, and so does the temper of the crowd. We saw ample evidence of this in earlier chapters of the book. But, even if markets were dominated during certain periods by irrational crowd behavior, the stock market might still well be approximated by a random walk. The original illustrative analogy of a random walk concerned a drunken man staggering around an empty field. He is not rational, but he's not predictable either.

Moreover, new fundamental information about a company (a big mineral strike, the death of the president, etc.) is also unpredictable. It will occur randomly over time. Indeed, successive appearances of news items must be random. If an item of news were not random, that is, if it were *dependent* on an earlier item of news, then it wouldn't be news at all. The weak form of the random-walk theory says only that stock prices cannot be predicted on the basis of past stock prices. Thus criticisms of the type quoted above are not valid.

The technical analyst will also cite chapter and verse that the academic world has certainly not tested every technical scheme that has been devised. That is quite correct. No economist or mathematician, however skillful, can prove conclusively that technical methods can never work. All that can be said is that the small amount of information contained in stock-market pricing patterns has not been shown to be sufficient to overcome the brokerage costs involved in acting on that information. Consequently, I have received a flood of letters condemning me for not mentioning, in my earlier editions of this book, a pet technical scheme that the writer is convinced actually works.

Being somewhat incautious, I will climb out on a limb and argue that no technical scheme whatever could work for any length of time. I suggest first that methods which people are convinced "really work" have not been adequately tested; and second, that even if they did work the schemes would be bound to destroy themselves.

Each year a number of eager people visit the gambling parlors of Las Vegas and Atlantic City and examine the last hundreds of numbers of the roulette wheel in search of some repeating pattern. Usually they find one. And so they stay until they lose everything because they do not retest the pattern.* The same thing is true for technicians.

If you examine past stock prices in any given period, you can almost always find some kind of system that would have worked in a given period. If enough different criteria for selecting stocks are tried, one will eventually be found that selects the best ones of that period.

Let me illustrate. Suppose we examine the record of stock prices and volume over the five-year period 1980 through 1984 in search of technical trading rules that would have worked

---

*Edward O. Thorp actually did find a method to win at blackjack. Thorp wrote it all up in *Beat the Dealer*. Since then casinos have started to use several decks of cards in order to make it more difficult for card counters, and as a last resort, they banish the counters from the gaming tables.

during that period. After the fact it is always possible to find a technical rule that works. For example, it might be that you should have bought all stocks whose names began with the letters X or I, whose volume was at least 3,000 shares a day, and whose earnings grew at a rate of 10 percent or more during the preceding five-year period. The point is that it is obviously possible to describe, after the fact, which categories of stocks had the best performance. The real problem is, of course, whether the scheme works in a different time period. What most advocates of technical analysis usually fail to do is to test their schemes with market data derived from other periods than those during which the scheme was developed.

Even if the technician follows my advice, tests his scheme in many different time periods, and finds it a reliable predictor of stock prices, I still believe that technical analysis must ultimately be worthless. For the sake of argument, suppose the technician had found that there was a reliable year-end rally, that is, every year stock prices rose between Christmas and New Year's Day. The problem is that once such a regularity is known to market participants, people will act in a way that prevents it from happening in the future.*

Any successful technical scheme must ultimately be self-defeating. The moment I realize that prices will be higher after New Year's Day than they are before Christmas I will start buying before Christmas ever comes around. If people know a stock will go up *tomorrow*, you can be sure it will go up *today*. Any regularity in the stock market that can be discovered and acted upon profitably is bound to destroy itself. This is the fundamental reason why I am convinced that no one will be successful in employing technical methods to get above-average returns in the stock market.

---

*If such a regularity was known to only one individual, he would simply practice the technique until he had collected a large share of the marbles. He surely would have no incentive to share a truly useful scheme by making it available to others.

Implications for Investors

The past history of stock prices cannot be used to predict the future in any meaningful way. Technical strategies are usually amusing, often comforting, but of no real value. This is the weak form of the random-walk theory, and it is the consistent conclusion of research done at universities such as Chicago, M.I.T., Yale, Princeton, and Stanford. It has been published mainly in investment journals, but also in more esoteric ones such as *Kyklos* and *Econometrica*. Technical theories enrich only the people preparing and marketing the technical service or the brokerage firms who hire technicians in the hope that their analyses may help encourage investors to do more in-and-out trading and thus generate commission business for the brokerage firm.

The implications of this analysis are simple. If past prices contain no useful information for the prediction of future prices, there is no point in following any technical trading rule for timing the purchases and sales of securities. A simple policy of buying and holding will be at least as good as any technical procedure. Discontinue your subscriptions to worthless technical services, and eschew brokers who read charts and are continually recommending the purchase or sale of securities.

There is another major advantage to a buy-and-hold strategy that I have not yet mentioned. Short-term trading (buying and selling within six months), to the extent that it is profitable at all, tends to generate short-term capital gains, which are taxed at regular income-tax rates. Buying and holding enables you to postpone or avoid gains taxes. By following any technical strategy, you are likely to realize most of your capital gains and pay larger taxes (as well as paying them sooner) than you would under a buy-and-hold strategy. Thus simply buying and holding a diversified portfolio suited to your objectives will enable you to save on investment expense, brokerage charges, and taxes; and, at the same time, to achieve an overall performance record at least as good as that obtainable using technical methods.

CHAPTER SEVEN

How Good Is Fundamental Analysis?

How could I have been so mistaken as to have trusted the experts? — John F. Kennedy (after the Bay of Pigs fiasco)

In the beginning he was a statistician. He wore a white, starched shirt and threadbare blue suit. He quietly put on his green eyeshade, sat down at his desk, and recorded meticulously the historical financial information about the companies he followed. The result: writer's cramp.

But then a metamorphosis began to set in. He rose from his desk, bought blue button-down shirts and gray flannel suits, threw away his eyeshade, and began to make field trips to visit the companies that previously he had known only as a collection of financial statistics. His title now became security analyst.

As time went on, his stature continued to grow. Portfolio managers increasingly relied on his reports and recommendations in deciding which stocks should be bought or sold. He became a bona fide *chartered financial analyst*, though old-timers still affectionately refer to him as a security analyst.

The Views from Wall Street and Academia

Some of Wall Street's portfolio managers actually invest on the basis of the charts and various technical schemes described in the last chapter. But even on Wall Street, technicians are considered a rather strange cult, and little faith is put in their recommendations. Thus the studies casting doubt on the efficacy of technical analysis would not be considered surprising by most professionals. At heart, the Wall Street pros are fundamentalists. The really important question is whether fundamental analysis is any good.

Two extreme views have been taken about the efficacy of fundamental analysis. The view of many on Wall Street is that fundamental analysis is becoming more powerful and skillful all the time. The individual investor has scarcely a chance against the professional portfolio manager and a team of fundamental analysts.

An opposite-extreme view is taken by much of the academic community. Some academicians have gone so far as to suggest that a blindfolded monkey throwing darts at the *Wall Street Journal* can select stocks with as much success as professional portfolio managers. They have argued that fund managers and their fundamental analysts can do no better at picking stocks than a rank amateur. Many have concluded that the value of professional investment advice is nil.

My own view of the matter is somewhat less extreme than that taken by many of my academic colleagues. Nevertheless, an understanding of the large body of research on these questions is essential for any intelligent investor. This chapter will recount the major battle in an ongoing war between academics and market professionals that has shaken Wall Street to its bedrock. Current field reports have the academics claiming victory and the professionals screaming "Foul."

Are Security Analysts Fundamentally Clairvoyant?

Forecasting future earnings is the security analysts' *raison d'être*. As a top Wall Street professional put it in his fraternity magazine, *Institutional Investor*: "Expectation of future earnings is still the most important single factor affecting stock prices." As we have seen, growth (in earnings and therefore in the ability to pay dividends) is the key element needed to estimate a stock's firm foundation of value. The analyst who can make accurate forecasts of the future will be richly rewarded. "If he is wrong," *Institutional Investor* puts it, "a stock can act precipitously, as has been demonstrated time and time again. Earnings are the name of the game and always will be."

To predict future directions, analysts generally start by looking at past wanderings. "A proven score of past performance in earnings growth is," one analyst told me, "a most reliable indicator of future earnings growth." If management is really skillful, there is no reason to think it will lose its Midas touch in the future. If the same adroit management team remains at the helm, the course of future earnings growth should continue as it has in the past, or so the argument goes.

Such thinking flunks in the academic world. Calculations of past earnings growth are no help in predicting future growth. If you had known the growth rates of all companies during, say, the 1960–70 period, this would not have helped you at all in predicting what growth they would achieve in the 1970–80 period. And knowing the fast growers of the seventies has not helped analysts find the fast growers of the eighties. This startling result was first reported by British researchers for companies in the United Kingdom in an article charmingly titled "Higgledy Piggledy Growth." Learned academicians at Princeton and Harvard applied the British study to U.S. companies—and, surprise, the same was true here!

"IBM," the cry immediately went up. "Remember IBM." I do remember IBM: a steady high grower for decades. It is an exception (though for how much longer is open to question). I also remember Polaroid and dozens of other firms that chalked up consistent large growth rates until the roof fell in. I hope you remember *not* the exception but rather the rule: there is no reliable pattern that can be discerned from past records to aid the analyst in predicting future growth.

A good analyst will argue, however, that there's much more to predicting than just examining the past record. Rather than measure every factor that goes into the actual forecasting process, John Cragg and I decided to concentrate on the end result: the prediction itself.

Donning our cloak of academic detachment, we wrote to nineteen major Wall Street firms engaged in fundamental analysis. The nineteen firms, which asked to remain anonymous, included some of the major brokerage firms, mutual fund management companies, investment advisory firms, and banks engaged in trust management. They are among the most respected names in the investment business.

We requested — and received — past earnings predictions on how these firms felt earnings for specific companies would behave over both a one-year and a five-year period. These estimates, made at several different times, were then compared with actual results to see how well the analysts forecast short-run and long-run earnings changes. The results were surprising.

Bluntly stated, the careful estimates of security analysts (based on industry studies, plant visits, etc.) do very little better than those that would be obtained by simple extrapolation of past trends, which we have already seen are no help at all. Indeed, when compared with actual earnings growth rates, the five-year estimates of security analysts were actually worse than the predictions from several naïve forecasting models.

For example, one placebo with which the analysts' estimates were compared was the assumption that every company in the economy would enjoy a growth in earnings approximating the long-run rate of growth of the national income. It often turned out that if you used this naïve forecasting model you would make smaller errors in forecasting long-run earnings growth than by using the professional forecasts of the analysts.

Our method of determining the efficacy of the security analyst's diagnoses of his companies is exactly the same as was used before in evaluating the technicians' medicine. We compared the results obtained by following the experts with the results from some naïve mechanism involving no expertise at all. Sometimes these naïve predictors work very well. For example, if you want to forecast the weather tomorrow you will do a pretty good job by predicting that it will be exactly the same as today. It turns out that while this system misses every one of the turning points in the weather, for most days it is quite reliable. How many weather forecasters do you suppose do any better?

When confronted with the poor record of their five-year growth estimates, the security analysts honestly, if sheepishly, admitted that five years ahead is really too far in advance to make reliable projections. They protested that while long-term projections are admittedly important, they really ought to be judged on their ability to project earnings changes one year ahead.

Believe it or not, it turned out that their one-year forecasts were even worse than their five-year projections. It was actually harder for them to forecast one year ahead than to estimate long-run changes.

The analysts gamely fought back. They complained it was unfair to judge their performance on a wide cross section of industries, since earnings for electronics firms and various "cyclical" companies are notoriously hard to forecast. "Try us on utilities," one analyst confidently asserted. So we tried it, and they didn't like it. Even the forecasts for the stable utilities were far off the mark. Those the analysts confidently touted as high growers turned out to perform much the same as the utilities for which only low or moderate growth was predicted. This led to the second major finding of our study: There is not one industry that is easy to predict.

Moreover, no analysts proved consistently superior to the

others. Of course, in each year some analysts did much better than average, but there was no consistency in their pattern of performance. Analysts who did better than average one year were no more likely than the others to make superior forecasts in the next year.

My findings with Cragg have been confirmed by several other researchers. For example, Michael Sandretto of Harvard and Sudhir Milkrishnamurthi of M.I.T. completed a massive study of the one-year forecasts of the most widely followed companies between 1977 and 1981. The number of companies monitored was about 1,000 each year, and, in general, estimates were available from five or six analysts for each company. All estimates were made for the then-current year, so that 1981 estimates had been made early in 1981. The staggering conclusion of the study was that the average annual error of the analysts was 31.3 percent over the five-year period. The error rates each year were remarkably consistent—the lowest error rate was 27.6 percent in 1978, the highest 33½ percent in 1981. Financial forecasting appears to be a science that makes astrology look respectable.

Amidst all these accusations and counterassertions, there is a deadly serious message. It is this: Security analysts have enormous difficulty in performing their basic function of forecasting earnings prospects for the companies they follow. Investors who put blind faith in such forecasts in making their investment selections are in for some rude disappointments.

Why the Crystal Ball Is Clouded

It is always somewhat disturbing to learn that a group of highly trained and well-paid professionals may not be terribly skillful at their calling. Unfortunately, this is hardly unusual. Similar types of findings could be made for most groups of professionals. There is, for example, a classic example in medicine. At a time when tonsillectomies were very fashionable, the American Child Health Association surveyed a group of 1,000 children, eleven years of age, from the public schools of New York City, and found that 611 of these had had their tonsils removed. The remaining 389 were then examined by a group of physicians, who selected 174 of these for tonsillectomy and declared the rest had no tonsil problem. The remaining 215 were reexamined by another group of doctors, who recommended 99 of these for tonsillectomy. When the 116 "healthy" children were examined a third time, a similar percentage were told their tonsils had to be removed. After three examinations, only 65 children remained who had not been recommended for tonsillectomy. These remaining children were not examined further because the supply of examining physicians ran out.

Numerous other studies have shown similar results. Radiologists have failed to recognize the presence of lung disease in about 30 percent of the X-ray plates they read, despite the clear presence of the disease on the X-ray film. Another experiment proved that professional staffs in psychiatric hospitals could not tell the sane from the insane. The point is that we should not take for granted the reliability and accuracy of any judge, no matter how expert. When one considers the low reliability of so many kinds of judgments, it does not seem too surprising that security analysts, with their particularly difficult forecasting job, should be no exception.

There are, I believe, four factors that help explain why security analysts have such difficulty in predicting the future. These are: (1) the influence of random events; (2) the creation of dubious reported earnings through "creative" accounting procedures; (3) the basic incompetence of many of the analysts themselves; and (4) the loss of the best analysts to the sales desk or to portfolio management. Each factor deserves some discussion.

1. THE INFLUENCE OF RANDOM EVENTS

A company is not an entity unto itself. Many of the most important changes that affect the basic prospects for corporate earnings are essentially random, that is, unpredictable.

Take the utility industry, to which I referred earlier. Presumably it is one of the most stable and dependable groups of companies. During the early 1960s almost every utility analyst expected Florida Power and Light to be the fastest-growing utility. The analysts saw a continued high population growth, increased demands for electric power among existing customers, and a favorable regulatory climate.

Everything turned out exactly as forecast except for one small detail. The favorable Florida regulatory climate turned distinctly unfavorable as the sixties progressed. The Florida Public Utilities Commission ordered Florida Power and Light to make several substantial rate cuts and the utility was not able to translate the rapid growth in demand for electric power into higher profits. As a result, the company closed the decade with a mediocre growth record, far below the ebullient forecasts. In the 1970s, similar kinds of mistakes were made as analysts failed to predict the increased fuel costs resulting from the tenfold increase in the international price of oil and the effect of the 1979 accident at Three Mile Island on the future of nuclear power. Thus, even the "stable" electric utility industry has proved extraordinarily difficult to predict.

U.S. government budgetary and contract decisions can have enormous implications for the fortunes of individual companies. So can the incapacitation of key members of management, the discovery of a major new product, the finding of defects in a current product, the shut-off of mideast oil, natural disasters such as floods and hurricanes, etc. The stories of unpredictable events affecting earnings are endless.

2. THE CREATION OF DUBIOUS REPORTED EARNINGS THROUGH "CREATIVE" ACCOUNTING PROCEDURES

A firm's income statement may be likened to a bikini—what it reveals is interesting but what it conceals is vital. National

Student Marketing, one of the concept stocks I mentioned in Chapter Three, led the beauty parade in this regard. Andrew Tobias described it all in *The Funny Money Game*.

In its fiscal 1969 report, National Student Marketing made generous use of terms such as "deferred new product development and start-up costs." These were moneys actually spent during 1969 but not charged against earnings in that year. "Unamortized costs of prepared sales programs" carried the ploy even further. These were advertising expenses that were not charged against earnings on the flimsy excuse that they would produce sales in the future. Subsidiary losses were easily handled: the companies were simply sold, removing their unfavorable results from the consolidated accounting statement. Actually it wasn't quite that simple, because the sales were consummated after the close of the fiscal year — but the accountants had no difficulty in arranging for the sale retroactively.

Since expenses were uncounted, why not count unearnings? No sooner said than done. These were duly noted in the sales column as unbilled receivables, on the justification that the actual billing of the sales could be expected to materialize in the future. Finally, came "the $3,754,103 footnote." Almost $4 million was added to net income in the form of earnings from companies whose acquisitions were "agreed to in principal and closed subsequent" to the end of fiscal 1969.

It turned out that even accepting the rest of the creative accounting, if you didn't count the earnings of companies that were not legally part of National Student Marketing in 1969, the company barely broke even. Of course, the imprimatur of a prestigious accounting firm was affixed to the bottom of a statement assuring the public that the accounts were prepared in accordance with "generally accepted accounting principles."*

---

*In 1972 the Securities and Exchange Commission charged National Student Marketing Corp., its auditors, two law firms, and fifteen individuals with violations of federal securities laws. Included in the SEC suit was a charge that the company had issued "materially false and misleading" financial statements. Randell, the company's chief executive officer, served a prison sentence. A partner of the accounting firm of Peat, Marwick, Mitchell & Co. was convicted of having made false and misleading statements.

The above is admittedly an extreme example, but the general problem is not uncommon. Seeming miracles can be accomplished with depreciation; the peculiarities of conglomerate accounting; the franchise accounting game; and the special features of the reports of land-sales companies, computer leasing companies, and insurance companies. It is small wonder that security analysts have trouble estimating reported future earnings.

3. THE BASIC INCOMPETENCE OF MANY OF THE ANALYSTS THEMSELVES

The overall performance of analysts in many respects reflects the limit of their abilities. Their record with regard to STP Corporation is certainly a good example.

In early 1971, Andy Granatelli's STP was the darling of the Wall Street fraternity. Report after report indicated why it was likely to enjoy a large, long-term growth rate. Analysts pointed to its consistent pattern of growth over ten years. On the argument that the future would be more of the same, and that STP could continue to create its destiny through its marvelously successful advertising campaign, the Wall Street fraternity gave STP an estimated 20 percent growth rate for earnings in future years. As STP's stock price rose, analysts recommended the shares with greater and greater enthusiasm. Needless to say, but said nevertheless, STP management actively encouraged this enthusiasm.

Few analysts bothered to ask about the company's major product, STP oil treatment, which apparently accounted for three-quarters of the firm's revenues and earnings. What did the product really do? Could one really believe that STP helped cars start faster in winter and made engines run longer, quieter, and cooler in summer?

Admittedly, some analysts had a queasy feeling, but this was carefully reasoned away. For example, in the May 17 issue of the *Wall Street Transcript*, one analyst was quoted as saying: "The risk is that it is difficult to prove what exactly the product accomplishes, and people fear that the FTC might attack the company on an efficacy basis. We feel there is a very low probability of that happening and in the meantime consumers think the product works and that's the important thing. It is sort of a 'cosmetic company' for the car." If ever there was a castle in the air, STP certainly qualified.

While the above analyst was being quoted, *Consumer Reports* was completing its report on STP. This was published in July 1971 and stated that STP was a worthless oil thickener, not a panacea that would make ailing engines healthy again. Indeed, the consumer magazine reported that "STP can change the viscosity of a new car's oil to a considerably thicker grade than certain auto manufacturers recommend." The magazine went on to say that the major auto manufacturers positively discouraged the practice of using such additives, and suggested that STP might modify the properties of a car's engine oil so much that the new-car warranty terms might be affected.

The stock fell abruptly and the company's consistent record of past earnings growth came to an untimely end. As one analyst confided after the debacle, "I guess we just didn't ask the right questions."

To be perfectly blunt, many security analysts are not particularly perceptive, critical, or competent. I learned this early in the game as a young Wall Street trainee. In attempting to learn the techniques of the pros, I tried to duplicate some analytic work done by a metals specialist named Louie. Louie had figured that for each 1¢ increase in the price of copper, the earnings for a particular copper producer would increase by $1 per share. Since he expected a 3¢ increase in the price of copper, he reasoned that this particular stock was "an unusually attractive purchase candidate."

In redoing the calculation, I found that Louie had misplaced a decimal point. A penny increase in the price of copper would increase earnings by 10¢, not by $1. When I pointed this out to Louie (feeling sure he would want to put out a correction immediately) he simply shrugged his shoulders and declared,

"Well, the recommendation sounds more convincing if we leave the report as is." Attention to detail was clearly not the forte of this particular analyst. From then on I referred to him as Sloppy Louie (not to denigrate the excellent fish restaurant of the same name near the New York financial district).

To balance this inattention to detail and careful work, we have those who glory in it. Take Railroad Roger, for example. Roger will accurately recount every conceivable statistic on track miles and freight carloadings for hours on end. But Roger does not have the faintest clue what the rails will earn next year, or which should be favored for purchase. Oil analyst Doyle performs in a similar manner. His knowledge concerning refinery capacity and allowables in Texas is encyclopedic, but he lacks the critical acumen to translate this into judgments useful for investment decision-making.

Many analysts, however, emulate Louie. Generally too lazy to make their own earnings projections, they prefer to copy the forecasts of other analysts or to swallow the ones released by corporate managements without even chewing. Then it's very easy to know whom to blame if something goes wrong. "That ***!!! treasurer gave me the wrong dope." And it's much easier to be wrong when your professional colleagues had all agreed with you. As Keynes put it, "Worldly wisdom teaches that it is better for reputation to fail conventionally than to succeed unconventionally."

Corporate management goes out of its way to ease the forecasting task of the analyst. Let me give you a personal example: A two-day field trip was arranged by a major corporation to brief a whole set of Wall Street security analysts on its operations and future programs.

We were picked up in the morning by the company's private plane for visits and briefings at three of the company's plants. In the evening we were given first-class accommodations and royally wined and dined. After two more plant visits the next day, we had a briefing, replete with slide show, indicating a "most conservative five-year forecast" of robustly growing earnings.

At each stop we were showered with gifts — and not only the usual souvenir mock-ups of the company's major products. We also received a variety of desk accessories for the office, a pen and pencil set, cigarette lighter, tie bar, cuff links, and a tasteful piece of jewelry to "take home to the wife or mistress, as the case may be." Throughout each day liquor and wine flowed in abundance. As one bleary-eyed analyst confided at the end of the trip, "It's very hard not to have a warm feeling for this company."

I do not mean to imply that most Wall Street analysts typically receive payola for touting particular stocks. Indeed, from my own experience, I would judge that the standards of ethics in Wall Street are very high. Sure, there are crooks, but I would guess far fewer than in other professions.

I do imply that the *average* analyst is just that — a well-paid and usually highly intelligent person who has an extraordinarily difficult job and does it in a rather mediocre fashion. Analysts are often misguided, sometimes sloppy, perhaps self-important, and at times susceptible to the same pressures as other people. In short, they are really very human beings.

4. THE LOSS OF THE BEST ANALYSTS TO THE SALES DESK OR TO PORTFOLIO MANAGEMENT

My fourth argument against the profession is a paradoxical one: many of the best security analysts are not paid to analyze securities. They are either very high-powered institutional salesmen; efficient new-business getters, successful in bringing new underwriting business to their firms; or get promoted to be prestigious portfolio managers.

Brokerage houses that pride themselves on their research prowess project an aura of respectability by sending a security analyst to chaperone the regular salesman on a call to a financial institution. Institutional investors like to hear about a new investment idea right from the horse's mouth, and so the regular salesman usually sits back and lets the analyst do the talking. Thus most of the articulate analysts find their time is spent with institutional clients, not with financial reports and corporate treasurers. They also find that their monetary rewards are heavily dependent upon their ability to bring commission business to the firm.

Another magnet away from the study of stocks is the ability of some analysts to attract to their firm profitable underwriting clients, that is, companies who need to borrow money or sell new common stock to raise funds for expansion. The analyst on a field trip who is looking for new, small, expanding companies as potential investment recommendations may put a great deal of effort into selling his firm's investment banking services. I have seen many a security analyst make his reputation by his ability to attract such clients to the firm. He may not come up with good earnings forecasts or select the right stocks for investment, but he brings the bacon home to his firm and that is the name of the game.

Finally, both the compensation and prestige structures within the securities industry induce many analysts away from research work into portfolio management. It's far more exciting and remunerative to "run money" in the line position of portfolio manager than only to advise in the staff position of security analyst. Small wonder that many of the best-respected security analysts do not remain long in their jobs.

Do Security Analysts Pick Winners?
The Performance of the Mutual Funds

I can almost hear the chorus in the background as I write these words. It goes something like this: The real test of the analyst lies in the performance of the stocks he recommends. Maybe Sloppy Louie, the copper analyst, did mess up his earnings forecast with a misplaced decimal point; but if the stocks he recommended made money for his clients, his lack of attention to detail can surely be forgiven. "Analyze investment performance," the chorus is saying, "not earnings forecasts."

Fortunately, the records of one group of professionals — the mutual funds — are publicly available. Better still for my argument, many of the men and women at the funds are the best and highest-paid analysts and portfolio managers in the business. They stand at the pinnacle of the investment profession.

They allegedly are the first to learn and act on any new fundamental information that becomes available. By their own admission they can clearly make above-average returns. As one investment manager recently put it: "It will take many years before the general level of competence rises enough to overshadow the startling advantage of today's aggressive investment manager." "Adam Smith" echoes a similar statement:

> All the players in the Game are getting rapidly more professional. . . . The true professionals in the Game — the professional portfolio managers — grow more skilled all the time. They are human and they make mistakes, but if you have your money managed by a truly alert mutual fund or even by one of the better banks, you will have a better job done for you than probably at any time in the past.

Statements like these were just too tempting to the lofty-minded in the academic world. Given the wealth of available data, the time available to conduct such research, and the overwhelming desire to prove academic superiority in such matters, it was only natural that academia would zero in on mutual fund performance.

Again the evidence from several studies, including a series conducted at the Wharton School of Finance, is remarkably uniform. Investors have done no better with the average mutual fund than they could have done by purchasing and holding an unmanaged broad stock index. In other words, over long periods of time mutual fund portfolios have not outperformed randomly selected groups of stocks. While funds may have very good records for certain short time periods, there is generally no consistency to superior performance. The only dependable relationship in mutual fund performance is the tendency for funds assuming greater risks to earn, on average, a larger long-run rate of return.

One of the best documented propositions in the field of investment is that on average investors receive higher rates of return for bearing greater risk. Risk, as will be discussed in Chapter Eight, is considered to be the relative volatility of returns. An investment promising a stable and dependable 9 percent each year is less risky than (and preferable to) one that may return 36 percent in a year when the market is strong and lose 18 percent in a year when the market falls. At least this seems to be the view of the majority of investors. Return in this context is composed of both dividends and any appreciation (or depreciation) in the market value of the shares held.

Few, if any, investors can fail to be concerned with the downside risk of their investments, especially if they may be forced to sell during a bear market. And because downside risk is so universally distasteful, investors who hold portfolios of riskier shares, whose price swings are wider, must be and actually are compensated with a somewhat higher long-run return.

The differences that exist in mutual fund returns can be explained almost entirely by differences in the risk they have taken. The chart on the following page illustrates this relationship over the 1957–80 period for a representative group of mutual funds.

Risk is measured by the relative sensitivity of the fund's performance to swings in the general market. A volatility number of 1.2 suggests that the fund was 1.2 times as volatile as the market index—it tended to fluctuate about 20 percent more than the market. A fund that tends to do very well when the market goes up but falls out of bed when the market falters gets a high risk rating. A fund with more stable returns from year to year gets a low risk rating. The chart also shows the rate of return for the market as measured by the Standard & Poor's 500-Stock Index, which by definition gets a volatility rating of 1.0.

The chart shows that by and large the riskiest funds—the growth-oriented ones—have had the largest average return. But these are also the funds whose annual returns were most

Performance of Selected Mutual Funds, 1957-80

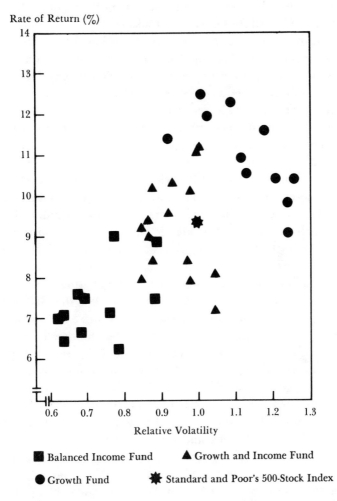

Rate of Return (%)

Relative Volatility

■ Balanced Income Fund ▲ Growth and Income Fund

● Growth Fund ✳ Standard and Poor's 500-Stock Index

volatile and that fell most sharply when the market turned sour. The safest funds—those balanced with short and intermediate-term fixed-income securities—tended to have the lowest but most stable returns. To be sure, over the whole period (including up and down markets) the growth funds outdistanced their safer counterparts and even tended to do better than a broad stock-market average. But this was not a matter of skill—added risk was the price of that performance. Randomly selected portfolios of riskier stocks also tended to outdistance the market. Indeed, you could have bought the stocks making up the market average (say, the S&P 500) on margin (that is, borrowing some of the funds needed to pay for the purchase) and increased both your risk and your return. If you held one of the supposedly better-performing but riskier funds, don't ascribe this to any genius on the fund manager's part. Your extra return was simply a just reward due you for bearing extra risk.

In addition to the scientific evidence that has been accumulated, several less formal tests have verified this finding. In June 1967, the editors of *Forbes* magazine, for example, intrigued with the results of academic studies, chose a portfolio of common stocks by throwing darts at the stock-market page of the *New York Times*. They struck 28 names and constructed a simulated portfolio consisting of a $1,000 investment in each stock. Seventeen years later in the summer of 1984, that $28,000 portfolio (with all dividends reinvested) was worth $131,697.61. The 370 percent gain easily beat the broad market indices. Moreover, the 9.5 percent annual compounded rate of return has been exceeded only by a minuscule number of professional money managers. Does this mean that the wrist is mightier than the brain? Perhaps not, but I think that the *Forbes* editors raised a very valid question when they wrote: "it would seem that a combination of luck and sloth beats brains."

How can this be? Every year one can read the performance rankings of mutual funds. These *always* show many funds beating the averages—some by significant amounts. The problem is that there is no consistency to the performances. A manager who has been better than average one year has only a 50 percent chance of doing better than average the next year. Just as past earnings growth cannot predict future earnings, neither can past fund performance predict future results. Fund managements are also subject to random events—they may grow fat, become lazy, or break up. An investment approach that works very well for one period can easily turn sour the next. One is tempted to conclude that a very important factor in determining performance ranking is our old friend Lady Luck. To shed further light on this issue, the table on pages 166 and 167 shows the top twenty funds of 1968 and then follows their record over the next six years.

I mentioned in Part One that performance investing was a product of the 1960s and became especially prominent during the 1967–68 strong bull market. Capital preservation had given way to capital productivity. The fund managers who turned in the best results for the period were written up in the financial press like sports celebrities. When the performance rankings were published in 1967 and 1968, the go-go funds with their youthful gunslingers as managers and concept stocks as investments were right at the top of the pack, outgunning all the competition by a wide margin.

The game ended unceremoniously with the bear market that commenced in 1969 and continued until 1971. The go-go funds suddenly went into reserve. It was fly now and pay later for the performance funds. Their portfolios of volatile concept stocks were no exception to the financial law of gravitation. They went down just as sharply as they had gone up. The legendary brilliance of the fund managers turned out to be mainly a legend of their own creation. The top funds of 1968 had a perfectly disastrous performance in the ensuing years (I was not able to extend my table beyond 1974 because by 1975 many of the funds were no longer in business).

The Mates Fund, for example, was number one in 1968. At the end of 1974, the Mates Fund sold at about one-fifteenth of its 1968 value and Mates finally threw in the towel. He then left the investment community to enter a business catering to a new fad. In New York City he started a singles' bar, appropriately named "Mates."

It seems clear that one cannot count on consistency of performance. Unlike Martina Navratilova, portfolio managers do not *consistently* outdistance their rivals. (In fact, sometimes even Martina loses.) But I must be fair: there are exceptions to

Some Results of the Performance Derby

1968 Rank	Fund	1969 Rank[a]	1970 Rank[a]	1971 Rank[a]	1972 Rank[a]	1973 Rank[a]	1974 Rank[a]	1968 Net Asset Value[b] per Share	1974 Net Asset Value per Share
1	Mates Investment Fund	312	424	512	465	531	400	15.51	1.12
2	Neuwirth Fund	263	360	104	477	397	232	15.29	6.24
3	Gibraltar Growth Fund[c]	172	456	481				17.27	
4	Insurance Investors Fund[d]	77	106	317	417	224		7.45	
5	Pennsylania Mutual	333	459	480	486	519	521	11.92	1.09
6	Puerto Rican Investors Fund[c]	30	308	387	435			19.34	
7	Crown Western-Dallas	283	438	207	244	330	133	13.86	4.66
8	Franklin Dynatech Series	342	363	112	120	453	453	14.47	4.56
9	First Participating Fund[e]	49	283	106	27	220	310	19.25	13.47
10	Connecticut Western Mutual Fund[f]	5	202					127.27	
11	Enterprise Fund	334	397	133	364	250	416	11.88	3.84

12 Ivy Fund	357	293	233	161	312	443	12.37	4.58
13 Century Shares Trust	120	55	62	62	127	428	13.09	8.48
14 Mutual Shares Corp.	284	272	152	452	62	4	22.18	15.44
15 Putnam Equities Fund	376	384	45	54	354	211	17.05	6.42
16 Financial Industrial Income Fund	244	222	277	231	35	90	8.40	4.73
17 Consumers Investment[c]	354						6.21	
18 Columbia Growth Fund	33	322	27	370	332	253	14.23	9.05
19 Templeton Growth Fund	1	241	163	1	81	84	4.00	6.23
20 Schuster Fund	129	231	253	425	445	434	12.29	4.86

Source: Lipper Analytical Division, Lipper Analytical Services, Inc.

[a] Out of 381 funds surveyed in 1969, 463 in 1970, 526 in 1971, 537 in 1972, 536 in 1973, and 527 in 1974.

[b] The net asset values for 1968 have been adjusted for all subsequent splits.

[c] No longer surveyed by Lipper.

[d] Insurance Investors Fund later changed name to First Sierra Fund. No longer surveyed by Lipper.

[e] First Participating Fund is now American General Growth Fund.

[f] Connecticut Western is now Channing Bond Fund, which is no longer surveyed by Lipper.

the rule. Note portfolio manager number nineteen. The Templeton Growth Fund has been a superior performer not only during the period covered in the table but in other periods as well. It is an excellent counterexample to the rule—but such examples are very rare. Indeed, the number of funds that have outperformed randomly selected portfolios with equivalent risk is no larger than might be attributed to chance.

In any activity in which large numbers of people are engaged, while the average is likely to predominate, the unexpected is bound to happen. The very small number of really good performers we find in the investment management business is not at all inconsistent with the laws of chance. Indeed, as I mentioned earlier, the fact that good past performance of a mutual fund is no help whatever in predicting future performance only serves to emphasize this point. The preceding table shows just how inconsistent fund performance can be.

Perhaps the laws of chance should be illustrated. Let's engage in a coin-tossing contest. Those who can consistently flip heads will be declared winners. The contest begins and 1,000 contestants flip coins. Just as would be expected by chance, 500 of them flip heads and these winners are allowed to advance to the second stage of the contest and flip again. As might be expected, 250 flip heads. Operating under the laws of chance, there will be 125 winners in the third round, 63 in the fourth, 31 in the fifth, 16 in the sixth, and 8 in the seventh.

By this time, crowds start to gather to witness the surprising ability of these expert coin-tossers. The winners are overwhelmed with adulation. They are celebrated as geniuses in the art of coin-tossing—their biographies are written and people urgently seek their advice. After all, there were 1,000 contestants and only 8 could consistently flip heads. The game continues and there are even those who eventually flip heads nine and ten times in a row.* The point of this analogy is not to indicate

---

*If we had let the losers continue to play (as mutual fund managers do, even after a bad year), we would have found several more contestants who flipped eight or nine heads out of ten and were therefore regarded as expert tossers.

that investment fund managers can or should make their decisions by flipping coins, but that the laws of chance do operate
and they can explain some amazing success stories.

As long as there are averages, some people will beat them.
With large numbers of players in the money game, chance will
— and does — explain some super performance records. The very
great publicity given occasional success in stock selection reminds me of the famous story of the doctor who claimed he had
developed a cure for cancer in chickens. He proudly announced
that in 33 percent of the cases tested remarkable improvement
was noted. In another third of the cases, he admitted, there
seemed to be no change in condition. He then rather sheepishly
added, "And I'm afraid the third chicken ran away."

While the preceding discussion has focused on mutual
funds, it should not be assumed that the funds are simply the
worst of the whole lot of investment managers. In fact, the
mutual funds have had a somewhat *better* performance record
than many other professional investors. The records of life
insurance companies, property and casualty insurance companies, foundations, college endowments, state and local trust
funds, personal trusts administered by banks, and individual
discretionary accounts handled by investment advisors have all
been studied, although not in nearly the same detail as mutual
funds. This research suggests that there are no sizable differences in investment performance among these professional
investors or between these groups and the market as a whole.
As in the case of the mutual funds there are some exceptions,
but again they are very rare. *No scientific evidence has yet
been assembled to indicate that the investment performance of
professionally managed portfolios as a group has been any better than that of randomly selected portfolios.*

Many people asked me how this thesis — first published in
1973 — has held up. The answer is, "Very well indeed. While
there continue to be some exceptions to the thesis, as I freely
admitted in 1973, history has been very kind to random walkers.
The table below makes the case as well as any. In the fifteen-
year period to 1984, over two-thirds of the professionals who

manage pension-fund common-stock portfolios were outperformed by the unmanaged Standard & Poor's 500-Stock Index.* And, as we have just read, the Forbes Dart Board Fund significantly outperformed both the unmanaged averages and the professionally managed funds.

Pension Funds Outperformed by S&P 500-Stock Index

Time Period	Return Median Pension Fund (Percent)	Return S&P 500 (Percent)	Percentage of Accounts Outperformed by S&P 500
15 years to 1984	6.7	7.7	68
20 years to 1984	7.5	8.3	66

Can Any Fundamental System Pick Winners?

Research has also been done on whether above-average returns can be earned by employing trading systems based on press announcements of new fundamental information. The answer seems to be a clear no.

Systems have been devised in which a news event such as the announcement of a stock split or an unexpectedly large increase in earnings triggers a *buy* signal. But the evidence points mainly toward the efficiency of the market in adjusting so rapidly to new information that it is impossible to devise successful trading strategies on the basis of such news announcement.** Research indicates that, on average, stock prices react well in advance of unexpectedly good or unexpectedly bad

*These data were provided by SEI Funds Evaluation (formerly A. G. Becker).

**These tests are often referred to as tests of the "semi-strong" form of the random-walk hypothesis. As mentioned earlier, the "weak" form asserts that past price information cannot be exploited to develop successful trading strategies. The "semi-strong" form says that no publicly announced news event can be exploited by investors to obtain above-average returns.

earnings reports. In other words, the market is usually sufficiently efficient at anticipating published earnings announcements that investment strategies involving purchases or sales of stocks after the publication of those announcements do not appear to offer any help to the general investor. While it is true some studies have found that stock price reactions to earnings announcements are not always complete, whatever abnormalities exist do not occur *consistently* over time and have been small enough when they did occur that only a professional broker-dealer would have earned abnormal profits. Similarly, no new information is obtained from announcements of stock splits. While it is true that companies announcing stock splits have generally enjoyed rising stock prices in the period prior to the announcement of the splits, the relative performance of the stocks after the announcement turns out to be precisely in line with that of the general market. The research indicates that splits are a consequence, not a cause, of rising stock prices and no useful investment strategy can be undertaken on the basis of news of impending stock splits. These studies lend support to the old Wall Street maxim, "A pie doesn't grow through its slicing."

There has also been a good deal of research on the usefulness of dividend increases as a basis for selecting stocks that will give above-average performance. The argument is that an increase in a stock's dividend is a signal by management that it anticipates strong future earnings. Dividend increases, in fact, are usually an accurate indicator of increases in future earnings. There is also some tendency for a strong price performance to follow the dividend announcement. However, any rise in price resulting from the dividend increase, while perhaps not immediately reflected in the price of stock was reflected reasonably completely by the end of the announcement month.

The Verdict on Market Timing

Many professional investors move money from cash to equities or to long-term bonds based on their forecasts of fundamental economic conditions. Indeed, several institutional investors now sell their services as "asset allocators" or "market timers." The words of John Bogle, chairman of the Vanguard Group of Investment Companies, in a speech given in 1984 are closest to my views on the subject of market timing. Bogle said: "In 30 years in this business, I do not know anybody who has done it successfully and consistently, nor anybody who *knows* anybody who has done it successfully and consistently. Indeed, my impression is that trying to do market timing is likely, not only *not* to add value to your investment program, but to be counterproductive."

Bogle illustrates his argument by documenting the horrendous record of private pension plans in varying the percentage of assets they allocate to equities. The following chart shows the annual returns of the Standard & Poor's 500 Stock Index and the percentage of pension plan acquisitions of financial assets flowing into equities each year. In every major stock-market cycle, pension funds have taken the incorrect course in allocating assets to equities. For instance, in the market runup in 1971-72, pension plans dramatically increased the percentage of assets going to equities—from a "norm" of 70 percent of cash flow in 1968-70 to 120 percent in 1971-72, immediately preceding the great bear market of 1973-74. Then, soured by their experience in that crashing market, they allocated just 22 percent of their 1974 asset purchases to equities, just at a time when stocks were cheap, and they should have been increasing equity exposure to benefit from the bull market of 1975-76. In 1981-82, pension funds reduced their purchases of equities to just 30 percent of cash flow, apparently frightened by the modest decline in the market in 1981. Then they roared back into the market in 1983, largely *after* the market had exploded upward. The benefits of a steady 60-70 percent equity allocation policy clearly would have been large.

Another example of the difficulty of market timing is provided by two covers from *Business Week*, one of the most respected business periodicals. On August 13, 1979, when the

Pension Fund Purchases of Equities
vs. Equity Market Performance

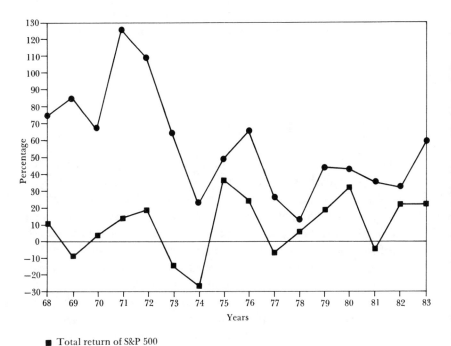

■ Total return of S&P 500
● Pension Fund Purchases of Equities as a
  Percentage of Total Pension Fund Acquisitions

S&P Index stood at 105, *Business Week* ran a cover story on
"The Death of Equities," and on May 9, 1983, after a 60 percent rise in the market, they ran another cover story, "The
Rebirth of Equities." The economist and highly successful investor, John Maynard Keynes, rendered the appropriate ver-
dict fifty years ago:

> We have not proved able to take much advantage of a general
> systematic movement out of and into ordinary shares as a whole
> at different phases of the trade cycle. . . . As a result of these
> experiences I am clear that the idea of wholesale shifts is for vari-

ous reasons impracticable and indeed undesirable. Most of those who attempt to sell too late and buy too late, and do both too often, incurring heavy expenses and developing too unsettled and speculative a state of mind, which, if it is widespread, has besides the grave social disadvantage of aggravating the scale of the fluctuations.

The Semi-strong and Strong Forms of the Random-Walk Theory

The academic community had rendered its judgment. Fundamental analysis is no better than technical analysis in enabling investors to capture above-average returns. Nevertheless, given its propensity for splitting hairs, the academic community soon fell to quarreling over the precise definition of fundamental information. Some said it was what is known now; others said it extended to the hereafter. It was at this point that what began as the strong form of the random-walk theory split into two. As we have seen, the "semi-strong" form says that no published information will help the analyst to select undervalued securities. The argument here is that the structure of market price already takes into account any public information that may be contained in balance sheets, income statements, dividend declarations, etc.; professional analyses of these data will at best be useless. The "strong" form says that absolutely nothing that is known or even knowable about a company will benefit the fundamental analyst. Not only all the news that is public but also all the information that it is possible to know about the company has already been reflected in the price of the stock.

The basic problem, both forms of the theory say, is that security analysts are very good at interpreting whatever new information does become available and acting on it quickly. Information is disseminated rapidly today, and it gets reflected almost immediately in market prices. The fact that they all react so quickly, makes it extremely difficult for the analysts to realize a significant profit in the stock market on the basis of fundamental analysis.*

Nobel laureate Paul Samuelson sums up the situation as follows:

> If intelligent people are constantly shopping around for good value, selling those stocks they think will turn out to be overvalued and buying those they expect are now undervalued, the result of this action by intelligent investors will be to have existing stock prices already have discounted in them an allowance for their future prospects. Hence, to the passive investor, who does not himself search out for under- and overvalued situations, there will be presented a pattern of stock prices that makes one stock about as good or bad a buy as another. To that passive investor, chance alone would be as good a method of selection as anything else.

This is a statement of the random-walk, or efficient-market, theory. The "narrow" (weak) form of the theory said that technical analysis — looking at past stock prices — could not help investors. The "broad" (semi-strong and strong) forms state that fundamental analysis is not helpful either: All that is known concerning the expected growth of the company's earnings and dividends, all of the possible favorable and unfavorable developments affecting the company that might be studied by the fundamental analyst, are already reflected in the price of the company's stock. Thus throwing darts at the financial page will produce a portfolio that can be expected to do as well as any managed by professional security analysts. In a nutshell, the broad form of the random-walk theory states:

> Fundamental analysis cannot produce investment recommendations that will enable an investor consistently to outperform a buy-and-hold strategy in managing a portfolio.

---

*It might actually be very inconvenient for professional analysts if it could be shown that they did get above-average returns. This would imply that some other group (presumably the public) was earning below-average returns. Think of the reformers who would press to restrict the pros' activities so as to protect the public.

The random-walk theory does not, as some critics have proclaimed, state that stock prices move aimlessly and erratically and are insensitive to changes in fundamental information. On the contrary, the point of the random-walk theory is just the opposite: the market is so efficient — prices move so quickly when new information does arise — that no one can consistently buy or sell quickly enough to benefit.

Even the legendary Benjamin Graham, heralded as the father of fundamental security analysis, reluctantly came to the conclusion that fundamental security analysis could no longer be counted on to produce superior investment returns. Shortly before he died in 1976, he was quoted in an interview in the *Financial Analysts Journal* as follows:

> . . . I am no longer an advocate of elaborate techniques of security analysis in order to find superior value opportunities. This was a rewarding activity, say, 40 years ago, when Graham and Dodd was first published; but the situation has changed. . . . [Today] I doubt whether such extensive efforts will generate sufficiently superior selections to justify their cost. . . . I'm on the side of the "efficient market" school of thought. . . .

Soft Spots in the Semi-strong and Strong Forms: Exceptions to the Rule

Are there no exceptions to the rule of the efficient market? Well, a few. While the preponderance of statistical evidence supports the view that market efficiency is high, some gremlins are lurking about that harry the efficient-market theory and make it impossible for anyone to state that the theory is conclusively demonstrated. Four of these nasty little exceptions are described below.

1. INSIDER TRADING

Corporate insiders typically do well when trading stocks of their own companies. Stocks purchased by insiders often outperform the stocks in a randomly selected group. Moreover, secondary distributions by "knowledgeable" sellers have often preceded significant price declines.

The random-walk theory recognizes that it is possible for insiders acting on the basis of information about an important mineral strike to make profits at the expense of public investors not privy to that information. Such things have happened in the past with too much frequency. But situations like that involving Texas Gulf Sulphur, where insiders allegedly profited from news of mineral discoveries at the expense of the public, are now less likely to occur than in the past.

In recent years, the Securities and Exchange Commission has taken an increasingly tough stand against anyone profiting from information not generally available to the public. The SEC has put the investment community on notice that corporate officials and anyone else acting on material nonpublic information do so at their own peril. More recently it has extended this warning to *any* investor acting on this information, even if he hears about it thirdhand—such as through his broker. It is small wonder that many a company president who thinks he has told a visiting security analyst some relevant piece of information he has not made available to others will immediately issue a public press release to rectify the situation.

Thus tightened rules on disclosure make time lags in the dissemination of new information much shorter than they may have been in previous years. Of course, the more quickly information is disseminated to the public at large, the more closely the market may be expected to conform to the random-walk model. Still, the evidence on insider trading does suggest that the very strongest form of the theory may not be valid.

2. VALUE LINE RECOMMENDATIONS

Some studies have demonstrated that, for a certain period of time, following the advice of the *Value Line Investment Survey* would have produced above-average returns for investors. This is bad news indeed for random walkers. We reply by pointing out that to some extent the higher returns can be explained by the risk level of the stocks *Value Line* selected. Moreover, one random walker was so mean as to design a study that questions the dependability of those above-average results. The stock selections of the *Survey* have been far less impressive in recent years and the investment results for the funds actually managed by *Value Line* have been distinctly mediocre.

There has also been a self-fulfilling aspect to *Value Line's* apparent success. The behavior of investors acting on the recommendations has often pushed market prices well above the previously published prices as of the official date of the recommendation. It remains to be seen if *Value Line* stock selections can consistently beat the averages in the future.

3. LOW P/E STRATEGIES

Other studies have suggested that, during most time periods from the 1960s on, stocks with low price-earnings multiples outperformed those with high price-earnings multiples. Were risk-adjusted returns on low P/E stocks to continue to exceed those on high P/E securities, the semi-strong form of the theory would be seriously weakened. I believe that the low multiples were often an indication of greater risk, however. I also feel, as I emphasized earlier, that "earnings" are not always what they seem. The "low" P/E of Continental Illinois in 1983 promptly shot up when Continental's earnings collapsed. Finally, as was shown in Chapter Four, price-earnings multiples of growth stocks had plunged relative to the Standard & Poor's average by the 1980s. Hence, in the mid-1980s a strategy of buying low-multiple stocks might not work the same way as it did in the 1970s.

4. SIZE AND OTHER EFFECTS

Another recently uncovered anomaly is now generally referred to as the "size effect." Returns on the stocks of small firms have been substantially higher than returns for the stocks of larger firms, even after attempts are made to adjust for risk. As we shall see in Part Three, however, risk is difficult to conceptualize and even harder to measure. Thus one must always be cautious of findings that may be no more than additional support for the quite reasonable stock-market maxim that the assumption of additional risk should be rewarded by extra return. Nevertheless, the magnitude of the size effect has puzzled supporters of the stronger forms of the efficient-market theory and has led to a rash of new "small-company funds" being offered to individual and to institutional investors.

As further study has been made of this phenomenon, the following findings have resulted. First, the "size effect" varies over time and may be negative in some periods. For example, from mid-1983 to mid-1984, small company stocks did substantially *worse* than the general market, as was documented in Chapter Three. This was also true of the five-year period from 1969 through 1973. Thus, investors could not simply buy a portfolio of small-company stocks and be assured of a higher rate of return over any specific time period.

Second, it has been shown that a large part of the abnormally high return from stocks of small companies occurs in the first few days of January. This is known as the "January effect" and suggests that tax effects are at work. Some investors may sell securities at the end of the calendar year to establish short-term capital losses for income-tax purposes. If this selling pressure depresses stock prices prior to the end of the year, it would seem reasonable that the bounce-back during the first week in January could create abnormal returns during that period. While this effect could be applicable for all stocks, it would be larger for small firms because stocks of small companies are more volatile and less likely to be in the portfolios of tax-exempt institutional investors and pension funds. One might suppose that traders would take advantage of any excess returns during this period. Unfortunately, transactions costs of trading in the stocks of small companies are substantially higher than for larger companies (because of the high bid-asked spreads) and there appears to be no way a commission-paying ordinary investor could exploit this anomaly.

Another strange anomaly has been called "the weekend effect." From 1953 through 1977, traders who purchased stocks on Monday just before the close and sold before Friday's close would have obtained extraordinary returns *before transactions costs*. In other words, there is some justification for the expression "blue Monday on Wall Street." It is hard to understand why such a phenomenon would continue to exist, however, and even if it did, transactions costs would wipe out any gain for the ordinary investor.

A Personal Viewpoint

Just to show how truly contrary a former analyst turned academic can be, I am now going to present my personal thoughts. But first, let's briefly recap the diametrically opposed viewpoints. The view of many of the managers themselves is that professionals certainly outperform all amateur and casual investors in managing money. Much of the academic community, on the other hand, believes that professionally managed investment portfolios cannot outperform randomly selected portfolios of stocks with equivalent risk characteristics. Random walkers claim that the stock market adjusts so quickly and perfectly to new information that amateurs buying at current prices can do just as well as the pros. Thus the value of professional investment advice is nil—at least insofar as it concerns choosing a stock portfolio.

I walk a middle road. I believe that investors might reconsider their faith in professional advisors, but I am not as ready as many of my academic colleagues to damn the entire field. While it is abundantly clear that the pros do not consistently beat the averages, I still worry about accepting all the tenets of the efficient-market theory, in part because the theory rests on several fragile assumptions. The first is that perfect pricing exists. As the quote from Paul Samuelson indicates, the theory holds that, at any time, stocks sell at the best estimates of their intrinsic values. Thus, uninformed investors buying at the existing prices are really getting full value for their money, whatever securities they purchase.

This line of reasoning is uncomfortably close to that of the "greater-fool" theory. We have seem ample evidence in Part One that stocks sometimes do not sell on the basis of anyone's estimate of value (as hard as this is to measure)—that purchasers are often swept up in waves of frenzy. The market pros were largely responsible for several speculative waves from the 1960s through the 1980s. The existence of these broader influences on market prices at least raises the possibility that investors may not want to accept the current tableau of market prices as being the best reflection of intrinsic values.*

Another fragile assumption is that news travels instantaneously. I doubt that there will ever be a time when all useful inside information is immediately disclosed to everybody. Indeed, even if it can be argued that all relevant news for the major stocks followed by institutional investors is quickly reflected in their prices, it may well be that this is not the case for all the thousands of small companies that are not closely followed by the pros. Moreover, the efficient-market theory implies that no one possesses monopolistic power over the market and that stock recommendations based on unfounded beliefs do not lead to large buying. But brokerage firms specializing in research services to institutions wield considerable power in the market and can direct tremendous money flows in and out of stocks. In this environment it is quite possible that erroneous beliefs about a stock by some professionals can for a considerable time be self-fulfilling.

---

*Robert Shiller has argued, for example, that variations in aggregate stock prices are much too large to be justified by the variation in subsequent dividend payments.

Finally, there is the enormous difficulty of translating known information about a stock into an estimate of true value. We have seen that the major determinants of a stock's value concern the extent and duration of its growth path far into the future. Estimating this is extraordinarily difficult, and there is considerable scope for an individual with superior intellect and judgment to turn in a superior performance.

But while I believe in the possibility of superior professional investment performance, I must emphasize that the evidence we have thus far does not support the view that such competence exists; and while I may be excommunicated from some academic sects because of my only lukewarm endorsement of the semi-strong and particularly the strong form of the efficient-market theory, I make no effort to disguise my heresy in the financial church. It is clear that if there are exceptional financial managers, they are very rare. This is a fact of life with which both individual and institutional investors have to deal.

PART THREE

The New Investment Technology

CHAPTER EIGHT

Modern Portfolio and Asset-Pricing Theory

> . . . Practical men, who believe themselves to be quite
> exempt from any intellectual influence, are usually the slaves
> of some defunct economist. Madmen in authority, who hear
> voices in the air, are distilling their frenzy from some
> academic scribbler of a few years back. —J. M. Keynes,
> *General Theory of Employment, Interest, and Money.*

Throughout this book, I have attempted to explain the theories used by professionals—simplified as the firm-foundation and castle-in-the-air theories—to predict the valuation of stocks. As we have seen, many academics have earned their reputations by attacking these theories. While not denying that these theories tell us a good deal about how stocks are valued, the academics maintain that they cannot be relied upon to yield extraordinary profits.

As graduate schools continued to grind out bright young economists and statisticians, the attacking academics became so numerous that it seemed obvious—even to them—that a new strategy was needed. Ergo, the academic community busily went about erecting its own theories of stock-market valuation. That's what Part Three is all about: the academic playground called the "new investment technology." Some people prefer to name it "capital-asset pricing theory." Neither title conveys the heart of the matter, which is that when all is said and done, risk is the only variable worth a damn in the market.

Academic research, remember, has taken a random walk. The stock market is such an efficient creature that nothing and no one can predict its future course in a superior manner. And, because of the actions of the pros, the prices of individual stocks quickly reflect all the information that is available. Thus, the odds of selecting superior stocks or anticipating the general direction of the market are even. Your guess is as good as that of the ape, your stockbroker, or even mine.

Hmmm. "I smell a rat," as Samuel Butler wrote long ago. Money is being made on the market; some stocks do outperform others. Common sense attests that some people can and do beat the market. It's not all chance. The academics agree; but the method of beating the market, they say, is not to exercise superior clairvoyance but rather to assume greater risk. As was briefly discussed in Chapter Seven, risk has its reward. Risk, and risk alone, determines the degree to which returns will be above or below average, and thus decides the valuation of any stock relative to the market.

Part Three deals with the new investment technology and its star performer, beta. Being an academic, I hold to the biased viewpoint that this material is important and every intelligent investor should be acquainted with the theories and models it includes. They explain how to reduce risk through diversification and present some of the ways to measure it. Even the investment professionals have latched on to much of the new investment technology. So, sit down in a straight-backed chair, prop your eyelids open, and read on. There is a lot to do in these chapters, and necessarily the discussion must be a bit more formal than in previous pages. (That means it *could* put you to sleep.) The wide-awake reader will be rewarded, however, with an understanding of a good deal of modern financial theory and of what lies behind the specific prescriptions for the investment strategy presented in Part Four.

Defining Risk: The Dispersion of Returns

Risk is a most slippery and elusive concept. It's hard for investors — let alone economists — to agree on a precise definition. The *American Heritage Dictionary* defines risk as the possibility of suffering harm or loss. If I buy one-year Treasury bills to yield 10 percent and hold them until they mature, I am virtually certain of earning a 10 percent monetary return, before income taxes. The possibility of loss is so small as to be considered nonexistent. If I hold common stock in my local power and light company for one year on the basis of an anticipated 12 percent dividend return, the possiblity of loss is greater. The dividend of the company may be cut, and, more important, the market price at the end of the year may be much lower, causing me to suffer a serious net loss. Risk is the chance that expected security returns will not materialize and, in particular, that the securities you hold will fall in price.

Once academics accepted the idea that risk for investors is related to the chance of disappointment in achieving expected security returns, a natural measure suggested itself — the probable variability or dispersion of future returns. Thus, financial risk has generally been defined as the variance or standard deviation of returns. Being long-winded, we use the accompanying exhibit to illustrate what we mean. A security whose returns are not likely to depart much, if at all, from its average (or expected) return is said to carry little or no risk. A security whose returns from year to year are likely to be quite volatile (and for which sharp losses are typical in some years) is said to be risky.

Exhibit

EXPECTED RETURN AND VARIANCE:
MEASURES OF REWARD AND RISK

This simple example will illustrate the concept of expected
return and variance and how they are measured. Suppose you
buy a stock from which you expect the following overall returns
(including both dividends and price changes) under different
economic conditions:

Business Conditions	Probability of Occurrence	Expected Return
Normal economic conditions	1 chance in 3	10 percent
Rapid real growth	1 chance in 3	30 percent
Recession with inflation (Stagflation)	1 chance in 3	−10 percent

If, on average, a third of past years have been "normal,"
another third characterized by rapid growth, and the
remaining third characterized by "stagflation," it might be
reasonable to take these relative frequencies of past events and
treat them as our best guesses (probabilities) of the likelihood of
future business conditions. We could then say that an investor's
expected return is 10 percent. A third of the time the investor
gets 30 percent, another third 10 percent, and the rest of the
time he suffers a 10 percent loss. This means that, *on average*,
his yearly return will turn out to be 10 percent.

$$\text{Expected Return} = \frac{1}{3}(.30) + \frac{1}{3}(.10) + \frac{1}{3}(-.10) = .10.$$

The yearly returns will be quite variable, however, ranging
from a 30 percent gain to a 10 percent loss. The "variance" is a
measure of the dispersion of returns. It is defined as the average
squared deviation of each possible return from its average (or
expected) value, which we just saw was 10 percent.

Variance $= \frac{1}{3}(.30-.10)^2 + \frac{1}{3}(.10-.10)^2 + \frac{1}{3}(-.10-.10)^2$

$\qquad\quad = \frac{1}{3}(.20)^2 + \frac{1}{3}(.00)^2 + \frac{1}{3}(-.20)^2 = .0267.$

The square root of the variance is called the *standard deviation*. In this example, the standard deviation equals .1634.

———————————————

Dispersion measures of risk such as variance and standard deviation have failed to satisfy everyone. "Surely riskiness is not related to variance itself," the critics say. "If the dispersion results from happy surprises—that is, from outcomes turning out better than expected, no investors in their right minds would call that risk."

It is, of course, quite true that only the possibility of downward disappointments constitutes risk. Nevertheless, as a practical matter, as long as the distribution of returns is symmetric—that is, as long as the chances of extraordinary gain are roughly the same as the probabilities for disappointing returns and losses—a dispersion or variance measure will suffice as a risk measure. The greater the dispersion or variance, the greater the possibilities for disappointment.

While the pattern of historical returns from individual securities has not usually been symmetric, the returns from well-diversified portfolios of stocks do seem to be distributed approximately symmetrically. The following chart shows the twenty-five year distribution of monthly security returns for a portfolio consisting of equal dollar amounts invested in 100 stocks. It was constructed by dividing the range of returns into equal intervals (of approximately $1\frac{1}{4}$ percent) and then noting the frequency (the number of months) with which the returns fell within each interval. On average the portfolio returned about 0.9 percent per month or 10.7 percent per year. In periods when the market declined sharply, however, the portfolio also plunged, losing as much as 13 percent in a single month.

For symmetric distributions such as this one, a helpful rule of thumb is that two-thirds of the monthly returns tend to fall within one standard deviation of the average return and 95

Distribution of Monthly Returns for a 100-Security Portfolio,
January 1945–June 1970

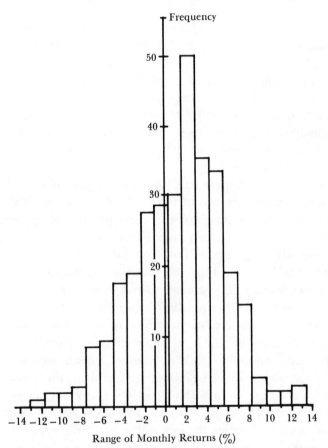

Range of Monthly Returns (%)

Source: Modigliani and Pogue, "An Introduction to Risk and Return,"
Financial Analysts Journal, March–April 1974.

percent of the returns fall within two standard deviations. Recall
that the average return for this distribution was just under 1
percent per month. The standard deviation (our measure of
portfolio risk) turns out to be about 4½ percent per month. Thus,
in two-thirds of the months the returns from this portfolio were

between 5½ percent and minus 3⅓ percent, and 95 percent of the returns were between 10 and –8 percent. Obviously, the higher the standard deviation (the more spread out are the returns), the more probable it is (the greater the risk) that at least in some periods you will take a real bath in the market. That's why a measure of variability such as standard deviation* is so often used and justified as an indication of risk.

Documenting Risk: A Long-Run Study

One of the best-documented propositions in the field of finance is that, on average, investors have received higher rates of return for bearing greater risk. The most thorough study has been done by Roger Ibbotson and Rex Sinquefield. Their data cover the period 1926 through 1983. The results are shown in the following table. Appearances notwithstanding, the table was not designed to show one Manhattan skyline and a series of Eiffel Towers. What Ibbotson and Sinquefield did was to take several different investment forms—stocks, bonds, and Treasury bills—as well as the Consumer Price Index, and measure the percentage increase or decrease each year for each item. A rectangle was then erected on the baseline to indicate the number of years the returns fell between 0 and 5 percent; another rectangle indicated the number of years the returns fell between 5 and 10 percent; and so on, for both positive and negative returns. The result is a chart which shows the dispersion of returns and from which the standard deviation can be calculated.

A quick glance shows that over long periods of time, common stocks have, on average, provided relatively generous total rates of return. These returns, including dividends and capital gains, have exceeded by a substantial margin the returns from long-term corporate bonds. The stock returns have also tended

---

*Standard deviation and its square, the variance, are used interchangeably as risk measures. They both do the same thing and it's purely a matter of convenience which one we use.

Selected Performance Statistics, 1926–83

Series	Annual (Geometric) Mean Rate of Return	Number of Years Returns Are Positive	Number of Years Returns Are Negative	Highest Annual Return (and Year)	Lowest Annual Return (and Year)	Standard Deviation of Annual Returns	Distribution
Common Stocks	9.6%	39	19	54.0% (1933)	−43.3% (1931)	21.4	
Long-term Corporate Bonds	4.2	44	14	43.8 (1982)	−8.1 (1969)	7.6	
U.S. Treasury Bills	3.1	57	1	14.7 (1981)	−0.0 (1940)	3.2	
Consumer Price Index	3.0[a]	48	10	18.2 (1946)	−10.3 (1932)	5.0	

Source: Ibbotson and Sinquefield, *Stocks, Bonds, Bills, and Inflation*, 1984.
[a] Annual rate of price increase.

to be well in excess of the inflation rate as measured by the annual rate of increase in consumer prices. Thus, stocks have also tended to provide positive "real" rates of return, that is, returns after washing out the effects of inflation. The data show, however, that common-stock returns are highly variable, as indicated by the standard deviation and the range of annual returns, shown in adjacent columns of the table. Returns from equities have ranged from a gain of over 50 percent (in 1933) to a loss of almost the same magnitude (in 1931). Clearly, the extra returns that have been available to investors from stocks have come at the expense of assuming considerably higher risk.

There have also been several periods of five years or longer when common stocks have actually produced negative rates of return. Much of the decade of the 1970s was extremely poor for stock-market investors. The 40 percent decline in the broad stock-market averages from January 1973 through February 1974 is the most dramatic change in stock prices during a brief period since the 1930s. From late 1976 through early 1978 the market had another serious sinking spell, with the popular averages down more than 20 percent. Still, over the long pull, investors have been rewarded with higher returns for taking on more risk.

The patterns evident in Ibbotson and Sinquefield's table also appear when the returns and risks of individual stock portfolios are compared. Indeed, as was shown in the preceding chapter, the differences that exist in the returns from different funds can be explained almost entirely by differences in the risk they have taken. However, given the rate of return they seek, there are ways in which investors can reduce the risks they take. This brings us to the subject of modern portfolio theory, which has revolutionized the investment thinking of professionals.

Reducing Risk: Modern Portfolio Theory (MPT)

Portfolio theory begins with the premise that all investors are like my wife—they are risk-averse. They want high returns and guaranteed outcomes. The theory tells investors how to combine stocks in their portfolios to give them the least risk possible, consistent with the return they seek. It also gives a rigorous mathematical justification for the time-honored investment maxim that diversification is a sensible strategy for individuals who like to reduce their risks.

The theory was invented in the 1950s by Harry Markowitz. His book, *Portfolio Selection*, was an outgrowth of his Ph.D. dissertation at the University of Chicago. Markowitz is a scholarly academic "computenick" type with a most varied background. His experience has ranged from teaching at UCLA to designing a computer language at RAND Corporation and helping General Electric solve manufacturing problems by computer simulations. He has even practiced money management, serving as president of Arbitrage Management Company, which ran a "hedge fund."* What Markowitz discovered was that portfolios of risky (volatile) stocks might be put together in such a way that the portfolio as a whole would actually be less risky than any one of the individual stocks in it.

The mathematics of modern portfolio theory (also known as MPT) is recondite and forbidding; it fills the journals and incidentally, keeps a lot of academics busy. That in itself is no small accomplishment. Fortunately, there is no need to lead you through the labyrinth of quadratic programming to understand the core of the theory. A single illustration will make the whole game clear.

Let's suppose we have an island economy with only two businesses. The first is a large resort with beaches, tennis courts, a

---

*Basically what Markowitz did was to search with the computer for situations where a convertible bond sold at a price that was "out of line" with the underlying common stock. He admitted, however, that it was "no great trick" and that competitors would be joining him in increasing numbers. "Then when we start tripping over each other, buying the same bonds almost simultaneously, the game will be over. Two, three years at most." I spoke to Harry three years later, and he admitted that convertible hedges were no longer attractive in the market. Consequently, he had moved on to do hedging operations on the Chicago Board Options Exchange.

golf course, and the like. The second is a manufacturer of umbrellas. Weather affects the fortunes of both. During sunny seasons the resort does a booming business and umbrella sales plummet. During rainy seasons the resort owner does very poorly, while the umbrella manufacturer enjoys high sales and large profits. The following table shows some hypothetical returns for the two businesses during the different seasons:

	Umbrella Manufacturer	Resort Owner
Rainy Season	50%	-25%
Sunny Season	-25%	50%

Suppose that, on average, one-half the seasons are sunny and one-half are rainy (i.e., the probability of a sunny or rainy season is $\frac{1}{2}$). An investor who bought stock in the umbrella manufacturer would find that half the time he earned a 50 percent return and half the time he lost 25 percent of his investment. On average, he would earn a return of $12\frac{1}{2}$ percent. This is what we have called the investor's *expected return*. Similarly, investment in the resort would produce the same results. Investing in either one of these businesses would be fairly risky, however, because the results are quite variable and there could be several sunny or rainy seasons in a row.

Suppose, however, that instead of buying only one security an investor with two dollars diversified and put half his money in the umbrella manufacturer's and half in the resort owner's business. In sunny seasons, a one-dollar investment in the resort would produce a fifty-cent return, while a one-dollar investment in the umbrella manufacturer would lose 25 cents. The investor's total return would be 25 cents (50 cents minus 25 cents), which is $12\frac{1}{2}$ percent of his total investment of two dollars.

Note that during rainy seasons exactly the same thing happens — only the names are changed. Investment in the umbrella manufacturer produces a good 50 percent return while the investment in the resort loses 25 percent. Again, however, the diversified investor makes a $12\frac{1}{2}$ percent return on his total investment.

This simple illustration points out the basic advantage of diversification. Whatever happens to the weather, and thus to the island economy, by diversifying investments over both of the firms an investor is sure of making a 12½ percent return each year. The trick that made the game work was that while both companies were risky (returns were variable from year to year), the companies were affected differently by weather conditions. (In statistical terms, the two companies had a negative covariance).* As long as there is some lack of parallelism in the fortunes of the individual companies in the economy, diversification will always reduce risk. In the present case, where there is a perfect negative relationship between the companies' fortunes (one always does well when the other does poorly), diversification can totally eliminate risk.

Of course, there is always a rub, and the rub in this case is that the fortunes of most companies move pretty much in tandem. When there is a recession and people are unemployed, they may buy neither summer vacations nor umbrellas. There-

---

*Statisticians use the term *covariance* to measure what I have called the degree of parallelism between the returns of the two securities. If we let R stand for the actual return from the resort and $\bar{R}$ be the expected or average return, while U stands for the actual return from the umbrella manufacturer and $\bar{U}$ is the average return, we define the covariance between U and R (or COV_{UR}) as follows:

$$COV_{UR} = \text{Prob. rain (U, if rain } -\bar{U}) \text{ (R, if rain } -\bar{R}) + \text{ prob. sun}$$
$$\text{(U, if sun } -\bar{U}) \text{ (R, if rain } -\bar{R}).$$

From the preceding table of returns and assumed probabilities we can fill in the relevant numbers:

$$COV_{UR} = \frac{1}{2}(.50 - .125)(-.25 - .125) + \frac{1}{2}(-.25 - .125)(.50 - .125)$$
$$= -.141.$$

Whenever the returns from two securities move in tandem (when one goes up the other always goes up) the covariance number will be a large positive number. If the returns are completely out of phase, as in the present example, the two securities are said to have negative covariance.

fore, one should not expect in practice to get the neat kind of total risk elimination just shown. Nevertheless, since company fortunes don't always move completely in parallel, investment in a diversified portfolio of stocks is likely to be less risky than investment in one or two single securities.

It is easy to carry the lessons of this illustration to actual portfolio construction. Suppose you were considering combining General Motors and its major supplier of new tires in a stock portfolio. Would diversification be likely to give you much risk reduction? Probably not. It may not be true that "as General Motors goes, so goes the nation" but it surely does follow that if General Motors' sales slump, G.M. will be buying fewer new tires from the tire manufacturer. In general, diversification will not help much if there is a high covariance between the returns of the two companies.

On the other hand, if General Motors were combined with a government contractor in a depressed area, diversification might reduce risk substantially. It usually has been true that as the nation goes, so goes General Motors. If consumer spending is down (or if an oil crisis comes close to paralyzing the nation) General Motors' sales and earnings are likely to be down and the nation's level of unemployment up. Now, if the government makes a habit during times of high unemployment of giving out contracts to the depressed area (to alleviate some of the unemployment miseries there) it could well be that the returns of General Motors and those of the contractor do not move in phase. The two stocks might have very little or, better still, negative covariance.

The example may seem a bit strained, and most investors will realize that when the market gets clobbered just about all stocks go down. Still, at least at certain times, some stocks do move against the market. Gold stocks are often given as an example of securities that do not typically move in the same direction as the general market. The point to realize in setting up a portfolio is that while the variability (variance) of the returns from individual stocks is important, even more important in judging the risk of a portfolio is covariance, the extent to which the securities move in parallel. It is this covariance that plays the critical role in Markowitz's portfolio theory.

True diversification depends on having stocks in your portfolio that are not all dependent on the same economic variables (consumer spending, business investment, housing construction, etc.). Wise investors will diversify their portfolios not by names or industries but by the determinants that influence the fluctuations of various securities.

The following chart illustrates the theory quite nicely. Looking first at the top line of the figure, marked "U.S. Stocks," we see that as the number of securities in the portfolio increases, the

The Benefits of Diversification

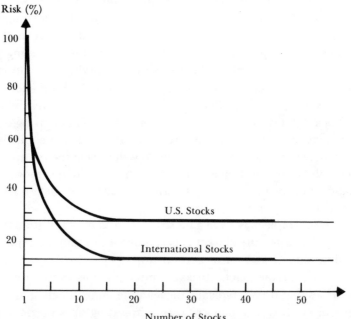

Source: Solnik, "The International Pricing of Risk," *Journal of Finance*, May 1974.

total portfolio risk is reduced. By the time the portfolio contains about 20 equal-sized and well-diversified issues, the total risk (standard deviation of returns) of the portfolio is reduced by about 70 percent. Further increase in the number of holdings do not produce any significant further risk reduction. Of course, we are assuming that the stocks in the portfolio are widely diversified. Clearly, 20 oil stocks or 20 electric utilities would not produce an equivalent amount of risk reduction.

Having learned the twin lessons that diversification reduces risk and that diversification is most helpful if one can find securities that don't move in tandem with the general market, investors in the 1980s have sought to apply these principles on the international scene. Since the movement of foreign economies is not always synchronous with that of the U.S. economy, we should expect some additional benefits from including foreign companies in the portfolio. The potential benefits of international diversification are illustrated in the bottom line of the figure. Here, the stocks are drawn not simply from the U.S. stock market but also from the United Kingdom, France, Germany, Italy, Belgium, the Netherlands, and Switzerland. As expected, the international diversified portfolio tends to be less risky than the one of corresponding size drawn purely from stocks directly traded on the NYSE.

Modeling Risk: The Capital-Asset Pricing Model (CAPM)

Portfolio theory has important implications for how stocks are actually valued. If investors seek to reduce risk in anything like the manner Harry Markowitz described, the stock market will tend to reflect these risk-reducing activities. This brings us to what is called the "capital-asset pricing model," a creation devised by Stanford professor William Sharpe, the late Harvard professor John Lintner, and others.

I've mentioned that the reason diversification cannot usually produce the miracle of risk elimination, as it did in my mythical island economy, is that usually stocks tend to move up and down together. Still, diversification is worthwhile—it can eliminate some risks. What Sharpe and Lintner did was to focus directly on what part of a security's risk can be eliminated by diversification and what part can't.

Can you imagine any stockbroker saying, "We can reasonably describe the total risk in any security (or portfolio) as the total variability (variance or standard deviaiton) of the returns from the security"? He'd probably scare away the few individual customers who are left. But we who teach are under no such constraints, and we say such things often. We go on to say that part of total risk or variability may be called the security's *systematic risk* and that this arises from the basic variability of stock prices in general and the tendency for all stocks to go along with the general market, at least to some extent. The remaining variability in a stock's returns is called *unsystematic risk* and results from factors peculiar to that particular company; for example, a strike, the discovery of a new product, and so on.

Systematic risk, also called market risk, captures the reaction of individual stocks (or portfolios) to general market swings. Some stocks and portfolios tend to be very sensitive to market movements. Others are more stable. This relative volatility or sensitivity to market moves can be estimated on the basis of the past record, and is popularly known by the Greek letter beta.

You are now about to learn all you ever wanted to know about beta but were afraid to ask. Basically, beta is the numerical description of systematic risk. Despite the mathematical manipulations involved, the basic idea behind the beta measurement is one of putting some precise numbers on the subjective feelings money managers have had for years. The beta calculation is essentially a comparison between the movements of an individual stock (or portfolio) and the movements of the market as a whole.

The calculation begins by assigning a beta of 1 to a broad market index, such as the NYSE index or the S&P 500. If a stock has a beta of 2, then on average it swings twice as far as the market. If the market goes up 10 percent, the stock rises 20 percent. If a stock has a beta of 0.5, it tends to be more stable than the market (it will go up or down 5 percent when the market rises or declines 10 percent). Professionals often call high-beta stocks aggressive investments and label low-beta stocks as defensive.

Now the important thing to realize is that *systematic risk cannot be eliminated by diversification*. It is precisely because all stocks move more or less in tandem (a large share of their variability is systematic) that even diversified stock portfolios are risky. Indeed, if you diversified perfectly by buying a share in the S&P index (which by definition has a beta of 1) you would still have quite variable (risky) returns because the market as a whole fluctuates widely.

Unsystematic risk is the variability in stock prices (and therefore, in returns from stocks) that results from factors peculiar to an individual company. Receipt of a large new contract, the finding of mineral resources on the company's property, labor difficulties, the discovery that the corporation's treasurer has had his hand in the company till—all can make a stock's price move independently of the market. The risk associated with such variability is precisely the kind that diversification can reduce. The whole point of portfolio theory was that, to the extent stocks don't move in tandem all the time, variations in the returns from any one security will tend to be washed away or smoothed out by complementary variation in the returns from other securities.

The following chart, similar to the one on page 198, illustrates the important relationship between diversification and total risk. Suppose we randomly select securities for our portfolio that tend on average to be just as volatile as the market (the average betas for the securities in our portfolio will always be equal to 1). The chart shows that as we add more and more securities the total risk of our portfolio declines, especially at the start.

When ten securities are selected for our portfolio, a good deal of the unsystematic risk is eliminated, and additional diversification yields little further risk reduction. By the time 20 well-

How Diversification Reduces Risk

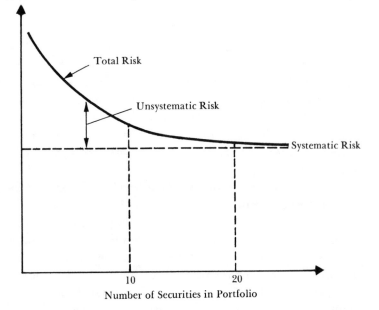

Risk of Portfolio
(Standard Deviation of Return)

Total Risk

Unsystematic Risk

Systematic Risk

10   20

Number of Securities in Portfolio

Source: Modigliani and Pogue, *op. cit.*

diversified securities are in the portfolio, the unsystematic risk is substantially eliminated and our portfolio (with a beta of 1) will tend to move up and down essentially in tandem with the market. Of course, we could perform the same experiment with stocks whose average beta is 1½. Again, we would find that diversification quickly reduced unsystematic risk, but the remaining systematic risk would be larger. A portfolio of 20 or more stocks with an average beta of 1½ would tend to be 50 percent more volatile than the market.

Now comes the key step in the argument. Both financial theorists and practitioners agree that investors should be compensated for taking on more risk by a higher expected return.

Stock prices must therefore adjust to offer higher returns where more risk is perceived, to insure that all securities are held by someone. Obviously, risk-averse investors wouldn't buy securities with extra risk without the expectation of extra reward. But not all of the risk of individual securities is relevant in determining the premium for bearing risk. The unsystematic part of the total risk is easily eliminated by adequate diversification. So there is no reason to think that investors will be compensated with a risk premium for bearing unsystematic risk. The only part of total risk that investors will get paid for bearing is systematic risk, the risk that diversification cannot help. Thus, the capital-asset pricing model says that returns (and, therefore, risk premiums) for any stock (or portfolio) will be related to beta, the systematic risk that cannot be diversified away.

The proposition that risk and reward are related is not new. Finance specialists have agreed for years that investors do need to be compensated for taking on more risk. What is different about the new investment technology is the definition and measurement of risk. Before the advent of the capital-asset pricing model, it was believed that the return on each security was related to the total risk inherent in that security. It was believed that the return from a security varied with the instability of that security's particular performance, that is, with the variability or standard deviation of the returns it produced. The new theory says that the *total* risk of each individual security is irrelevant. It is only the systematic component of that total instability that is relevant for valuation.

While the mathematical proof of this proposition would stun even a Yoda, the logic behind it is fairly simple. Consider a case where there are two groups of securities — Group I and Group II — with 20 securities in each. Suppose that the systematic risk (beta) for each security is 1; that is, each of the securities in the two groups tends to move up and down in tandem with the general market. Now suppose that, because of factors peculiar to the individual securities in Group I, the total risk for each of them is substantially higher than the total risk for each security in

Group II. Imagine, for example, that in addition to general market factors the securities in Group I are also particularly susceptible to climatic variations, to changes in exchange rates, and to natural disasters. The specific risk for each of the securities in Group I will therefore be very high. The specific risk for each of the securities in Group II, however, is assumed to be very low, and hence the total risk for each of them will be very low. Schematically, this situation appears as follows:

Group I (20 Securities)	Group II (20 Securities)
Systematic risk (beta) = 1 for each security	Systematic risk (beta) = 1 for each security
Specific risk is high for each security	Specific risk if low for each security
Total risk high for each security	Total risk low for each security

Now, according to the old theory, commonly accepted before the advent of the capital-asset pricing model, returns should be higher for a portfolio made up of Group I securities than for a portfolio made up of Group II securities, because each security in Group I has a higher total risk, and risk, as we know, has its reward. The advent of the new investment technology changed that sort of thinking. Under the capital-asset pricing model, returns from both portfolios should be equal. Why?

First, remember the chart on page 198. (The forgetful can turn the pages back to take another look.) There we saw that as the number of securities in the portfolio approached 20, the total risk of the portfolio was reduced to its systematic level. All of the unsystematic risk had been eliminated. The conscientious readers will now note that in our schematic illustration, the number of securities in each portfolio is 20. That means that the unsystematic risk has essentially been washed away: an unexpected weather calamity is balanced by a favorable exchange rate, and so forth. What remains is only the systematic risk of each stock in the portfolio, which is given by its beta. But in these two groups each of the stocks has a beta of 1. Hence, a portfolio of Group I securities and a portfolio of Group II securities will perform exactly the same with respect to risk (standard deviation) even though the stocks in Group I display higher total risk than the stocks in Group II.

The old and the new views now meet head on. Under the old system of valuation, Group I securities were regarded as offering a higher return because of their greater risk. The capital-asset pricing model says there is no greater risk in holding Group I securities if they are in a diversified portfolio. Indeed, if the securities of Group I did offer higher returns, then all rational investors would prefer them over Group II securities and would attempt to rearrange their holdings to capture the higher returns from Group I. But by this very process they would bid up the prices of Group I securities and push down the prices of Group II securities until, with the attainment of equilibrium (when investors no longer want to switch from security to security), the portfolio for each group had identical returns, related to the systematic component of their risk (beta) rather than to their total risk (including the unsystematic or specific portions). Because stocks can be combined in portfolios to eliminate specific risk, only the undiversifiable or systematic risk will command a risk premium. Investors will not get paid for bearing risks that can be diversified away. This is the basic logic behind the capital-asset pricing model.

In a big fat nutshell, the proof of the capital-asset pricing model (henceforth to be known as CAPM because we economists love to use letter abbreviations) can be stated as follows:

> If investors did get an extra return (a risk premium) for bearing unsystematic risk, it would turn out that diversified portfolios made up of stocks with large amounts of unsystematic risk would give larger returns than equally risky portfolios of stocks with less unsystematic risk. Investors would snap at the chance to have these higher returns, bidding up the prices of stocks with large unsystematic risk and selling stocks with

equivalent betas but lower unsystematic risk. This process would continue until the prospective returns of stocks with the same betas were equalized and no risk premium could be obtained for bearing unsystematic risk. Any other result would be inconsistent with the existence of an efficient market.

The key relationship of the theory is shown in the following chart. As the systematic risk (beta) of an individual stock (or portfolio) increases, so does the return an investor can expect. If an investor's portfolio has a beta of zero, as might be the case if all his funds were invested in a bank savings certificate (beta would be zero since the returns from the certificate would not vary at all with swings in the stock market), the investor would receive some modest rate of return, which is generally called the risk-free rate of interest. As the individual takes on more risk, however, the return should increase. If the investor holds a portfolio with a beta of 1 (as, for example, holding a share in one of the broad stock market averages) his return will equal the general return from common stocks. This return has over long periods of time exceeded the risk-free rate of interest, but the investment is a risky one. In certain periods the return is much less than the risk-free rate and involves taking substantial losses. This, as we have said, is precisely what is meant by risk.

The diagram shows that a number of different expected returns are possible simply by adjusting the beta of the portfolio. For example, suppose the investor put half of his money in a savings certificate and half in a share of the market averages. In this case he would receive a return midway between the risk-free return and the return from the market and his portfolio would have an average beta of 0.5.* The CAPM then asserts very simply that to get a higher average long-run rate of return you should just increase the beta of your portfolio. An investor can get a portfolio with a beta larger than 1 either by buying high-beta stocks or by purchasing a portfolio with average volatility on margin. (See the following illustration.) There was an actual fund proposed by a West Coast bank that would have allowed an

---

*In general, the beta of a portfolio is simply the weighted average of the betas of its component parts.

Risk and Return According to the Capital-Asset Pricing Model*

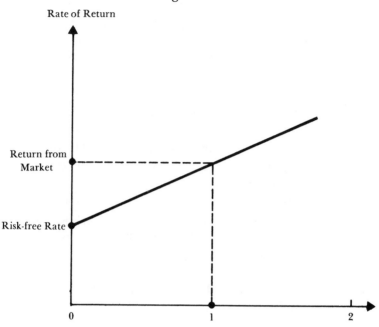

Systematic Risk (Beta)

*Those who remember their high school algebra will recall that any straight line can be written as an equation. The equation for the straight line in the diagram is

Rate of Return = Risk-free Rate + Beta (Return from Market — Risk-free Rate).

Alternately, the equation can be written as an expression for the risk premium, that is, the rate of return on the portfolio or stock over and above the risk-free rate of interest.

Rate of Return — Risk-free Rate = Beta (Return from Market — Risk-free Rate).

The equation says that the risk premium you get on any stock or portfolio increases directly with the beta value you assume. Some readers may wonder what relationship beta has to the covariance concept that was so critical in our discussion of portfolio theory. The beta for any security is essentially the same thing as the covariance between that security and the market index as measured on the basis of past experience.

investor to buy the S&P average on margin, thus increasing both
his risk and potential reward. Of course, in times of rapidly
declining stock prices, such a fund would have enabled an
investor to lose his shirt in a hurry. This may explain why the
fund found few customers in the 1970s.

Just as stocks had their fads, so beta came into high fashion by
the early 1970s. The *Institutional Investor*, the glossy prestige
magazine that spent most of its pages chronicling the accomplish-
ments of professional money managers, put its imprimatur on
the movement in 1971 by featuring on its cover the letters BETA
on top of a temple and including as its lead story "The Beta Cult!
The New Way to Measure Risk." The magazine noted that
money men whose mathematics hardly went beyond long division
were now "tossing betas around with the abandon of Ph.D.s in
statistical theory." Even the Securities and Exchange Commission
gave beta its approval as a risk measure in its Institutional
Investors Study Report.

Illustration of Portfolio Building[a]

Desired Beta	Composition of Portfolio	Expected Return From Portfolio
0	$1 in risk-free asset	10%
$\frac{1}{2}$	$.50 in risk-free asset $.50 in market portfolio	$\frac{1}{2}(.10) + \frac{1}{2}(.15) = .125,$ or $12\frac{1}{2}\%$[b]
1	$1 in market portfolio	15%
$1\frac{1}{2}$	$1.50 in market portfolio borrowing $.50 at an assumed rate of 10 percent	$1\frac{1}{2}(.15) - \frac{1}{2}(.10) = .175,$ or $17\frac{1}{2}\%$

[a]Assuming expected market return is 15 percent and risk-free rate is 10 percent.
[b]We can also derive the figure for expected return using directly the formula
that accompanies the preceding chart:

$$\text{Rate of Return} = .10 + \frac{1}{2}(.15 - .10) = .125, \text{ or } 12\frac{1}{2}\%.$$

In Wall Street the early beta fans boasted that they could earn higher long-run rates of return simply by buying a few high-beta stocks. Those who thought they were able to time the market thought they had an even better idea. They would buy high-beta stocks when they thought the market was going up, switching to low-beta ones when they feared the market might decline. To accommodate the enthusiasm for this new investment idea, beta measurement services proliferated among brokers, and it was a symbol of progressiveness for an investment house to provide its own beta estimates. The beta boosters in the Street oversold their product with an abandon that would have shocked even the most enthusiastic academic scribblers intent on spreading the beta gospel.

CHAPTER NINE

The Current State of the Art: Beyond Beta

Everything should be made as simple as possible, but not
more so. — Albert Einstein

In Shakespeare's *Henry IV*, Glendower boasts to
Hotspur, "I can call spirits from the vasty deep." "Why, so can I
or so can any man," says Hotspur, unimpressed; "but will they
come when you do call for them?" Anyone can theorize about
how security markets work, and the capital-asset pricing model is
just another theory. The really important question is: Does it
work?

Certainly many institutional investors have embraced the
beta concept, if only in an attempt to play down the flamboyant
excesses of the past. Beta is, after all, an academic creation.
What could be more staid? Simply creating a number that
describes a stock's risk, it appears almost sterile in nature. True,
it requires large investments in computer programs, but the
closet chartists love it. Even is you don't believe in beta, you have
to speak its language because back on the nation's campuses, my

colleagues and I have been producing a long line of Ph.D.'s and M.B.A.'s who spout its terminology.

By September 1980, according to a *Wall Street Journal* article, beta had become so popular that it underlay the investment rationale for $65 billion in U.S. pension funds. Beta also appears to provide a method of evaluating a portfolio manager's performance. If the realized return is larger than that predicted by the overall portfolio beta, the manager is said to have produced a positive alpha. During the 1970s, lots of money in the market sought out the manager who could deliver the largest alpha.

But is beta a useful measure of risk? Do high-beta portfolios always fall farther in bear markets than low-beta ones? Is it true that high-beta portfolios will provide larger long-term returns than lower-beta ones, as the capital-asset pricing model suggests? Do present methods of calculating beta on the basis of past history give any useful information about future betas? Does beta alone summarize a security's total systematic risk, or do we need to consider other factors as well? In short, does beta really deserve an alpha? These are subjects of intense current debate among practitioners and academics, and not all the evidence is in as yet. This chapter reviews the available evidence and discusses the current state of thinking on the new investment technology.

Batting for Beta: The Supporting Evidence

Tests of the capital-asset pricing model have tried to ascertain if security returns are in fact directly related to beta, as the theory asserts. I have already presented some data on this question in previous chapters. Here I would like to present some additional evidence.

The enthusiasm for beta and for the CAPM in which it is wrapped has been fueled by charts, such as the following, that show the relationship between the performance of a large number of professionally managed funds and the beta measure

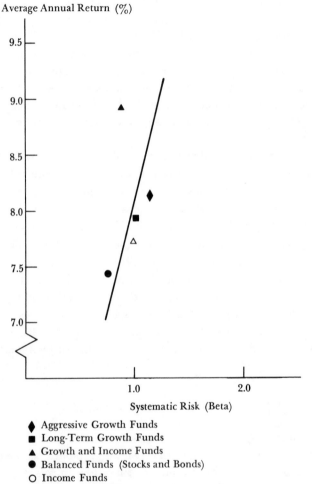

Average Annual Return vs. Risk: Selected Institutional
Investors (15 Years, 1969-1983)

Average Annual Return (%)

◆ Aggressive Growth Funds
■ Long-Term Growth Funds
▲ Growth and Income Funds
● Balanced Funds (Stocks and Bonds)
○ Income Funds
△ Stocks (S&P 500)

of relative volatility. It is because the numbers are averages of
many funds that the relationship between risk and reward is so
tight. Still, the results appear to be quite consistent with the
theory. The portfolio returns have varied positively with beta in

(almost) a straight-line manner, so that over the long pull, high-beta portfolios have provided larger total returns than low-risk ones.

The next two charts break down the fifteen-year performance into two subperiods: (1) the ten years when the market went up and (2) the five years when it went down. Again, the relationship is exactly as predicted by the theory. In "up" years, the high-beta portfolios well outdistanced the low-beta ones. (Since the market was up on average from 1969 through 1983, this same relationship held over the whole period.) In "down" years, however, the high-beta portfolios did considerably worse than the low-volatility ones. It was the high-beta portfolios that took the real drubbings in the bear-market periods of the 1970s. Of course, this is precisely what we mean by the concept of risk, and this is why betas for diversified portfolios appear to be useful risk measures.

The possibility of obtaining higher returns over the long pull from higher-beta portfolios is perfectly consistent with the random-walk and efficient-market notions I have discussed earlier. The former theories assert that there is no way to gain superior performance (that is, extra returns) *for a given level of risk*. The beta advocates say that the only way to gain extra returns is to take on more risk. But this is hardly an inefficiency in the market. It is the natural expectation in a market where most participants dislike risk and therefore must be compensated (rewarded) to bear it.

Being Bearish on Beta: Some Disquieting Results

Like just about everything in life, beta may work well some of the time, but it certainly doesn't live up to its press billings all of the time. Burrowing away at the statistical base of the capital-asset pricing model, the beta bears have uncovered major flaws. The evidence contradicting this fundamental part of the new investment technology has sent some practitioners and

Average Annual Return vs. Risk: Selected Institutional
Investors (10 "Up" Years, 1969–1983)

Average Annual Return (%)

● Aggressive Growth Funds
■ Long-Term Growth Funds
▲ Growth and Income Funds
□ Balanced Funds (Stocks and Bonds)
○ Income Funds
△ Stocks (S&P 500)

Average Annual Return vs. Risk: Selected Institutional Investors (5 "Down" Years, 1969–1983)

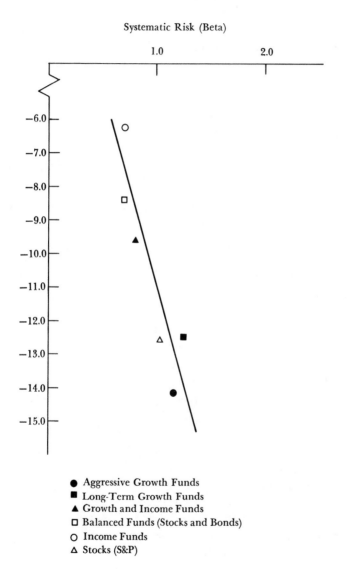

Systematic Risk (Beta)

● Aggressive Growth Funds
■ Long-Term Growth Funds
▲ Growth and Income Funds
□ Balanced Funds (Stocks and Bonds)
○ Income Funds
△ Stocks (S&P)

academics off in search of ways to improve the CAPM. But judging from a cover story in the July 1980 *Institutional Investor*, many of those who in the past swore by the model are now disavowing it altogether. The story noted, "It took nearly a decade for money managers to learn to love beta. Now it looks like they were sold a bill of goods." While this reaction may be a bit too strong, we do need to examine the academic studies that have led to beta's fall from grace.

ACADEMIC ATTACK 1: THEORY DOES NOT MEASURE
UP TO PRACTICE

Recall that the CAPM could be reduced to a very simple formula:

Rate of Return = Risk-free Rate + Beta (Return from Market — Risk-free Rate).

Thus, a security with a zero beta should give a return exactly equal to the risk-free rate. Unfortunately, the actual results don't come out that way.

This damning accusation is the finding from an exhaustive study of all the stocks on the New York Stock Exchange over a thirty-five-year period. The securities were grouped into ten portfolios of equal size, according to their beta measures for the year. Thus, Portfolio I consisted of the 10 percent of the NYSE securities with the highest betas. Portfolio II contained the 10 percent with the second-highest betas, etc. The chart below shows the relation between the average monthly return and the beta for each of the ten different portfolios (shown by the black dots on the chart) over the entire period. The market portfolio is denoted by O, and the solid line is a line of best fit (a regression line) drawn through the dots. The dashed line connects the average risk-free rate of return with the rate of return on the market portfolio. This is the theoretical relationship of the CAPM that was described in the last chapter.

If the CAPM were absolutely correct, the theoretical and the actual relationship would be one and the same. But practice, as

Systematic Risk (Beta) vs. Average Monthly Return for Ten Different-Risk Portfolios, and the Market Portfolio for 1931-65

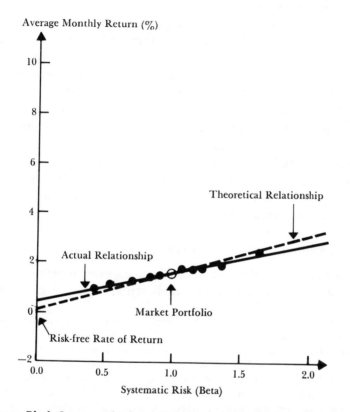

Source: Black, Jensen, and Scholes, "The Capital Asset Pricing Model: Some Empirical Tests," in *Studies in the Theory of Capital Markets,* ed. Jensen, 1972.

can quickly be seen, is not represented by the same line as theory on the chart. Note particularly the difference between the rate of return on an actual zero-beta common stock or portfolio of stocks and the risk-free rate. From the chart, it is clear that the measured zero-beta rate of return exceeds the risk-free rate. Since the zero-beta portfolio and a portfolio of riskless assets such as Treasury bills have the same systematic risk (beta), this result implies that something besides a beta measure of risk is being valued in the market. It appears that some unsystematic (or at least some non-beta) risk makes the return higher for the zero-beta portfolio.

Furthermore, the actual risk-return relationship examined by Black, Jensen, and Scholes appears to be flatter than that predicted by the CAPM; low-risk stocks earn higher returns, and high-risk stocks earn lower returns, than the theory predicts. (This is a phenomenon much like that found at the race track, where long shots seem to go off at much lower odds than their true probability of winning would indicate, whereas favorites go off at higher odds than is consistent with their winning percentages). Shrewd old Adam Smith recognized this way back in 1776 when he wrote, "The ordinary rate of profit always rises more or less with the risk. It does not, however, seem to rise . . . so as to compensate it completely."*

ACADEMIC ATTACK 2: BETA IS A FICKLE SHORT-TERM PERFORMER

The devergence of theory from evidence is even more striking in the short run: for some short periods, it may happen that risk and

---

*Fischer Black attempted to explain these discrepancies between theory and evidence by pointing out that with uncertain inflation, the future real value of any dollar return is also uncertain. Hence, what we have been calling the risk-free rate is actually a risky real rate of return. Indeed, when inflation is taken into account a truly riskless asset does not exist. It is therefore not surprising that the procedure of drawing a line from some supposedly risk-free return through the market portfolio (as in the theoretical relationship depicted in the chart above) does not represent the actual relationship between returns and beta.

Black argues that the true relationship between risk and return can be described by the following equation:

Rate of Return = Zero-beta Return + Beta (Return from Market − Zero-beta Return).

He finds that the data better support this version of the CAPM. It is, however, still subject to many of the other problems that are discussed in the rest of this chapter.

return are *negatively* related. In 1972, for example, which was an "up" market year, it turned out that safer (lower-beta) stocks went up *more* than the more volatile securities. *Fortune* magazine commented dryly on this well-publicized failure, "The results defied the textbooks." What happened was that in 1972 styles changed in Wall Street as institutional investors eschewed younger, more speculative companies, the "faded ladies" of the late 1960s, and became much more enamored of the highest-quality, most stable leading corporations in the so-called "first tier" of stocks. This was the Nifty Fifty craze chronicled in Chapter Three. It became clear that beta could not be used to guarantee investors a predictable performance over a period of a few months or even a year.

Black, Jensen, and Scholes found a similar type of anomaly for the entire period from April 1957 through December 1965. Their results are shown in the chart below.

Not only does the zero-beta return exceed the riskless rate here, but during this period of nearly nine years, securities with higher risk produced *lower* returns than less-risky (lower-beta) securities. Substantial deviations from the relationship predicted by the CAPM were also found for many subperiods.

If we maintain that beta summarizes the total systematic risk of securities, we must accept three uncomfortable conclusions: (1) in some short periods, investors may be penalized for taking on more risk; (2) in the long run, investors are not rewarded enough for high risk and are overcompensated for buying securities with low risk; and (3) in all periods, some unsystematic risk is being valued by the market. Any of these results is a serious contradiction of the CAPM.

ACADEMIC ATTACK 3: ESTIMATED BETAS ARE UNSTABLE

Another problem the theory encounters is the instability of measured betas. One might well be skeptical about the wisdom of relying on beta estimates based on historical data. Beta really looks suspiciously like a tool of technical analysis in academic

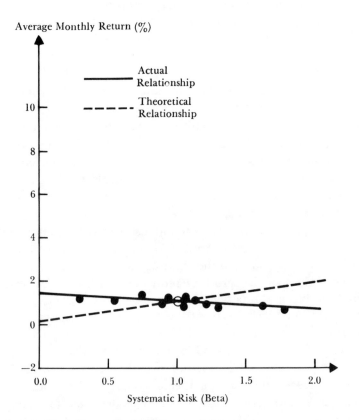

Source: Black, Jensen, and Scholes, *op. cit.*

dress—a bastard cousin of the technicians' charts. And as far as individual securities go, historical betas—used as a basis for predicting future betas and, hence, expected security returns—do not seem to be much more reliable as predictors of security performance than any of the devices cooked up by technical analysts.

In order to see how beta familiarity breeds contempt, we should know how beta is bred in the first place. The typical procedure in estimating betas for an individual stock is to measure the relationship between the security's past return and the return from the market as a whole. For example, suppose that in the last quarter AT&T's total return (including both dividends and capital gains) was 5 percent and the market return (similarly measured) was 10 percent. We plot this pair of returns on a graph, as is done below.

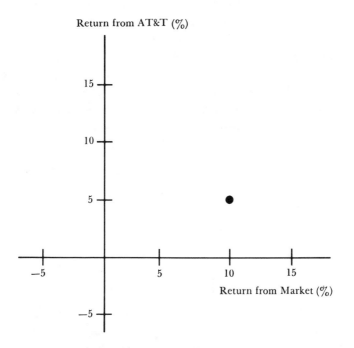

We can continue the process by measuring the rate of return for AT&T and for the S&P 500 (our proxy for the market) in many other past three-month periods, and we can plot these observations on the same graph. After many pairs of returns for AT&T and for the market have been plotted, a line of best fit (a regression line) is drawn to represent the average relationship between the returns from AT&T and those from the S&P 500.*

*The regression line is also called a "least squares" line, since it is estimated by finding the line that minimizes the sum of the squared vertical distances from each of the black dots to the line.

The slope of the regression line (i.e., the ratio between the vertical and horizontal sides of a right triangle having the regression line as its hypotenuse) is our measure of the security's historical beta. This historical beta is then used as an estimate of the security's future beta. In this example, we get a beta estimate for AT&T of ½, or 0.5. This means that AT&T has been about half as volatile as the overall market, and the assumption is that it will continue to be so in the future. It is clear why this last assertion may be wrong. After the divesture of 1983 and with deregulation of the telecommunications industry, AT&T is not the same company as it previously was. Even without such major changes affecting the characteristics of the company's stock, some unforseen event(s), not reflected in past returns, may decisively affect the security's future returns.

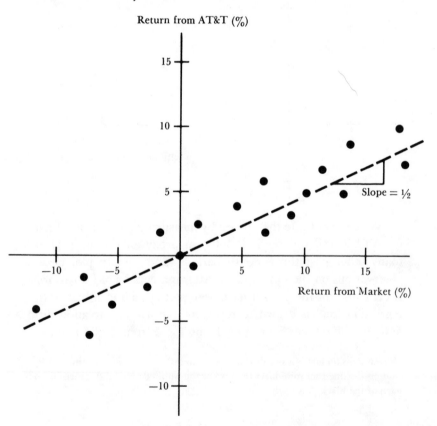

To illustrate this hazard in measuring an individual stock's beta, consider the following example: During some periods in the 1960s, Mead Johnson and Company (now part of Bristol-Myers Company) had a measured beta that was negative; it tended to move against the market, and thus appeared to be precisely the kind of stock investors would seek to reduce the risks of their portfolio. But looking behind the reasons for this measured beta's being less than zero did not give one very much comfort that the beta for the future—which is after all what is really relevant— would turn out to be anything like the beta from the past.

What happened in the Mead Johnson case was that in 1962 the Company came out with a marvelous new product that became an instant bestseller. The product, called "Metrecal," was a liquid dietary supplement. Consumers were urged to have a can of Metrecal rather than their normal lunch. Metrecal would provide all the vitamins and nutrients needed for health with few of the calories that usually went along with lunch. And so, in 1962, as Americans became more diet-conscious, drinking Metrecal became quite a fad, and the earnings and stock price of Mead Johnson climbed sharply at precisely the time the stock market was taking one of its worst baths since the Great Depression.

Like most fads, the Metrecal boom did not last very long; by 1963 and 1964, just when the general stock market was recovering, Americans got pretty sick and tired of drinking Metrecal for lunch, and the big boost in earnings and stock prices that Mead Johnson had earlier enjoyed began to fade away.

Later in the 1960s, just about the time the market took another slump, Mead Johnson came out with another new product. This one was called "Nutrament." Nutrament was a dietary supplement that was supposed to put on weight, and skinny teenagers bought it by the case to improve their appearance. Yes, you guessed it! Nutrament was the same product as Metrecal except that if you drank Nutrament *in addition* to lunch you could put on weight, rather than lose it. Again, Mead Johnson prospered while the market slumped, and it is this unusual combination of circumstances that produced the negative betas of the period.

The problem is, of course, whether such a fortuitous string of events could reasonably be anticipated to occur in the future. On a priori grounds we would expect not. Indeed, what was in fact measured was anything but a systematic relationship with the market. Of course, this is precisely the problem in predicting betas on the basis of past experience. Any changes in the economy, in the characteristics of an individual company, or in the competitive situation facing the company can be expected to change the sensitivity of the company's stock to market fluctuations. It would be surprising to discover that betas of individual stocks did not vary widely over time. In fact, they do vary. The Mead Johnson example is not just an isolated case, the exception that proves the rule.

Marshall Blume has conducted several tests of the stability of historical beta estimates. He has found that the smaller the number of securities in the portfolio, the weaker the relationship between portfolio betas for consecutive periods. Some of his results are shown in the table below. For a portfolio of one security, the earlier beta is a very poor predictor of the beta in the second period: past betas are not useful predictors of future betas for individual stocks. Not surprisingly, the table also shows that better predictive power is obtained from betas calculated for portfolios containing larger numbers of stocks. Thanks to the law of large numbers, a number of inaccurate beta estimates on individual stocks can be combined to form a much more accurate estimate of the risk of the portfolio as a whole. While the beta estimates for some securities will be much too high, the estimates for many others will be too low.

Mutual-fund betas are not quite as easy to predict from period to period as betas for unmanaged portfolios because fund managers will often deliberately change the risk composition of the portfolio. Still, the general investment objective of the fund (e.g., growth, stability, etc.) does put a limit on the degree of change possible, and mutual-fund betas also tend to be far more stable from period to period than are the betas for individual stocks. Still, the general conclusion that should be drawn from

Correlations of Betas for July 1954–June 1961 with Betas
for July 1961–June 1968

Number of Securities in Portfolio	Correlation Coefficient[a]	Coefficient of Determination[b]
1	.60	.36
2	.73	.53
4	.84	.71
7	.88	.77
10	.92	.85
20	.97	.95
35	.97	.95
50	.98	.96

Source: Blume, "On the Assessment of Risk," *Journal of Finance,* March 1971.
[a]The correlation coefficient is a number between zero and 1 showing how closely betas in one period match betas in the next period. A correlation coefficient of 1 indicates perfect predictability—the beta in the base period can be used to predict the beta in the second period with complete accuracy. A correlation coefficient of zero indicates that no relationship whatsoever exists between betas in successive periods.
[b]The coefficient of determination (R^2) is the square of the correlation coefficient. It tells what percentage of the variability of betas in the second period can be "explained" by betas in the base period.

this discussion is that historical betas may be quite imperfect indicators of future betas. The people who oversold beta as a useful tool in predicting the behavior of individual stocks did the new investment technology a great disservice. In judging risk, beta cannot substitute for brains.

Many beta boomers, however, have gone to great lengths to legitimize their technical bastard. One of the most celebrated of these is Barr Rosenberg, a professor at Berkeley, whose new investment technology work and California lifestyle were celebrated in a cover story in *Institutional Investor* during the late 1970s. What Rosenberg has done is to come up with a better beta mousetrap. Instead of calculating betas from past history, Rosenberg calculates what he calls "fundamental betas" based on the fundamental characteristics of each company, such as its earnings history, relative size, financial structure, and so forth. (Think of Chrysler, a *relatively* small company in a cyclical industry, in debt up to its eyeballs. No wonder the stock is so volatile.) These risk estimates became known as "Barr's bionic betas."

An academic turned entrepreneur, Rosenberg formed his own firm, Barr Rosenberg and Associates (or just BARRA, as the name appears on the official company T-shirt). Along with his reputation as the guru of the new investment technology, Barr presents the perfect image. He is into Zen, attends Esalen, and intones a Sanskrit chant before dinner. He believes in telepathy and clairvoyance. Each year, he spends three months on the Hawaiian island of Kauai for work and meditation. Although quiet and unassuming, he projects a kind of authority and omniscience. While the pros have not all jumped to embrace Rosenberg's techniques, he has won several converts among the cadre of institutional investors. Unfortunately, however, Rosenberg's betas are still based on historical accounting information and thus are still subject to the same kind of instability problems as are conventional betas.

ACADEMIC ATTACK 4: BETA IS EASILY ROLLED OVER

Perhaps the most devastating criticism of beta has been delivered by Richard Roll. Like Rosenberg, he is a financial theorist from California. The resemblance ends there. The personalities of the two men clash. Barr is a guru, while *Institutional Investor* has characterized Richard Roll as "ebullient and 'laid back'— teaching his UCLA course in jeans and a shirt open to the waist . . . —with a taste for fast motorcycles and (aggressive) skiing"; and their theories clash, too. Roll has focused his attack on the CAPM, the model Rosenberg has painstakingly defended.

Roll says that it is impossible to observe the market's return. Because, in principle, the market includes *all* stocks, a variety of other financial instruments, and even nonmarketable assets such as an individual's investment in education, the S&P index (or any other index used to represent the market) is a very imperfect market proxy at best. And when we measure market risk using an imperfect proxy, we may obtain a quite imperfect estimate of market sensitivity. Roll showed that by changing the market index against which betas are measured, one can obtain quite different measures of the risk level of individual stocks or portfolios. As a consequence, one would make very different predictions about the expected returns from the stocks or portfolios. He further demonstrated that by changing market indexes (from, say, the S&P 500 to the much broader Wilshire 5000) one could actually reverse the risk-adjusted performance rankings (alphas) of fund managers. But if betas differ according to the market proxy that are measured against, and if you never can get a measure of the "true" market portfolio, then, in effect, the CAPM has not been (and cannot be) adequately tested.

Obviously, these problems with the CAPM have been the subject of intense debate among practitioners and academics. If beta cannot produce an alpha, what's an investor or academic to do? *Institutional Investor,* the magazine which was early in chronicling the ascendancy of the CAPM and beta, turned full circle. In the summer of 1980, it ran another cover story on beta, this one with the title "Is Beta Dead?" The story quoted a letter the magazine had just received from a writer known only as "Deep Quant."* The letter began, "There is a very big story breaking in money management. The Capital-Asset Pricing Model is dead." The Magazine went on to quote one "turncoat quant" as follows: "If Roll is right, advanced mathematics will become to investors what the *Titanic* was to sailing," and so the whole set of tools making up the new investment technology— including even modern portfolio theory (MPT)—came under a cloud of suspicion.

---

*"Quant" is the Wall Street nickname for the quantitatively inclined financial analyst who devotes attention largely to the new investment technology.

Does it bother you at all that when you say MPT quickly it comes out "empty"?

Source: *Pensions and Investments,* September 15, 1980.

Searching for the Investment Grail

My own guess is that the "turncoat quant" is wrong. The
unearthing of serious cracks in the CAPM will not lead to an
abandonment of mathematical tools in financial analysis and a
return to traditional security analysis. The evidence that supports
the efficiency of capital markets and the existence of a positive
relationship between risk and return is far too abundant for anyone to reject the new investment technology out of hand. And
since academics and practitioners have already made substantial
progress in building better theories of the risk-return relationship, the practical consequence of the failures of the CAPM is
likely to be *more* discriminating risk measurement, with the use
of even more quantitative tools in risk analysis—not less. In this
section, I will give the flavor of some of the new approaches to
security pricing that have been developed as alternatives to the
CAPM, and will present their practical meaning to investment
analysts.

THE QUANT QUESTS: RECENT WORK ON RISK MEASUREMENT

One of the pioneers in the field of risk measurement is the Yale School of Management's finance wunderkind, Stephen Ross. Ross has developed a new theory of pricing in the capital markets called "APT," or Arbitrage Pricing Theory. APT has had wide influence both in the academic community and in the practical world of portfolio management. To understand the logic of the newest APT work on risk measurement, one must remember the correct insight underlying the CAPM: The only risk that investors should be compensated for bearing is the risk that cannot be diversified away. Only systematic risk will command a risk premium in the market. But the systematic elements of risk in particular stocks and portfolios may be too complicated to be capturable by a measure of beta — the tendency of the stocks to move more or less than the market. This is especially so since any particular stock index is a very imperfect representative of the general market. Hence, many quants now feel that beta may fail to capture a number of important systematic elements of risk.

Let's take a look at several of these other systematic risk elements. Changes in national income, for one, may affect returns from individual stocks in a systematic way. This was shown in our illustration of a simple island economy, in the preceding chapter. Also, changes in national income mirror changes in the personal income of individuals, and the systematic relationship between security returns and salary income can be expected to have a significant effect on individual behavior. For example, the laborer in a Ford plant will find a holding of Ford common stock particularly risky, since job layoffs and poor returns from Ford stock are likely to occur at the same time. Changes in national income may also reflect changes in other forms of property income and may therefore be relevant for institutional portfolio managers as well.

Changes in interest rates also systematically affect the returns from individual stocks and are important nondiversifiable risk elements. To the extent that stocks tend to suffer as interest rates go up, equities are a risky investment, and those stocks that are particularly vulnerable to increases in the general level of interest rates are especially risky. Thus, many stocks and fixed-income investments will tend to move in parallel, and these stocks will not be helpful in reducing the risk of a bond portfolio. Since fixed-income securities are a major part of the portfolios of many institutional investors, this systematic risk factor is particularly important for some of the largest investors in the market. Clearly, then, investors who think of risk in its broadest and most meaningful sense will be sensitive to the tendency of certain stocks to be particularly affected by changes in interest rates.

Changes in the rate of inflation will similarly tend to have a systematic influence on the returns from common stocks. This is so for at least two reasons. First, an increase in the rate of inflation tends to increase interest rates and thus tends to lower the prices of equities, as just discussed. Second, the increase in inflation may squeeze profit margins for certain groups of companies — public utilities, for example, which often find that rate increases lag behind increases in costs. On the other hand, inflation may benefit the prices of common stock in the natural-resource industries. Thus, again there are important systematic relationships between stock returns and economic variables that may not be captured adequately by a simple beta measure of risk.

Statistical tests of the influence on security returns of several systematic risk variables have shown promising results. Better explanations than those given by the CAPM can be obtained for the variation in returns among different securities by using, in addition to the traditional beta measure of risk, a number of systematic risk variables, such as sensitivity to changes in national income, in interest rates, and in the rate of inflation. Of course, the evidence supporting many-risk-factor models of security pricing has only begun to accumulate. It is not yet certain how these new theories will stand up to more extensive examination. Still, the preliminary results are definitely encouraging.

If, however, one wanted for simplicity to select the one risk measure most closely related to expected returns, the traditional beta measure would not be my first choice. In my own work with John Cragg, the best single risk proxy turned out to be the extent of disagreement among security analysts' forecasts for each individual company. Companies for which there is a broad consensus with respect to the growth of future earnings in dividends seem to be considered less risky (and hence have lower expected returns) than companies for which there is little agreement among security analysts. It is possible to interpret this result as contradicting modern asset pricing theory, which suggests that individual security variability *per se* will not be relevant for valuation. The dispersion of analysts' forecasts, however, may actually serve as a particularly useful proxy for a variety of systematic risks.

Consider, for example, two companies. One, a machinery manufacturer, is heavily in debt and extremely sensitive to systematic influences. The other, an all-equity pharmaceutical firm, is quite insensitive to economic conditions. It could be that Wall Street analysts agree completely on how economic conditions will affect the companies, but differ greatly on their economic forecasts. If so, there could be a big dispersion in earnings forecasts for the machinery manufacturer (because of the difference in economic forecasts and the extreme sensitivity of the company to economic conditions) and very small differences in the forecasts for the drug company (because economic conditions have little effect on that company). Thus, if two different analysts have very different forecasts for GNP, inflation, and interest rates, a highly debt-leveraged company in a heavy industry would be greatly affected by differences in underlying economic forecasts, while the unleveraged drug company might show no effect whatsoever. Hence, differences in analysts' forecasts could be a most useful proxy for systematic risk in the broadest sense of the term.

While we still have much to learn about the market's evaluation of risk, I believe it is fair to conclude that risk is unlikely to be captured adequately by a single beta statistic, the risk measure of the CAPM. It appears that several other systematic risk measures affect the valuation of securities. In addition, as was indicated in the previous chapter, there is some evidence that security returns are related to size (smaller firms tend to have higher rates of return) and also to price earnings multiples (firms with low P/Es tend to produce higher returns). Whether individual risk plays any role at all in the valuation process is still, however, an open question.

My results with Cragg can be interpreted as showing that individual security variability does play a role in the valuation process. This would not be hard to explain. Because of transactions and information costs, a large number of individual portfolios may not be diversified. Individuals own between one-half and two-thirds of all NYSE stocks and an even larger fraction of stocks traded on other exchanges. Thus, these security holders might well be concerned with the variability of individual stocks. Even well-diversified institutional investors may worry about the behavior of individual stocks when they must report to finance committees the breakdown of their performance results over the preceding period. Still, there is a powerful argument on the other side. Any role in the valuation process that may consistently be provided by individual security variability will create an arbitrage opportunity for investors able to diversify widely. It is difficult to believe that these arbitrage opportunities will not eventually be exploited. Returning to the theme we played earlier, eventually "true value will out."

THE YIELD YEN: A CASE HISTORY OF THE IMPORTANCE OF OTHER SYSTEMATIC RISK INFLUENCES

Is the quant quest for better risk measures an assault on windmills — a useless exercise that succeeds only in enabling academics to continue to play with their computers? NO! It has important implications for protecting investors. Take, for example, the yield yen. The yield yen, which attracted a considerable following in the investment community by the 1980s, is a proposal for what is called a yield-tilted index fund.

The reasoning behind this proposal seems appealingly plausible. Since dividends are generally taxed more highly than capital gains, and since the market equilibrium is presumably achieved on the basis of after-tax returns, the equilibrium pre-tax returns ought to be higher for stocks that pay high dividends than for securities that produce lower dividends and correspondingly higher capital gains. Hence, the tax-exempt investor should specialize in buying high-dividend-paying stocks. In order to avoid the assumption of any greater risk than is involved in buying the market index, however, this tax-exempt investor is advised to purchase a yield-tilted index fund; that is, a very broadly diversified portfolio of high-dividend-paying stocks that mirrors the market index in the sense that it is constructed to have a beta coefficient exactly equal to 1.

Even on a priori grounds one might question the logic of the yield-tilted index fund. The validity of the proposal rests on the premise that the major market participants prefer to receive income through capital gains rather than through dividends. But many of the largest investors in the market (such as pension and endowment funds) are tax exempt, and others (such as corporations) actually pay a higher tax on capital gains than on dividend income.* It is far from clear that the most important investors in the stock market prefer to receive income in the form of capital gains. Therefore, the market may not price high-dividend-paying stocks so that they offer especially attractive returns to tax-exempt institutions. But apart from these a priori arguments, the statistical results just reviewed can be interpreted as providing another argument against the yield-tilted index fund.

If the traditional beta calculation does not provide a full description of systematic risk, a yield-tilted index fund may well fail to mirror the market index. Specifically, during periods when inflation and interest rates rise, high-dividend stocks may be particularly vulnerable. Public-utility common-stocks are a good example. Although they are known as low-beta stocks, they are likely to have systematic risk with respect to interest rates and inflation. This is so not only because they are good substitutes for fixed-income securities but also because public utilities are vul-

---

*For corporate investors, 85 percent of dividend income is excluded from taxable income, while capital gains are taxed at normal gains rates.

nerable to a profits squeeze during periods of rising inflation, as a result of regulatory lags and increased borrowing costs. Hence, the yield-tilted index fund with a beta of 1 may not mirror the market index when inflation accelerates.

The actual experience of yield-tilted index funds during the 1979–80 period was far from reassuring. The performance of these funds was significantly worse than that of the market. At other times, high yield stocks have significantly outperformed the market. Of course, we should not reject a model simply because of its failure over any specific short-term period. Nevertheless, I believe that an understanding of the wider aspects of systematic risk, as analyzed here, can potentially help to prevent serious investment errors.

A Summing Up

Part Three has been an academic exercise in the modern theory of capital markets. The stock market appears to be an efficient mechanism that adjusts quite quickly to new information. Neither technical analysis, which analyzes the past price movements of stocks, nor fundamental analysis, which analyzes more basic information about the prospects for individual companies and the economy, seems to yield consistent benefits. It appears that the only way to obtain higher long-run investment returns is to accept greater risks — and those risks can be horrendous, as any investor who has lived through the great bear markets of the late 1960s and 1970s can tell you.

Unfortunately, a perfect risk measure does not exist. Beta, the risk measure from the capital-asset pricing model, looks nice on the surface. It is a simple, easy-to-understand measure of market sensitivity, and differences in long-run rates of return from portfolios are clearly related to that single risk factor. Unfortunately, beta also has its warts. The actual relationship between beta and rate of return does not correspond to the relationship predicted in theory. Moreover, the relationship is undependable in the short run and has even failed to work in periods as long as seven or eight years. Finally, beta is not stable from period to period, and it is sensitive to the particular market proxy against which it is measured.

I have argued here that no single measure is likely to capture adequately the variety of systematic risk influences on individual stocks and portfolios. Returns are sensitive to general market swings, to changes in interest and inflation rates, to changes in national income, and, undoubtedly, to other economic factors. And if the best single risk estimate were to be chosen, the traditional beta measure would not be the only possibility. The mystical perfect risk measure is still beyond our grasp.

To the great relief of assistant professors who must publish or perish, there is still much debate within the academic community on risk measurement, and much more empirical testing needs to be done. Undoubtedly, there will yet be many improvements in the techniques of risk analysis, and the quantitative analysis of risk measurement is far from dead. My own guess is that future risk measures will be even more sophisticated — not less so. Nevertheless, we must be careful not to accept beta or any other measure as an easy way to assess risk and to predict future returns with any certainty. You should know about the best of the modern techniques of the new investment technology — they can be useful aids. But there is never going to be a handsome genie who will appear and solve all our investment problems. And even if he did, we would probably foul it up — as did the little lady in the following favorite story of Robert Kirby of Capital Guardian Trust:

> She was sitting in her rocking chair on the porch of the retirement home when a little genie appeared and said, "I've decided to grant you three wishes."
>
> The little old lay answered, "Buzz off, you little twerp, I've seen all the wise guys I need to in my life."
>
> The genie answered, "Look, I'm not kidding. This is for real. Just try me."
>
> She shrugged and said, "Okay, turn my rocking chair into solid gold."

When, in a puff of smoke, he did it, her interest picked up noticeably. She said, "Turn me into a beautiful young maiden."

Again, in a puff of smoke, he did it. Finally, she said, "Okay, for my third wish turn my cat into a handsome young prince."

In an instant, there stood the young prince, who then turned to her and asked, "Now aren't you sorry you had me fixed?"

A Practical Guide for Random Walkers and Other Investors

CHAPTER TEN

A Fitness Manual for Random Walkers

> In investing money, the amount of interest you want should
> depend on whether you want to eat well or sleep well. —
> J. Kenfield Morley, *Some Things I Believe*

Part Four is a how-to-do-it guide for your random
walk down Wall Street. In this chapter, I shall offer general
investment advice that should be useful to all investors, even if
they don't believe that security markets are highly efficient. In
Chapter Eleven, I present some personal reflections on why you
should invest in stocks and bonds and why I believe they are a
good inflation hedge that should continue to serve you very
well throughout the remainder of the 1980s.

In the final chapter, I outline three specific strategies for
equity investors who believe at least partially in the random-
walk theory or who are convinced that even if real expertise
does exist, they are unlikely to find it. I have yet to see any
compelling evidence that past stock prices can be used to predict future stock prices, and I am convinced that new informa-

tion quickly gets reflected in market prices. I can't, however, keep in step with a "strong" random walker. While markets are reasonably efficient, I doubt that there will ever be a time when no one possesses any useful nonpublic information. Moreover, I have seen enough castles in the air to leave me skeptical about the market's vaunted ability to price all assets perfectly at all times. In economic jargon, I am a weak or semi-strong random walker, and, as such, I believe useful techniques and unique investment opportunities often exist.

Remember, you'll need the highest possible returns on your investment funds to keep up with inflation. If inflation proceeds at, say, a 6 percent rate, the price level will double and your dollars will lose half their value in just twelve years. Hence, if you are sensible, you will take your random walk only after you have made detailed and careful plans with regard to all your investments, including your cash reserves. Even if stock prices move randomly, you shouldn't. Think of the advice that follows as a set of warm-up exercises that will enable you to reduce your income taxes and risk and at the same time increase your returns.

Exercise 1: Cover Thyself with Protection

Disraeli once wrote that "patience is a necessary ingredient of genius." It's also a key element in investing; you can't afford to pull your money out at the wrong time. You need staying power to increase your odds of earning attractive long-run returns. That's why it is so important for you to have noninvestment resources, such as medical and life insurance, to draw on should any emergency strike you or your family. It isn't always the guy in the well-known TV commercial who is hit by misfortune and calls "Hello, Prudential." It could happen to you.

Up until a couple of years ago, there were only two broad categories of life insurance products available: high-premium whole-life and low-cost term insurance. The standard whole-life insurance policy combines an insurance scheme with a type of savings plan; the latter was supposed to be attractive because the savings accumulate tax-free. But when double-digit inflation battered the U.S. economy, insurance buyers had second thoughts about the saving aspect of whole-life policies. Many of the assets of these policies had been invested in pre-inflation bonds and the yields on the savings part of the policies were as low as 3 or 4 percent per year. Since older whole-life policies generally allowed you to borrow the amount saved at attractive interest rates as low as 4 or 5 percent, consumers in the early 1980s borrowed over $45 billion against the cash value of their policies and many invested these dollars in money-market funds paying double-digit yields. Other consumers just gave up totally on whole-life policies and switched to term insurance, which I recommended in earlier editions. Term insurance provides death benefits only and provides no buildup of cash value. By 1981, this form of insurance accounted for more than half the volume of individual life sales.

Into this changing insurance market stepped two new products: universal life and variable life. As this edition goes to press, some companies appear to be trying to cover all bases and are planning to offer "universal-variable" policies. With a universal life insurance policy you can raise or lower the premium or death benefit according to your changing needs. You do this by, in effect, buying more or less term insurance, which is what provides for death benefits. In addition, interest rates on the cash value are allowed to change with market interest rates, rather than being tied to an insurance company's portfolio yield at the time you buy your policy. With variable life, the premium does not vary but the rate on which your cash value builds up does. This is possible because you choose the investment medium in which your cash values are invested. In effect, it is like having money with a mutual fund family. If you choose the right investment plan (say a growth stock fund during a period when they are booming) you come out ahead. The "universal-variable" policies that are planned give the policyholder universal's flexibility in premiums and death benefits and variable's menu of investment choices.

Increasingly, however, there is less difference between these "new wave" policies and ordinary whole life. Many traditional whole-life policies are now becoming somewhat more "interest sensitive." But, as with any cash value policy, your early premiums go mainly for sales commissions and other overhead rather than for buildup of cash value. Thus, not all your money goes to work. Hence, I continue to favor the do-it-yourself approach. Buy term insurance for protection — invest the difference yourself (preferably in tax-deferred plans such as IRAs).

Many people, however, will not regularly and consistently invest what they have saved by paying lower insurance premiums. If you are not confident of your ability to set up and maintain an investment program but nevertheless want to be sure there will be a certain amount of money available to your family when you die, you do need to buy permanent whole-life insurance, and you may find one of the flexible new wave policies useful.

But if you have the discipline to save, my advice is to buy renewable term insurance; you can keep renewing your policy without the need for a physical examination. So-called decreasing term insurance, renewable for progressively lower amounts, should suit many families best, since as time passes (and the children and family resources grow), the need for protection usually diminishes. Unless you will incur heavy penalties for discontinuing your present coverage, have a special tax reason for buying permanent insurance, or are able to save money only when a bill from your insurance company forces you to do so, look for a term-insurance plan. You should understand, however, that term-insurance premiums escalate sharply when you reach the age of sixty or seventy or higher. If you still need insurance at that point, you will find that term insurance has become prohibitively expensive. But the major risk at that point is not premature death; it is that you will live too long and outlive your assets. You can increase those assets more effectively by buying term insurance and using the money you save for the investments I'll discuss below.

Take the time to shop around for the best deal. There is considerable variation in insurance-company rates, and you can often get a better deal by looking around.

In addition, you should keep some reserves in safe and liquid investments. That, surely, is to many the antithesis of investing. Why put money in a safe place when you could be picking the next winner on the stock market? To cover unforeseen emergencies, that's why! It's the height of folly to gamble that nothing will happen to you. Every family should have a reserve of funds to pay an unexpected medical bill or to provide a cushion during a time of unemployment.

The old rule of thumb was that a year's living expenses should be kept in assets that could be converted to cash quickly and without loss. If you are protected by medical and disability insurance, this emergency reserve can be reduced safely. Indeed, even some bank trust departments—the acme of conservative money management—now estimate that a reserve that will cover living expenses for three months is satisfactory. In no case, however, should you be without at least some assets near the safe and liquid end of the spectrum.

Exercise 2: Know Your Investment Objectives

This is a part of the investment process that too many people skip, with disastrous results. You must decide at the outset what degree of risk you are willing to assume and what kinds of investments are most suitable to your tax bracket. The securities markets are like a large restaurant with a variety of products, suitable for different tastes and needs. Just as there is no one food that is best for everyone, so there is no one investment that is best for all investors.

We would all like to double our capital overnight, but how many of us can afford to see half our capital disintegrate just as quickly? J. P. Morgan once had a friend who was so worried about his stock holdings that he could not sleep at night. The friend asked, "What should I do about my stocks?" Morgan replied, "Sell down to the sleeping point." He wasn't kidding. Every investor must decide the tradeoff he or she is willing to make between eating well and sleeping well. The decision is up to you. High investment rewards can be achieved only at the cost of substantial risk-taking. This has been one of the fundamental lessons of this book. So what's your sleeping point? Finding the answer to this question is one of the most important investment steps you must take.

To help raise your investment consciousness, I've prepared a sleeping scale on investment risk and expected rate of return, as of late 1984. At the stultifying end of the spectrum are a variety of short-term investments. A bank account appears to be the safest investment of all. You are *certain* to be able to withdraw every dollar you put in. The dollar value of your investment will never fluctuate. But even this investment does have a risk, because with continued inflation, you are, unfortunately, just about certain to lose out in real purchasing power even with the interest added, especially if you pay taxes on the interest. Next come special six-month certificates, money-market deposit accounts, and money-market funds—somewhat less flexible, but far more likely to offer inflation protection. If this is your sleeping point, you'll be interested in the information on these kinds of investments in Exercise 4.

Corporate bonds are somewhat riskier, and some dreams will start intruding in your sleep pattern if you choose this form of investment. In late 1984, the yield on good-quality, long-term public-utility bonds ranged from 13 to 15 percent when held to maturity. Should you sell before then, your return will depend on the level of interest rates at the time of sale. If they rise in yield, your bonds will fall to a price that makes their yield competitive with new bonds offering a higher stated interest rate. Thus, there is a chance of loss. Your capital loss could be enough to eat up a whole year's interest—or even more. On

The Sleeping Scale of Major Investment Choices

Sleeping Point	Type of Asset	Expected Rate of Return (1984) (before Income Taxes)	Length of Time Investment Must Be Held to Get Expected Rate of Return	Risk Level
Semicomatose state	Bank accounts	5–5½%	No specific investment period required. Many thrift institutions calculate interest from day of deposit to day of withdrawal.	No risk of losing what you put in. Deposits up to $100,000 guaranteed by an agency of the federal government. An almost sure loser with high inflation, however.
Long afternoon naps and sound night's sleep	Money-market deposit accounts	9–10%	No specific investment period required but check withdrawals limited to 3 per month.	No risk of losing what you put in. Deposits guaranteed as above. Rates geared to expected inflation. Will vary over time.
Sound night's sleep	Money-market funds	10–11%	No specific investment period required. Most funds provide check-writing privileges.	Very little since most funds are invested in bank certificates. Not usually guaranteed,

(continued on next page)

The Sleeping Scale of Major Investment Choices (*continued*)

Sleeping Point	Type of Asset	Expected Rate of Return (1984) (before Income Taxes)	Length of Time Investment Must Be Held to Get Expected Rate of Return	Risk Level
				however, although some funds buy only government securities. Rates geared to expected inflation. Will vary.
	Special six-month certificates	10½–11½%	Money must be left on deposit for the entire six months to take advantage of higher rate.	Early withdrawals subject to penalty. Rates geared to expected inflation. Will vary.
An occasional dream or two— some possibly unpleasant	Corporate bonds (good-quality public utilities)	13–15%	Investments must be made for the period until the maturity of the bond (20–30 years) to be assured of the stated rate. The bonds may be sold at any	Very little if held to maturity. Moderate to substantial fluctuations can be expected in realized return if bonds are sold prior to maturity. Rate geared to expected

			time, however, in which case the net return will depend on fluctuations in the market price of the bonds.	long-run inflation rate now. This may differ from *actual* rate over the term to maturity of the bond.
Some tossing and turning before you doze and vivid dreams upon awakening	Diversified portfolios of blue-chip common stocks (such as an index fund)	15% or more	No specific investment periods required, and stocks may be sold at any time. The 15% average expected return assumes a fairly long investment period and can only be treated as a rough guide based on current conditions.	Moderate to substantial. In any one year the actual return could in fact be negative. Diversified portfolios have at times lost 25% or more of their actual value. Contrary to some opinion — a good inflation hedge.
Nightmares not uncommon, but over the long run well rested	Diversified portfolios of relatively risky stocks (such as aggressive growth-oriented mutual funds)	16–17%	Same as above. The average expected return of 16–17% assumes a fairly long investment period and can only be treated as a rough guide based on current conditions.	Substantial. In any one year the actual return could be negative. Diversified portfolios of very risky stocks have at times lost 50% or more of their value. Good inflation hedge.

(*continued on next page*)

The Sleeping Scale of Major Investment Choices (*continued*)

Sleeping Point	Type of Asset	Expected Rate of Return (1984) (before Income Taxes)	Length of Time Investment Must Be Held to Get Expected Rate of Return	Risk Level
Vivid dreams and occasional night-mares	Real estate	Similar to common stocks	Only makes sense as a very long-term invest-ment. Heavy transac-tions costs in trading.	Can't sell in a hurry without substantial penalties. Hard to diver-sify. Very good inflation hedge if bought at reasonable price levels.
Bouts of insomnia	Gold	Impossible to predict	High returns could be earned in any new speculative craze as long as there are greater fools to be found.	Substantial. Believed to be a hedge against doomsday and hyper-inflation. Can, however, play a useful role in balancing a diversified portfolio.

the other hand, if interest rates fall, the price of your bonds will rise and you will get not only the promised percent interest but also a capital gain. Thus, if you sell prior to maturity, your actual yearly return could vary considerably, and that is why bonds are riskier than short-term instruments, which carry almost no risk of principal fluctuation. Generally, the longer a bond's term to maturity, the greater the risk and the greater the resulting yield.* You will find some useful information on how to buy both short- and long-term bonds in Exercises 4 and 5.

No one can say for sure what the returns on common stocks will be. But the stock market, as Oskar Morgenstern once observed, is like a gambling casino where the odds are rigged in favor of the players. Although stock prices do plummet, as they did so disastrously during the 1970s, the overall return of the past fifty years (including the 1970s) has been over 9 percent per year, including both dividends and capital gains. I believe that a portfolio of common stocks such as those that make up a typical mutual fund will have an average annual rate of return of 15 percent or more during the remainder of the 1980s. Excellent returns have been earned on common stocks during the first half of the 1980s. The actual yearly return in the future can and probably will deviate substantially from this target — in down years you may lose as much as 25 percent or more. Can you stand the sleepless nights in the bad years?

How about dreams in full color with quadraphonic sound? You may want to choose a portfolio of somewhat riskier (more

---

*This isn't always the case. In the early 1980s, for example, a period of unusually high interest rates, short-term securities actually yielded more than long-term bonds. The catch was that investors could not count on continually reinvesting their short-term funds at such high rates, and by later in the decade, short-term rates had declined sharply. Thus, investors can reasonably expect that continual investment in short-term securities will not produce as high a return as investment in long-term bonds. In other words, there is a reward for taking on the risk of owning long-term bonds even if short-term rates are temporarily above long-term rates.

volatile) stocks, like those in aggressive growth-oriented mutual funds. These are the stocks in younger companies in newer technologies, where the promise of greater growth exists. Such companies are likely to be more volatile performers, and portfolios of these issues can easily lose half of their value in a bad market year. But your average rate of return for the remainder of the 1980s could be in the neighborhood of 16–17 percent per year. Portfolios of riskier stocks have tended to outperform the market averages by small amounts. If you have no trouble sleeping during bear markets, and if you have the staying power to stick with your investments, an aggressive common stock portfolio may be just right for you.

Real estate is a very tricky and often sleepless investment for most individuals. Nevertheless, the returns from real estate have been quite generous, similar to those from common stocks. I'll argue in Exercise 6 that individuals who can afford to buy their own home are well advised to do so.

I realize that my table slights gold, art objects, commodities, and other more exotic investment possibilities. Many of these have done very well over the past decade and can serve a useful role in balancing a well-diversified portfolio of paper assets. Because of their substantial risk, and thus extreme volatility, it's impossible to describe them in the kind of terms applied to other investments; Exercise 7 reviews them in greater detail.

In all likelihood, your sleeping point will be greatly influenced by the way in which a loss would affect your financial survival. That is why the typical "widow" is often viewed in investment texts as unable to take on much risk. The widow has neither the life expectancy nor the ability to earn, outside her portfolio, the income she would need to recoup losses. Any loss of capital and income will immediately affect her standard of living. At the other end of the spectrum is the "aggressive young businesswoman." She has both the life expectancy and the earning power to maintain her standard of living in the face of any financial loss.

In addition, your psychological makeup will influence the degree of risk you are willing to assume. One investment advisor suggests that you consider what kind of Monopoly player you once were. Were you a plunger? Did you construct hotels on Boardwalk and Park Place? True, the other players seldom landed on your property, but when they did you could win the whole game in one fell swoop. Or did you prefer the steadier but moderate income from the orange monopoly of St. James Place, Tennessee Avenue, and New York Avenue? The answers to these questions may give you some insight into your psychological makeup with respect to investing, and may help you to choose the right categories of securities for you. Or perhaps the analogy breaks down when it comes to the money game, which is played for keeps. In any event, it is critical that you understand yourself before choosing specific securities for investment.

A second key step is to review how much of your investment return goes to Uncle Sam and how much current income you need. Check your last year's income-tax form (1040) and the taxable income you reported for the year. The table on the following page shows the 1984 marginal tax brackets (rates paid on the last dollar of income) as well as the tax advantage of municipal (tax-exempt) bonds. If you are in a high tax bracket, with little need for current income, you will prefer bonds that are tax-exempt and stocks that have low dividend yields but promise favorably taxed long-term capital gains (where 60 percent of realized gains may be excluded from income and taxes do not have to be paid until gains are realized — perhaps never, if the stocks are part of a bequest). On the other hand, if you are in a low tax bracket and need a high current income, you will be better off with taxable bonds and high-dividend-paying common stocks, so that you don't have to incur the heavy transactions charges involved in selling off shares periodically to meet current-income needs. Remember also that the first $200 of dividend income is tax-exempt for a couple filing a joint return. Almost everybody should own enough stock to gain this tax-free income. A $5000 investment in IBM with its (approxi-

The Tax-Free Edge of Municipal Bonds[a]
(for Investors with Differing Taxable Incomes—in Thousands)

Taxable Income	25%	26%	28%	30%	33%	34%	38%	42%	45%	48%	49%	50%
Single Return		$18.2– 23.5		$23.5– 28.8		$28.8– 34.1	$34.1– 41.5	$41.5– 55.3			$55.3– 81.8	over $81.8
Joint Return	$24.6– 29.9		$29.9– 35.2		$35.2– 45.8		$45.8– 60.0	$60.0– 85.6	$85.6– 109.4		$109.4– 162.4	over $162.4
% Tax Bracket	25%	26%	28%	30%	33%	34%	38%	42%	45%	48%	49%	50%
9	12.00	12.16	12.50	12.86	13.43	13.64	14.52	15.52	16.36	17.31	17.65	18.00
10	13.33	13.51	13.89	14.29	14.93	15.15	16.13	17.24	18.18	19.23	19.61	20.00
11	14.67	14.86	15.28	15.71	16.42	16.67	17.74	18.97	20.00	21.15	21.57	22.00

Source: Merrill Lynch.

[a]To see what a taxable-interest bond would have to yield to equal your take-home yield in a tax-free municipal bond, find your taxable-income bracket. Then find the yield in the left-hand column of a tax-free bond you might buy and read across until you find what percentage interest you would have to receive from a taxable security to equal that yield. For example, if your joint return income is $50,000, your marginal tax bracket is 38%. Thus, a 10.00% tax-free return is equal to a 16.13% taxable return. (Taxable income in thousands of dollars. Based on tax tables effective for 1984 income.)

mate) 4 percent yield will produce tax-free income for a couple if that is their only holding.

The two steps in this exercise — finding your risk level, and identifying your tax bracket and income needs — seem obvious. But it is incredible how many people go astray by mismatching the types of securities they buy with their risk tolerance and their income and tax needs. The confusion of priorities so often displayed by investors is not unlike that exhibited by a young woman whose saga was recently written up in a London newspaper:

RED FACES IN PARK

London, Oct. 30.
Secret lovers were locked in a midnight embrace when it all happened.

Wedged into a tiny two-seater sports car, the near-naked man was suddenly immobilised by a slipped disc, according to a doctor writing in a medical journal here.

Trapped beneath him his desperate girlfriend tried to summon help by sounding the hooter button with her foot. A doctor, ambulancemen, firemen and a group of interested passers-by quickly surrounded the couple's car in Regents Park.

Dr. Brian Richards of Kent said: "The lady found herself trapped beneath 200 pounds of a pain-racked, immobile man.

"To free the couple, firemen had to cut away the car frame," he added.

The distraught girl, helped out of the car and into a coat, sobbed: "How am I going to explain to my husband what has happened to his car?"

— Reuters.

Investors are often torn by a similar confusion of priorities. You can't seek safety of principal and then take a plunge with investment into the riskiest of common stocks. You can't shelter your income from high marginal tax rates and then lock in returns of 14 percent from taxable corporate bonds, no matter how attractive these may be. Yet, the annals of investment counselors are replete with stories of investors whose security holdings are inconsistent with their investment goals.

Exercise 3: Dodge Uncle Sam Whenever You Can

One of the best ways to obtain extra investment funds is to avoid taxes legally. We've already discussed tax-exempt bonds and the tax advantages of the first dollars of dividends and of long-term capital gains. But did you know that you pay no income taxes on money invested in a retirement plan (or on the earnings from this investment) until you actually retire and use the money? At that time you may be in a lower tax bracket—especially since what you collect from Social Security is tax free. Even if you are not then in a lower bracket, you will have paid no taxes on your retirement savings over the years. This exercise makes you fit enough to reap these benefits.

First, check to see if your employer has a pension or profit-sharing plan. If so, you are home free. But what if your employer doesn't have such a plan? If you're single, as of 1984 you can contribute up to $2,000 of your annual income a year to an Individual Retirement Account (IRA). If you're married and both you and your spouse work, you can contribute $4,000. If your spouse is not working, you can contribute $2,250. For self-employed people, Congress has created the Keogh plan. Since 1984 all self-employed individuals—from accountants to Avon ladies, barbers to real estate brokers, doctors to decorators—are permitted to establish such a plan, to which they can contribute as much as 20 percent of their income, up to $30,000 annually. If you moonlight from your regular job, you can establish a Keogh for the income you earn on the side. As with the IRA, the money paid into a Keogh is deductible from taxable income, and the earnings are not taxed until they are withdrawn. If you qualify for either of these plans, you'll be making a big mistake not to take advantage of this perfectly legal way to checkmate the Internal Revenue Service and maximize your retirement savings to help you cope with the ravages of inflation.

Millions of taxpayers are currently missing what is one of the truly good deals around. Unless we look at a few numbers, it's impossible to realize what a difference these plans can make. Let's say you're thirty-five years old and contribute $1000 to an IRA or Keogh plan this year, placing this sum in fixed-income investments yielding 11 percent. In thirty years (when you are sixty-five) your $1000 investment will have compounded tax free to $24,840.* Now suppose you withdraw the whole amount at age sixty-five, when you retire. If you are then in the 21 percent tax bracket, you will retain $19,624 *after all taxes*.

Consider now the alternative of not establishing a Keogh or IRA plan. Your $1000 will then be taxed at the regular rate. That means that if you are presently in the 32 percent bracket, you will retain only $680 for investment in 11 percent securities. What's more, each year's interest will be taxed, so that your net earnings rate, after a tax of 32 percent, will be only 7.48 percent. At age sixty-five you will end up with only $6158 *after taxes*, assuming you haven't blown the money on a good toot sometime along the way. In this conservative example, an IRA or Keogh plan allows you to end up with over three times as much income, after taxes, at retirement. And we've just looked at a single $1000 contribution; suppose you contribute $1000 every year, or better still, the maximum amount you can contribute to an IRA or Keogh. My advice is to save as much as you can through these tax-sheltered means. Use up any other savings you may have for current living expenses, if you must, so you can contribute the maximum allowed.

Is there a fly in the ointment? Yes, as the favorite expression of economists goes, "There ain't no such thing as a completely free lunch." You can't touch IRA or Keogh funds before turning fifty-nine and a half or becoming disabled. If you do, the amount withdrawn is taxed, and in addition you must pay a 10 percent penalty on it.

But even with this catch, I believe IRAs and Keoghs are a good deal. While 10 percent of what you withdraw is indeed a

---

*The calculation assumes you can continue to reinvest the interest earnings at the same 11 percent rate.

stiff penalty, it's really not too much to pay for having been able to compound your savings tax free and to defer taxes on the income you put into the plan. Certainly, the advantages of staying in the plan for a few years far outweigh the penalty, even if you do withdraw some funds.

The important point is that if you plan to have any money saved up by the time you are fifty-nine and a half, you may as well do your saving by means of a tax-free retirement fund. Whatever your savings and investment decisions, it's always better to keep the sums involved tax free.

What can Keogh and IRA funds be invested in? You name it—stocks, bonds, mutual funds, savings certificates, annuity contracts, and other investments. Your choice should depend on your risk preferences as well as the composition of your other investment holdings. You can choose from a wide variety of plans offered by savings institutions, securities dealers, insurance companies, and mutual funds. My own preference would be stock and bond funds, and I'll give you specific advice later on in choosing the best vehicle for you. You certainly don't want to invest in lower-yield tax-exempt securities, however, since your retirement fund will accumulate tax free anyway.

Any further questions regarding the plans? You can call your local office of the Internal Revenue Service for answers to specific questions. Also, IRS publications 560 (Keoghs) and 590 (IRAs) cover all the detailed regulations.

Another strategy to foil the tax collector is the use of tax-deferred annuities. A tax-deferred annuity is a contract between you and an insurance company, purchased with one or more payments; the funds deposited accumulate tax-deferred interest, and the money is used to provide regular income payments at some later time. Usually, this type of contract involves no risk to your principal; the insurance company guarantees return of your original deposit at any time. As with the IRA and the Keogh plan, you pay no income tax on the interest accrued during the accumulation period. Thus, all of your interest—as well as the principal—keeps working for you. When you start receiving payments from your annuity, a portion of each payment is considered to be a return of principal and is therefore tax free. Furthermore, if—like most people—you use the annuity to provide a regular income during retirement, you will most likely be in a lower tax bracket when you finally do pay the taxes. A deferred annuity can also avoid the cost and delay of probate in the event of death, since your funds pass automatically to your beneficiaries.

Exercise 4: Be Competitive; Let the Yield on Your Cash Reserve Keep Pace with Inflation

As I've already pointed out, some ready assets are necessary for pending expenses, such as college tuition, for possible emergencies, or even for psychological support. Thus, you have a real dilemma. You know that if you keep your money in a savings bank and get, say, $5\frac{1}{2}$ percent interest in a year in which the inflation rate exceeds $5\frac{1}{2}$ percent, you will lose real purchasing power. In fact, the situation's even worse because the interest you get is subject to regular income taxes. So what's a small saver to do?

The investor of substantial means has no problems. He or she can buy Treasury bills (short-term IOUs issued by the U.S. government) or large certificates of deposit (short-term IOUs issued by banks, called bank CDs). But these instruments are issued in denominations of $10,000 and $100,000, respectively. If you have only a small amount of liquid assets, you can't get into this market directly. So how does the small saver avoid getting shafted? How do you get a rate of return that protects you against inflation? That is what this exercise is all about.

There are four short-term investment instruments that can at least help you stand up to inflation. These are (1) money-market mutual funds; (2) money-market deposit accounts; (3) six-month bank certificates; and (4) tax-exempt money-market funds.

MONEY-MARKET MUTUAL FUNDS

In my judgment the money-market mutual funds (or money funds) provide the best instrument for many investors' needs. They combine safety, high yields, and the right to withdraw money with no penalty attached. Most funds allow you to write large checks against your fund balance, generally in amounts of at least $250. Interest earnings continue until the checks clear. These money funds are the best alternative to bank accounts, and they have been extraordinarily popular. A representative sample of these funds is shown in the table on pages 260 and 261.

These money funds invest in large bank CDs, commercial paper (short-term corporate IOUs), government securities, and other instruments. Their yield therefore fluctuates fairly closely with the available yield on these short-term securities. To date, this yield has always outpaced—by a significant margin—the interest offered on cash savings accounts. Since they pool the funds of many small investors, the money funds can buy larger issues, beyond the individual's financial reach. The funds sell for a dollar a share and aim to keep that principal constant. While there's no guarantee against a loss of principal, you shouldn't have trouble sleeping nights if you invest in any of the funds in my table. Even during the volatile market periods in the early 1980s, these funds were able to keep the principal value constant at a dollar, although in some cases this was accomplished only through not paying out all of the interest earnings of the fund for periods of several days. In judging the funds that are best for your sleeping scale you should know that those with longer average maturities and with riskier investments (such as Eurodollar CDs, described below) tend to offer somewhat higher returns as well as occasional dreams.

A Eurodollar is a dollar on deposit outside the U.S., and these certificates, even when issued by foreign branchs of U.S. banks, are not subject to the same regulations as dollars on deposit within the country. A foreign government can impose restrictions on foreign branches of U.S. banks. For example, it can impose exchange controls that block payment of the interest and principal on these certificates. However unlikely such an event may be, these investments do entail some additional risk. Is the extra interest worth it? That depends on your psychological makeup.

For those who deep in their hearts prefer the semi-comatose state of safety that banks provide, a new class of money-market funds has been formed. These are funds that invest only in federally guaranteed securities. As you might expect, they tend to yield less than comparable funds investing in bank obligations. Late in 1984, the differential in yields was between ½ and ¾ of 1 percent. Is the yield sacrifice worth the extra safety? Again, the answer depends on your psychological makeup.

My personal answer is to go with the higher yielding regular funds. While I would be the first to agree that money saved for a rainy day should not be allowed to go down the drain, I think that the risk of the prime quality funds is, as my lawyer friends like to put it, *de minimus*. Even funds that held obligations of the incontinent Continental Bank in 1984 got paid off in full. I should also tell you, however, that I am not a worrier. For those who are, a sample listing of funds investing in federally insured instruments is shown on the table on pages 262 and 263.

MONEY-MARKET DEPOSIT ACCOUNTS

The money funds became so popular that hundreds of billions of dollars were drained out of bank deposits into these higher yielding mutual funds. Needless to say, the banks sought ways to compete. And so, in another example of how deregulation benefits the consumer, the banks were allowed to offer money-market deposit accounts to individuals with $2,500 or more to invest. At the outset banks offered promotional rates that were well above the yields offered by the money funds. Indeed, initially some money-market deposit accounts had a yield advantage of two percentage points. Savvy consumers, chasing the prettiest rate in the market, deserted the money funds in droves.

Data on Selected Money-Market Funds

Fund	Date Originated	Minimum Initial Purchase	Minimum Subsequent Purchase	Minimum Amount for Check Withdrawal	Total Assets (in Millions) (8/29/84)	30-Day Average Yield (%) (8/29/84)	Average Maturity (Days) (8/29/84)	Distribution of Portfolio Holdings (Percent) (8/29/84)								
								U.S. Treasury	U.S. Other	Repos[b]	Certificates of Deposit	Banker's Acceptances	Commercial Paper	Eurodollar CDs	Yankee CDs	Other Non-Prime
Dreyfus Liquid Assets 666 Old Country Road Garden City, NY 11530 800/645-6561	1974	2,500	100	500	7,850	10.6	42	8	0	0	5	4	6	77		0
Fidelity Cash Reserves 82 Devonshire Street Boston, MA 02109 800/225-6190	1979	1,000	250	500	3,815	10.6	27	3	0	0	3	—	26	23		45
Dean Witter/Sears Liquid Assets 1 World Trade Center New York, NY 10048 800/221-2685	1975	5,000	1,000	500	5,713	11.1	47	0	2	0	21	15	45	0		17

Fund	Year				Assets	Yield									
Merrill Lynch Ready Assets 165 Broadway New York, NY 10080 800/221-7210 or call local office	1975	5,000	1,000	500	11,264	10.5	58	2	30	2	10	16	40	0	0
The Reserve Fund, Inc. (Primary Portfolio) 810 Seventh Avenue New York, NY 10010 800/223-5547 800/223-9864	1970	1,000	1,000	500	1,648	10.6	27	0	0	4	1	0	95	0	0
Vanguard Money Market Trust[a] (Prime Portfolio) P.O. Box 2600 Valley Forge, PA 19482 800/523-7025 (800/362-0530 in PA)	1974	1,000	100	250	1,294	11.2	33	0	0	1	22	13	64	0	0

Source: *Donoghue's Money Fund Report.* Current data on these funds can be obtained from Donoghue's Money Fund Service, P. O. Box 540, Holliston, MA 01746. Free sample copies of current reports are available on request. The yields are also listed weekly in many newspapers.

[a]I am on the Board of Directors of this fund.
[b]Securities held under repurchase agreements.

Data on Selected Money-Market Government Funds

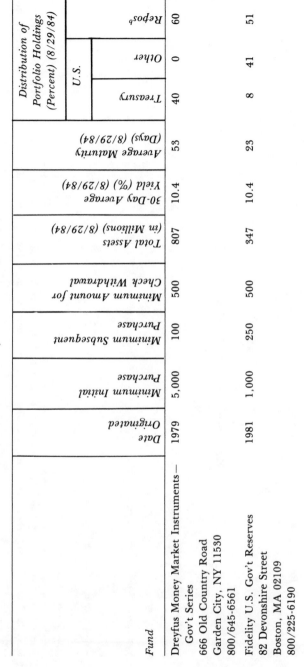

Fund	Date Originated	Minimum Initial Purchase	Minimum Subsequent Purchase	Minimum Amount for Check Withdrawal	Total Assets (in Millions) (8/29/84)	30-Day Average Yield (%) (8/29/84)	Average Maturity (Days) (8/29/84)	Distribution of Portfolio Holdings (Percent) (8/29/84)		
								U.S. Treasury	Other	Repos[b]
Dreyfus Money Market Instruments—Gov't Series 666 Old Country Road Garden City, NY 11530 800/645-6561	1979	5,000	100	500	807	10.4	53	40	0	60
Fidelity U.S. Gov't Reserves 82 Devonshire Street Boston, MA 02109 800/225-6190	1981	1,000	250	500	347	10.4	23	8	41	51

Dean Witter/Sears U.S. Gov't MM 1 World Trade Center New York, NY 10048 800/221-2685	1982	5,000	100	500	348	10.1	46	20	69	11
Merrill Lynch Gov't Fund 165 Broadway New York, NY 10080 800/221-7210 or call local office	1977	5,000	1,000	500	1,307	10.2	41	100	0	0
The Reserve Fund, Inc. (Gov't Portfolio) 810 Seventh Avenue New York, NY 10010 800/223-5547 800/223-9864	1981	1,000	1,000	500	278	10.6	2	0	0	100
Vanguard Money Market Trust[a] (Federal Portfolio) P.O. Box 2600 Valley Forge, PA 19482 800/523-7025 (800/362-0530 in PA)	1981	1,000	100	250	415	10.5	31	23	61	16

Source: *Donoghue's Money Fund Report*. Wiesenberger Financial Services, *Investment Companies and Their Securities*.

[a]I am on the Board of Directors of this fund.

[b]Securities held under repurchase agreements.

In 1984, however, the money funds enjoyed a renaissance. The banks, having reestablished themselves, quietly reduced the rates they were offering so that the money funds then had a ½ to 1 percentage point advantage over the deposit accounts. Money began to return to the funds and now both types of investments have hundreds of billions of consumers' dollars.

How should you decide between the two? Each has its own advantages. The banks enjoy important attractions. First, like other bank deposits, money-market deposit accounts are insured by an agency of the federal government. Thus, they score at the top of the scale for worried insomniacs. In addition, it's convenient to invest in money-market deposit accounts, since banks have branches, while money funds only have post office boxes and toll-free telephone numbers. But the money funds have their own advantages. Their yields tend to be a good deal higher than the bank accounts as noted above. Indeed, during periods when interest rates have been rising, the differential in favor of the money funds has tended to widen as the banks have been slow in raising posted rates. In addition, the money funds allow an unlimited number of checks to be written against balances (although each check must be written for at least $250 or $500 depending on the fund). The deposit accounts allow only three checks per month (for any amount).* Money funds also offer wire transfer facilities that permit money to be moved around overnight. Moreover, since money funds are typically part of a large mutual fund or brokerage complex, they are an ideal place to "park" cash at high earning rates awaiting movement into more permanent investments. Finally, it is possible to find money funds that invest only in tax-exempt securities so that high-bracket investors can earn considerably higher after-tax yields. I'll discuss these tax-exempt money funds below.

---

*Banks do offer so-called Super NOW deposit accounts that allow unlimited checking and these accounts can be very useful for investors who can meet the minimum deposit requirements. The interest rates on Super NOWs are, however, substantially below the returns on money-market deposit accounts.

Copyright © 1984 by The New York Times Company.
Reprinted by permission.

SIX-MONTH BANK CERTIFICATES

Banks also offer six-month certificates of deposit. Yields on these instruments are typically higher than either those on money-market deposit accounts or money funds. These certificates are government insured up to $100,000 per buyer ($200,000 with your spouse). Thus, the certificates are even safer than the money funds and are an excellent medium for investors who can tie up their liquid funds for at least six months.

The certificates do have a number of disadvantages, however. First, you need to have a substantial nest egg—$10,000—before you can buy. Second, you can't write checks against the certificates as you can with shares in the money funds. Most important, as in other aspects of life there is a substantial penalty for premature withdrawal. If you redeem your certificate prior to maturity, federal regulations stipulate a minimum penalty of the loss of one month's interest. Some banks impose even greater penalties. Third, the yield on bank certificates is subject to state and local taxes (Treasury bills, also obtainable for $10,000, are exempt from these).

CURRENT YIELDS

ASK ABOUT OUR
DAILY SPECIALS

Drawing by Lorenz, © 1984
The New Yorker Magazine, Inc.

TAX-EXEMPT MONEY-MARKET FUNDS

This instrument may be useful for some investors, particularly those who pay marginal tax rates of near 50 percent. A disadvantage of all the vehicles previously described is that the interest is fully taxable. Investors in very high brackets will find that, after taxes, even the highest of the yields offered will not compensate for inflation. This situation led to the establishment of the first tax-exempt money-market fund, the Vanguard Municipal Bond Fund short-term portfolio.

Vanguard invests in a portfolio of short-term high-quality tax-exempt issues. It thus produces daily tax-exempt income. Like the regular money-market funds, it provides instant liquidity and free checking for large bills ($250 or more). The minimum investment is $3000. There are now several tax-exempt money funds. Some sample funds are listed on pages 268 and 269. The yields on tax-exempt funds are considerably lower than those on taxable funds. Nevertheless, individuals in the highest tax brackets will find the earnings from this investment more attractive than the after-tax yield of the regular money funds.

Exercise 5: Investigate a Promenade through Bond Country

Let's face it, bonds were a lousy place to put your money during the 1960s and 1970s. Inflation had eaten away at the real value of the bonds with a vengeance. For example, savers who bought U.S. Savings Bonds for $18.75 in the early 1970s and redeemed them five years later for $25 found, much to their dismay, that they had actually lost real purchasing power. The trouble was that, while the $18.75 invested in such a bond five years before might have filled one's gas tank twice, the $25 obtained at maturity did little more than fill it once. In fact, an investor's real return was negative, as inflation had eroded purchasing power faster than interest earnings were compounding. Small wonder many investors view the "bond" as an unmentionable four-letter word.

In fact, the U.S. Savings Bond program, with its touching appeals to patriotism and good citizenship, has been a monumental ripoff. Interest rates on Series EE Savings Bonds were far below the inflation rates of the late 1960s and 1970s and were not much more than half what the government was paying on regular bonds sold on the open market. Fortunately, the government has recently improved the terms of U.S. Savings Bonds so that they can pay 85 percent of the rate the Treasury pays for funds in the open market. The bonds also have some tax advantages. Still, as I'll show you below, far more attractive investment opportunities are available.

Data on Selected Tax-Exempt Money-Market Funds

Fund	Date Originated	Minimum Initial Purchase	Minimum Subsequent Purchase	Minimum Amount for Check Withdrawal	Total Assets (in Millions) (8/29/84)	30-Day Average Yield (%) (8/29/84)	Average Maturity (Days) (8/29/84)
CMA Tax-Exempt Fund 165 Broadway New York, NY 10080 800/CMA-INFO	1981	20,000	None	None	3,150	5.8	70
Dean Witter/Sears Tax Free Daily Income Fund 1 World Trade Center New York, NY 10048 800/221-2685	1980	1,000	50	500	286	5.8	65

Fund	Year						
Dreyfus Tax-Exempt Money Market Fund, 666 Old Country Rd, Garden City, NY 11530, 800/645-6561	1980	5,000	100	500	1,704	5.7	77
Federated Tax-Free Trust, 421 Seventh Avenue, Pittsburgh, PA 15219, 800/245-4270	1980	25,000	None	No checking	3,116	5.8	62
Fidelity Tax-Exempt Money Market Trust, 82 Devonshire St., Boston, MA 02109, 800/225-6190	1980	10,000	500	500	2,324	5.8	33
Vanguard Municipal Bond Fund (Money Market)[a], P.O. Box 2600, Valley Forge, PA 19482, 800/523-7025 (800/362-0530 in PA)	1980	3,000	100	250	389	6.2	86

Source: *Donoghue's Money Fund Report.*
[a] I am on the Board of Directors of this fund.

Of course, other bonds have also been poor investments in recent years, since the interest rates they carried have often proved insufficient to offer adequate inflation protection. Investors ten to twenty years ago simply did not realize how high inflation could go. But remember Part Two. Markets are reasonably efficient, and investors now refuse to buy bonds unless their yields offer a reasonable degree of compensation for the expected loss in the dollar's purchasing power. In mid-1984 good-quality long-term bonds were yielding 14 percent in the open market. This yield translates freely into protection against a long-term inflation of 6 percent and provides a real rate of return above that inflation of about 8 percent. Of course, it is always possible that the actual long-run rate of inflation may be considerably greater than the 6 percent inflation premium that was implicit in this bond yield. But the 8 percent real return they promise gives an unusually generous margin of safety as I will argue in the next chapter.

In my view, there are four kinds of bond purchases you may especially want to consider: (1) the floating-rate note (a bond with particularly good principal stability since its interest rate floats each half year with the current level of interest rates); (2) zero-coupon bonds (that allow you to lock in high yields for a predetermined length of time; (3) bond mutual funds (that permit you to buy shares in bond portfolios); and (4) tax-exempt bonds (for those who are fortunate enough to be in high tax brackets).

HAVE NO FEAR OF FLOATING

One of the most interesting financial innovations of the 1970s, floating-rate notes provide the closest thing we have to inflation indexing in the financial markets. This is achieved through a contractual interest rate that automatically changes each half year in line with the market yields of Treasury bills. The premise, supported by economic evidence, is that Treasury-bill yields will rise and fall with the rate of inflation. Thus, floaters give investors a yield that tends to vary with the rate of inflation.

Floating-rate notes have several features that may make them an attractive investment for you. First, as noted, the semiannual interest payment floats with the Treasury-bill rate — e.g., 1 percent above the bill yield. Second, there is usually a minimum rate below which the interest cannot drop no matter how low Treasury-bill yields fall. Third, the issues are often convertible into long-term bonds at the option of the holder, although at rates somewhat below competitive long-term yields. Finally, the floaters are available in denominations of $1000. These features imply a considerable degree of capital stability for the floaters. Normal bonds (with fixed-interest payments) fall in price as market yields rise, so that new purchasers of the bonds will obtain yields that are competitive with the higher level of rates. Floaters issued with generous terms will remain fairly stable in price, however, since their contractual interest rate gets adjusted semiannually.

Some of the earlier floating-rate notes did not have terms as generous as those on more recent issues, nor were the rates of return they offered large investors as great as could be obtained by holding bank certificates of deposit directly. Hence, the early floaters tended to decline in price until their yields were competitive with those available in the open market.

The following table shows the prices and yields in mid-1984 of a representative sample of early issues. At the going market prices, these issues should provide good returns and excellent capital stability. Either these issues or more recent floaters, which now offer better premiums over Treasury-bill yields and more frequent changes in interest rates, will serve investors in low tax brackets very well. For that portion of their portfolio in stable assets, the floaters will provide an excellent measure of inflation protection. By the 1980s tax-exempt floaters became available. These are suitable for investors in high tax brackets, as I will argue below.

Representative Issues of Floating-Rate Notes

	Coupon When Issued	Mid-1984		
Issue and Maturity		Interest Coupon	Price	Current Yield (%)
Citicorp, 2004	11.05	10.35	90	11.5
Chase Manhattan, 2009	10.75	10.90	87	12.5

ZERO COUPON BONDS CAN GENERATE LARGE FUTURE RETURNS

Suppose you were told you could invest $10,000 now and be guaranteed by the government that you would get more than 10 times that amount back in 20 years. The ability to accumulate such a $100,000+ nest egg is possible through the use of zero coupon securities.

These securities are called zero coupons or simply zeros because owners receive no periodic interest payments as they do in a regular interest-coupon paying bond. Instead, these securities are purchased at deep discounts from their face value (for example, 10 cents on the dollar) and gradually rise to their face or par values over the years. If held to maturity, the holder is paid off the full stated amount of the bond. These securities are available on maturities ranging from a few months to almost thirty years. As of mid-1984, long-term zero coupon Treasury securities sold to yield about 12½ percent per year.

The first zero coupon obligations were created by major brokerage houses. They were introduced in 1982 by Merrill Lynch under the proprietary acronym TIGRs (Tigers), Treasury Investment Growth Receipts. Other brokerage houses followed suit and marketed similar products bearing such names as CATS, LIONS, COUGARS, and TEDDY BEARS. Small denomination zeros marketed by Merrill Lynch are known as "tiger cubs." In 1985, the Treasury itself began to provide zero coupon bonds directly. Zero coupon securities have also been offered by corporations, insurance companies, and banks.

They are available at somewhat higher yields than treasury zeros, but with not quite the same degree of safety.

The principal attraction of zeros is that the purchaser is faced with no reinvestment risk. It would, of course, be possible to duplicate a zero with a regular bond by taking the interest coupons and reinvesting them over the life of the issue. Indeed, the typical yield to maturity calculation assumes that interest payments are reinvested at a constant rate. In fact, however, the interest rate at which you could reinvest the coupons could fall, so that the realized yield to maturity could be a good bit lower. A zero coupon Treasury bond guarantees an investor that his or her funds will be continuously reinvested at the yield to maturity rate. Thus, the zeros offer a convenient way to lock in high yields for many years to come.

The main disadvantage of zeros is that the Internal Revenue Service requires that taxable investors declare annually as income a pro rata share of the dollar difference between the purchase price and the par value of the bond. This is not required, however, for investors who hold zeros in IRAs or Keogh plans. Here the investor can defer all taxes until retirement. Thus zero coupon securities are a superb vehicle for retirement plans.

Two warnings are in order. Often brokers will charge small investors fairly large commissions for the purchase of zero coupon bonds in small denominations. It would, therefore, be worthwhile to check the net yields available on, say, twenty-year zeros with two or three brokers to ascertain the best quotes. As I will discuss in Exercise 8 below, commission rates are not random and some comparison shopping could pay big yields. In addition, you should know that redemption at face value is guaranteed *only* if you hold the bonds to maturity. In the meantime, prices can be highly variable as interest rates change.

NO-LOAD BOND FUNDS ARE APPROPRIATE VEHICLES FOR INDIVIDUAL INVESTORS

Floating-rate notes provide capital stability and variable interest rates. Zero coupon securities provide guaranteed interest rates over a long term, but highly variable capital values if they are sold prior to maturity. Transactions costs could also be high if the bonds are sold prior to maturity. Open-end bond (mutual) funds are an intermediate vehicle; they give some of the long-term advantages of the zeros but are much easier and less costly to buy or sell. Those that I have listed on pages 276 and 277 all invest in long-term securities. While there is no guarantee that you can reinvest your interest at constant rates, these funds do offer long-run stability of income and are particularly suitable for investors who plan to live off their interest income.

Bond mutual funds typically hold a diversified portfolio of high-quality bonds. Purchasers of shares in such a fund in essence buy a pro rata share in all of the assets of the fund and are entitled to a pro rata share of the income. Thus, a small investor would be able to obtain the same kind of broad-scale diversification available to a large institutional investor.

These open-end funds issue shares in unlimited quantities and stand ready to redeem their shares at net asset value calculated each day on the basis of the market prices of the bonds they hold. Many funds charge an $8\frac{1}{2}$ percent loading fee or commission fee to invest in the fund. The funds that I recommend are all no-load; that is, there is neither a fee to buy into the fund nor a fee to redeem shares. Performance of bond mutual funds is totally unrelated to the fees they charge (including the expenses they incur in managing the investments). Thus, I recommend only no-load funds. There's no point in paying for something if you can get it free. Moreover, I prefer funds with low expense ratios.

The following table shows a sample of bond funds available from some of the largest mutual fund complexes. I list in the table two types of funds: those specializing in prime-quality corporate bonds and one that buys a portfolio of GNMA mortgage-backed bonds. In a separate table, I list those funds investing in tax-exempt bonds (which I will discuss in the next exercise).

All of the funds listed in my table are invested in prime-quality issues with minimal risk of default. I personally favor the GNMA fund. This fund invests exclusively in GNMA (Ginnie Mae) mortgage pass-through securities. These are bonds backed by a pool of government-insured mortgages (either VA or FHA), and are therefore a general obligation of the U.S. government. Interest and principal payments on the bonds come from the interest and principal repayments of the underlying mortgages. Not only is the security on these bonds of the highest quality, but also the yields are comparable to those on corporate bonds. Hence, I think that a Ginnie Mae fund is a particularly attractive investment in today's bond market.

TAX-EXEMPT BONDS ARE USEFUL FOR
HIGH-BRACKET INVESTORS

If you are in a very high tax bracket, taxable floaters, zeros, and taxable bond funds may not be right for you. You need the tax-exempt bonds issued by state and local governments and by various governmental authorities, such as port authorities or toll roads. The interest from these bonds doesn't even have to be reported on your federal tax form, and bonds from the state in which you live are typically exempt from any state income taxes.

This tax exemption gives a subsidy to state and local governments, since they can issue bonds at lower interest rates than if the bonds were fully taxable. Economists have argued that it's an inefficient subsidy (it would be cheaper, so this argument goes, for the U.S. Treasury just to pay the state and local governments to issue taxable bonds). But since that's the present law, there is no reason why you shouldn't take advantage of it.

By now, if you've carefully followed Exercise 2, you know whether municipal bonds are compatible with your tax bracket and your income needs. In mid-1984, good quality long-term corporate bonds were yielding about 14½ percent, and tax-exempt issues of comparable quality yielded about 11½ percent. Suppose your tax bracket (the rate at which your last dol-

Open-End Bond Funds

Fund	Sales Charge (%)	Year Organized	Minimum Amount, Initial Purchase ($)	Minimum Amount, Subsequent Purchases ($)	Expense Ratio (%) (1983)	Total Net Assets ($ Millions) (6/29/84)	% Change in Net Assets per Share with Capital Gains Accepted in Shares and Income Dividends Reinvested 1 Year (1983)	5½ Years (to 6/29/84)	% Yield Last 12 Months (6/29/84)	Payroll Deduction or Bank Draft Payment Plan Available	Keogh Plan Available	Individual Retirement Account Available
CORPORATE BOND FUNDS (PRIME QUALITY)												
Dreyfus A Bonds Plus 600 Madison Ave. New York, NY 10022 800/645-6561	None	1976	2,500	100	0.95	94.4	7.7	58.3	12.6	Yes	Yes	Yes
Fidelity Corporate Bond Fund 82 Devonshire St.	None	1971	2,500	250	0.81	133.7	6.5	44.6	12.5	No	Yes	Yes

Boston, MA 02109
800/225-6190

IDS Bond Fund 100 Roanoke Bldg. Minneapolis, MN 55402 612/372-3131	3.5	1974	2,000	100	0.61	1061.3	14.6	59.6	12.9	No	Yes	Yes
Vanguard Fixed Income Securities Fund-Investment Grade[a] P.O. Box 2600 Valley Forge, PA 19482 800/523-7025 (800/362-0530 in PA)	None	1978	3,000	50	0.75	91.4	6.9	51.3	13.8	Yes	Yes	Yes

GNMA FUND

Vanguard Fixed Income-GNMA Fund[a] P.O. Box 2600 Valley Forge, PA 19482 800/523-7025 (800/362-0530 in PA)	None	1980	3,000	50	0.58	200.2	9.7	N/A	12.9	Yes	Yes	Yes

[a]I am a director of this fund.

lar of income is taxed — not your average rate) is 40 percent.
The table below shows that the after-tax income is $280 higher
on the tax-exempt security, which is clearly the better investment for a person in your tax bracket. Even if you are in the 30-
percent bracket, tax-exempts may pay, depending on the exact
yields available in the market when you make your purchase.

Tax-Exempt vs. Taxable Bonds

Type of Bond	Interest Paid	Applicable Taxes (40% Rate)	After-Tax Income
11½% tax-exempt	$1150	$ 0	$1150
14½% taxable	1450	580	870

Look carefully at new long-term revenue bond issues of
various public authorities, such as port authorities, established
turnpikes, power authorities, etc. These bonds (called term
bonds) often serve as very attractive tax-exempt investment
vehicles. I suggest that you buy new issues rather than already
outstanding securities, because new-issue yields are usually a
bit sweeter than the yields of seasoned outstanding bonds. I
also suggest that to keep your risk within reasonable bounds,
you stick with issues rated at least A by Moody's and Standard
& Poor's rating services. These term bonds usually mature in
twenty years or more, but they often enjoy a good trading market after they have been issued. Thus, if you want to sell the
bonds later you can do so with reasonable ease, particularly if
you own at least $5000 worth of a single issue.

Avoid serial bonds. These are tax-exempt bonds that mature
serially over perhaps thirty different years or more. These are
usually tougher to sell than term bonds if you have to raise
funds prior to their maturity. Also, yields on serial issues (especially the shorter-term ones) usually tend to be lower than on

term bonds, in part because they are particularly attractive to institutions, like banks, that pay taxes at high corporate rates. Unless you have funds to invest for some specific period of time and want to match the maturity of the bond you buy with the timing of your fund requirements, these bonds are best left to institutional buyers. So ask your broker how the "new-issue calendar" looks. By waiting a week or so until a new high-yielding revenue term bond comes out, you may be able to improve your interest return substantially.

There is one nasty "heads I win, tails you lose" feature of bonds that you should know about. If interest rates go up, the price of your bonds will go down, as I noted earlier. But if interest rates go down, the issuer can often "call" the bonds away from you (repay the debt early) and then issue new bonds at lower rates.

To protect yourself, make sure your bonds have a call-protection provision that prevents the issuer from calling your bonds in order to issue new ones at lower rates. Many tax-exempt revenue issues offer about ten years of call protection. After that the bonds are callable, but typically at a premium over what you paid for them. Make sure to ask about call protection, especially during periods when interest rates are higher than usual.

There are good tax-exempt bond funds available as well. I have listed these in the table on pages 280 and 281. If you have substantial funds to invest in tax-exempts ($25,000 or more), however, I see little reason for you to make your tax-exempt purchases through a fund and pay the management fees involved. If you follow the rules already presented and confine your purchases to high-quality bonds, there is little need for you to diversify, purchasing many different securities. And you'll get more interest return if you invest directly. On the other hand, if you have just a few thousand to invest, you will find it costly to buy and sell small lots of bonds, and a fund will provide convenient liquidity and diversification for you.

Tax-Exempt Open-End Bond Funds

Fund	Sales Charge (%)	Year Organized	Minimum Amount, Initial Purchase ($)	Minimum Amount, Subsequent Purchases ($)	Expense Ratio (%) (1983)	Total Net Assets ($ Millions) (8/29/84)	% Change in Net Assets per Share with Capital Gains Accepted in Shares and Income Dividends Reinvested 1 Year (1983)	5½ Years (to 6/29/84)	% Yield Last 12 Months (6/29/84)	Payroll Deductions or Bank Draft Payment Plan Available
Dreyfus Tax-Exempt Bond Fund 600 Madison Ave. New York, NY 10022 800/645-6561	None	1976	2,500	100	0.73	1,864.3	11.6	17.0	9.7	Yes

Fidelity Municipal Bond Fund 82 Devonshire St. Boston, MA 02109 800/225-6190	None	1976	2,500	250	0.62	612.4	9.3	8.1	9.5	No
IDS Tax-Exempt Bond Fund 1000 Roanoke Bldg. Minneapolis, MN 55402 612/372-3131	5.0[b]	1976	2,000	100	0.66	427.6	10.5	14.6	9.0	No
Vanguard Municipal Bond Fund[a] P.O. Box 2600 Valley Forge, PA 19482 800/523-7025 (800/362-0530 in PA)	None	1978	3,000	50	0.48	249.1	9.5	7.4	9.8	Yes

Source: Wiesenberger Investment Companies Service.

[a]I am a director of this fund.

[b]Actually ranging from 0% to 50% depending on amount of purchase.

Exercise 6: Begin Your Walk at Your Own Home; Renting Leads to Flabby Investment Muscles

Remember Scarlett O'Hara? She was broke at the end of the Civil War, but she still had her beloved plantation, Tara. A good house, on good land, keeps its value no matter what happens to money. As long as the world's population continues to grow, the demand for real estate will be among the most dependable inflation hedges available. If you do own your own home, you will probably find that the house you live in is the best investment you ever made in your life.

One hundred years ago, Henry George sounded the call for real estate investment:

> Go, get yourself a piece of ground, and hold possession. . . . You need do nothing more. You may sit down and smoke your pipe; you may lie around like the lazzaroni of Naples or the leperos of Mexico; you may go up in a balloon, or down a hole in the ground and without doing one stroke of work, without adding one iota to the wealth of the community, in ten years you will be rich.

By and large, George's advice turned out to be pretty good.

Although the calculation is tricky, it appears that the returns on real estate have been quite generous. Real estate returns appear to be roughly comparable to the long-run returns from common stocks. Not only that, they appear to be less variable from year to year and thus more predictable than stock returns. But the real estate market is less efficient than the stock market. There may be hundreds of knowledgeable investors who study the worth of every common stock. Perhaps only a handful of prospective buyers assess the worth of a particular real estate property. Hence, individual pieces of property are not always appropriately priced. Finally, real estate returns seem to be higher than stock returns during periods when inflation is accelerating, but to do less well during periods of disinflation. In sum, real estate has proved to be a good investment providing generous returns and excellent inflation-hedging characteristics.

The natural real estate investment for most people is the single-family home or the condominium. You have to live somewhere, and buying has several tax advantages over renting. Because Congress wanted to encourage home ownership and the values associated with this, it gave the homeowner a number of tax breaks: (1) while rent is not deductible from income taxes, the two major expenses associated with home ownership — interest payments on your mortgage and property taxes — are fully deductible; (2) any realized gains in the value of your house are taxed at favorable capital-gains rates (if you have owned the house for over six months); (3) if you buy another, more expensive house, you can defer realizing capital gains; and (4) if you sell your house after age fifty-five, $100,000 of the gains are tax-exempt. In addition, ownership of a house is a good way to force yourself to save, and a house provides enormous emotional satisfaction. My advice is: Own your own home if you can possibly afford it.

How do you know if you can afford a home? The general rule of thumb is that a family should not spend more than 30 percent of its income on mortgage payments. With long-term fixed-ratio mortgages, that used to be easy to calculate. You told the lending institution how much you needed for how long and they would tell you what your monthly payments would be at the prevailing interest rate. When that rate hit 14 percent or more in the first half of the 1980s, however, the monthly payments effectively priced many families out of their pursuit of the American dream — an affordable home. Enter the red-hot adjustable-rate mortgage, known as the ARM. By 1984, two out of every three homes were financed with ARMs.

There are literally thousands of different variations of the adjustable-rate mortgage. Their basic feature is that the contract interest rate is subject to periodic adjustment based on the movements of a selected interest rate index, such as the rate on short-term treasury securities. In general, the initial rates on ARMs are considerably lower than on fixed-rate mortgages. However, the home buyer takes the risk of future increases in interest rates. Many mortgage experts have warned that if rates rise in the future, this could lead to "payment shock"—payments rising so sharply that they wreck the household budget or, at worst, that high rates could strong-ARM some families out of their homes.

Fortunately, ARMs are now usually available with a cap on interest payments. The cap typically limits yearly rate adjustments to, say, 1 to 2 percent and sets a lifetime or maximum cap on total increases at, say, 5 percent. While these caps are very useful for consumers, they can at times lead to a false sense of security. If, for example, the capped interest payments are not enough to cover interest-rate increases called for by the rise in the index interest rate on which the ARM is based, the home-buyer could be faced with something called "negative amortization." That awful-sounding term means that, if your payments don't cover all the interest due, the unpaid interest is added to your mortgage loan. Thus you've got more debt to pay off instead of less. The result is that you may be paying over a longer term or get a reduced net proceeds from the sale of your home.

As you can see, getting a home mortgage these days is not nearly as simple as it used to be. Personally, I favor ARMs, but as I've suggested in other places in the book, shopping around is absolutely essential. There are many variations and many different arrangements offered and it would be well worth your while to look for the best deal. My advice is to look for the lowest-priced ARM you can find provided you can get a good cap along the lines described above. Make sure that if interest rates rose to the cap limit, you could still afford your mortgage interest payments without wrecking your budget. In addition, look for a deal with no negative amortization and no pre-payment penalty. Despite a lot of the negative publicity about ARMs, they can be a very good deal for the home-buyer.

Once you find a successful investment, why not repeat it? For example, the rent from another well-located well-maintained single-family house or condominium can provide generous returns—especially if you know the property well. If you have the temperament to accept a 2:00 A.M. call from your neighbor complaining that the furnace doesn't work, you may even adore the house next door and purchase it as a rental property. You're likely to have the best knowledge of the market and the specific characteristics of the property in your own neighborhood. If the rent just covers your interest and taxes, you can come out well ahead. The depreciation of the house provides good tax writeoffs, and any rise in the value of the house will be taxed at favorable capital-gains rates.

Despite the recent rash of fabulous get-rich-quick stories about real estate investing, there are risks aplenty. A few deserve special mention. There is a maxim in the real estate field that there are three principles of real estate investment: location, location, and location. And location is a fickle thing. A country home without access to public transportation is no longer as desirable as it was in the early 1970s. Now that family size is shrinking, six- and seven-bedroom homes are no longer *de riguer*. There is also another real estate maxim: "The buyer needs 100 eyes; the seller not one." As mentioned above, the market can be inefficient and a particular property not appropriately priced. Keep in mind, too, that demographic trends that have helped inflate house prices will begin to diminish as the growth in household formation will slow considerably. There are also particular risks in specific real estate investments. For example, local restrictions can prevent you from building on land in which you have invested. Rent controls can turn a profitable apartment-house investment into a sour lemon, especially since property taxes go on whether you can rent on favorable terms or not. It's also important to remember that real estate cannot be sold quickly or inexpensively. Also, it's very difficult for an investor to obtain adequate diversification in real estate, since each unit typically involves a great deal of money.* Finally, the greatest risk facing real estate investment

*There are some Real Estate Investment Trusts (REITs) that work on the same principle as a closed-end fund and allow the investor to buy a diversi-

is the risk of disinflation. If the inflation rate continues to decelerate in the late 1980s, the returns from real estate are likely to be inferior to those from stocks and bonds.

Despite the risks, well-located real estate which is not excessively priced remains a useful investment medium — capable of producing generous returns and providing an excellent inflation hedge. Every investing household should plan to own its own home.

Exercise 7: Tiptoe through the Investment Fields of Gold and Collectibles

In the previous edition of this book, I took a very negative view of gold and other "things" as investment vehicles. At that time, gold had risen past $800 an ounce. Diamonds glittered, metals such as copper and silver shone, and collectibles such as art, rugs, and porcelains all became popular investment vehicles.

Publishers jumped on this golden bandwagon and a number of "how-to-beat-inflation" books came out, touting investments in "things" rather than paper securities. The premise was that since you and everybody else consume "things," if you want to preserve real purchasing power, you can do so by owning specific commodities. For example, if you eat TV dinners and drive Honda Accords, the way to preserve real purchasing power is to store away TV dinners and Hondas. There's something to this advice. Indeed, in countries which have suffered from hyperinflation, one can often see cars up on blocks in the backyards of middle-class neighborhoods, for it is by accumulating objects of this sort that people hedge their savings against inflation.

The problem is that "things" often don't yield a stream of

fied portfolio of holdings, often at a discount from book value. In principle I like these investments. Many of these trusts invest in mortgages rather than equity interests in real estate, however. Moreover, it is very difficult even for professionals (let alone individual investors) to evaluate these instruments.

benefits, such as dividend returns. Moreover, they can be costly to store and protect. They can even spoil. The Honda Accord in your backyard can rust, and the three-year-old TV dinner in your freezer may not taste very good. While agreeing that the notion of owning real assets is desirable, I tend to prefer the kind of assets that produce a return while they are giving inflation protection. That's why I like real estate and common stocks.

Still, there's no denying that for those who feed on economic paranoia, 1979, with its gold rush, was a banner year. People who early in the year pooh-poohed gold at a price of less than $300 an ounce swallowed awfully hard when they saw it rise to more than $600. In early 1980 gold continued to soar— approaching the $900-an-ounce mark. The doomsday groupies, on the other hand, were ecstatic, having long recom-

"I'm putting all my money into 'things.'"

Drawing by Geo. Price. © 1979 The New Yorker Magazine, Inc.

mended a portfolio consisting entirely of gold. The price of gold feeds on anxiety, and we certainly have had much cause for worry.

The problem, as I pointed out, was that gold is a sterile investment in a rational world. It does not yield dividends and can be costly to store and protect. Moreover, the sharp run-up in prices in 1979–80 was uncomfortably close in my mind to the price increases during the tulip-bulb craze described in Chapter Two. I said in 1980 that I am not panning gold for all time. "Investment in gold can help to reduce risks, because gold prices generally move counter to trends in the U.S. market. Moreover, anything can happen when it's tulip time in the market. If gold can sell at $900 an ounce, it can just as easily sell for $1800 an ounce (or $450 an ounce)." But I did conclude that at 1980s prices, gold was "an extraordinarily risky investment." I rested my case with the following calculation. "Suppose gold continues to rise and sells at the astronomical price of $3000 an ounce in December 1990. If you made your purchase at the January 1980 price, your total money return when you sell in 1990 will actually be less than that provided by an $11\frac{1}{2}$ percent bond."

From mid-1980 to mid-1984, an investment in gold lost over 20 percent a year. By early 1985, gold was selling at the much more reasonable price of less than $300 an ounce. Accordingly, my current attitude toward gold as an investment is somewhat more positive. While I would recommend against putting a major proportion of your assets into gold, there is a modest role for gold in a well-diversified portfolio. Returns from gold tend to be very little correlated with the returns from paper assets. Hence even modest holdings (say, 5 percent of the portfolio) can be of considerable help to an investor in reducing the variability of the total portfolio, as was clearly shown in Chapter Eight. Small gold holdings can easily be obtained now by purchasing shares in one of the specialized mutual funds concentrating on gold.

The volatile movements in gold prices remind me of the

story of the wiley Chinese merchant who made an excellent living trading in sardines. His business was so successful that he hired a bright young college graduate to assist him in his endeavors. One day when the young man was entertaining his in-laws for dinner he decided to bring home a couple of cans of sardines to have as an appetizer. Upon opening the first can he found, to his great chagrin, that the can was filled with sand. He then opened the second can and found that it, too, was filled with sand. Upon informing the Chinese merchant of his experience the next day the wiley trader simply smiled and said, "Oh, those cans are for trading, not for eating."

In a sense, this story is very similar to the situation that occurs in gold trading. Practically all gold trading is for the purpose of hoarding or speculating that the bullion can be sold later at a higher price. Almost none of the gold is actually used. While there is some small demand for such uses as dental work, jewelry, and a few other specialized industrial needs, the current inventory of gold is some fifty times its annual industrial requirement — not to mention the large amounts of yet-to-be-mined metal stored below ground. In this kind of market, no one can tell where prices will go. Prudence suggests — at best —a limited role for gold as a vehicle for obtaining broader diversification.

What about other collectibles? They have not had the kind of price correction that has occurred in the gold market and are generally not suitable as investment mediums for the lay-person. Diamonds, for example, are often described as everybody's best friend. But, there are enormous risks and disadvantages for individual investors. One must remember that buying diamonds involves large commission costs. Furthermore, there are fads in the way diamonds are cut. Despite assurances to the contrary, you will seldom be able to buy at true wholesale prices. It's also extraordinarily hard for an individual to judge quality, and I can assure you that the number of telephone calls you get from folks wishing to sell diamonds will greatly exceed the calls from those who want to buy them.

Another popular current strategy is investment in collectibles. Thousands of salesmen are touting everything from Renoir to rugs, Tiffany lamps to rare stamps, art deco to airsick bags. I think there's nothing wrong in buying "things" you can love—and God knows people do have strange tastes—but my advice is buy those things because you love them, not because you expect them to appreciate in value. Contrary to popular belief, the inflation-adjusted value of art objects and collectibles does not generally increase. In addition, enormous commissions are paid when you buy and sell. Suppose you buy some collectibles from a dealer for $1000; the dealer keeps 50 percent, which, after sales tax and various charges, leaves $400 for the original seller. Suppose in five years the market value increases to four times what the seller got, from $400 to $1600. Now suppose you sell your collectibles at auction. The auction house may take its commission of $350 and send you a check for $1250. In this scenario, then, you've made a profit of 25 percent in five years, less than the rate on bank passbook savings—and these calculations are based on the assumption that your collectibles appreciated to an astronomical 400 percent of their original value, certainly an unlikely event.

Ask yourself why everyone is so willing to part with things whose value is supposedly increasing. And don't forget that fakes and forgeries are common. A portfolio of collectibles also often requires hefty insurance premiums and endless maintenance charges—so you are making payments instead of receiving dividends or interest. To earn money collecting, you need great originality and taste. You must buy first-class objects when no one else wants them, not inferior schlock when a vast uninformed public enthusiastically bids it up. In my view, most people who think they are collecting profit are really collecting trouble.

Two other popular instruments these days are commodities and stock options. You can buy not only gold but also contracts for the delivery of a variety of commodities from grains to metals. It's a fast market where professionals can benefit greatly but individuals who don't know what they are doing can easily get clobbered. Similarly, stock options can provide investors with a variety of risk-enhancing as well as risk-reducing strategies. But again, it's an extremely complex market and I fear that most individual investors who are not highly trained in the evaluation of options contracts will make much money for their brokers but little, if any, for themselves. My advice to the non-professional investor: Don't go against the grain, and don't exercise all your options.

Exercise 8: Remember that Commission Costs Are Not Random; Some Are Cheaper than Others

With the advent of competitive commission rates, it has now become possible to buy your brokerage services at wholesale prices. A number of brokers around today will execute your stock orders at discounts of as much as 75 percent off the standard commission rates charged by the leading brokerage houses. The discount broker provides a plain-pipe-rack service. If you want your hand held, if you want opinions and investment suggestions, if you want a broker you can call for quotations and other information, the discount broker is *not* for you. If, however, you know exactly what you want to buy, the discount broker can get it for you at much lower commission rates than the standard full-service house.

It's not too hard to find discount brokers. Just read the financial pages of your daily or Sunday paper and you'll find their ads with such catchy headlines as "Full commissions are for the herds" and "There's nothing discount about [our service] except [our] commission rates." Purely for the execution of stock-market orders you can use a discounter with complete confidence. The discounters all belong to the Security Investors Protection Corporation, which insures all accounts up to $100,000. By 1984 the discounters had garnered over 25 percent of the individual investor market.

Exercise 9: Diversify Your Investment Steps

In these warm-up exercises, we have discussed a number of investment instruments—from fixed property to floating-rate notes. The most important part of our walk down Wall Street will take us to the corner of Broad Street—to a consideration of sensible investment strategies with respect to common stocks. A guide to this part of our walk is contained in the final two chapters, since I believe common stocks should form the cornerstone of most portfolios. Nevertheless, in our final warm-up exercise we recall the important lesson of modern portfolio theory—the advantages of diversification.

A biblical proverb states that "in the multitude of counselors there is safety." The same can be said of investments. Diversification reduces risk and makes it far more likely that you will achieve the kind of good average long-run return that meets your investment objective. Therefore, within each investment category you should hold a variety of individual issues, and while common stocks should be a major part of your portfolio, they should not be the sole investment instrument. Whatever the investment objectives, the investor who's wise diversifies.

A Final Check-up

Now that you have completed your warm-up exercises, let's take a moment for a final check-up. The theories of valuation worked out by economists and the performance recorded by the professionals lead to a single conclusion: There is no sure and easy road to riches. High returns can be achieved only through higher risk-taking (and perhaps through acceptance of lesser degrees of liquidity). The sleeping scale of investment choices presented earlier in this chapter should have shown you clearly that you must make for yourself the difficult decision as to how much risk you can tolerate. This is perhaps your most important investment decision.

Once you've done your warm-up exercises and decided where your sleeping point is, you are ready to begin your walk. You need a clear notion of how you want to allocate your funds among the different types of securities (money-market funds, bonds, stocks) marketed by the financial community. The next chapter discusses paper assets as a general investment medium and should help you decide what portion of your capital should be placed in common stocks and bonds.

CHAPTER ELEVEN

The Continuing Case for Investment in Paper Assets

> No man who is correctly informed as to the past will be disposed to take a morose or desponding view of the present. — Thomas B. Macaulay, *History of England*

In 1980 I published an investment manual called *The Inflation Beater's Investment Guide*. The thesis of that book was that investors should be very cautious in forming forward-looking investment strategies solely with the aid of a rearview mirror. While the inflationary 1970s produced highly unsatisfactory investor returns on common stocks and bonds and outstanding returns on hard assets such as gold, I suggested that a different investment philosophy was needed for the 1980s. I proposed that the 1980s were likely to be the age of paper assets, and I strongly recommended eschewing metals and collectibles, which had risen spectacularly in the 1970s, in favor of stocks and bonds. I repeated that message in the 1981 edition of *Random Walk*. I am always cautious about people who say, "I told you so," and I don't make an exception for myself either. While it is true that the investment climate during the first half of the 1980s has been reasonably kind to my investment thesis, the decade is only half over, and the final returns are far from in. Nevertheless, I am going to stick to my guns. I may be a random walker, but I'm also a direct talker. I think my support of paper assets is based on fundamental reasons and I believe they are still the most sensible investment medium for you. The chapter tells you why.

First I will review the inflationary history of the 1970s and explain why bonds and, more surprisingly, common stocks failed to provide protection against accelerating inflation. Next, I will repeat yet again the paper asset thesis I made in 1980. Finally, and this is where you must stay awake, I want to survey the bond and stock markets as of the mid-1980s and offer recommendations for the remainder of the decade.

The Acceleration of Inflation in the Late 1960s and 1970s

From the late 1960s through the early 1980s the major influence on the securities markets was the sharp and unanticipated upward ratcheting of the underlying or core rate of inflation in the U.S. economy. By the core rate of inflation (prop your eyes open now), I mean the rate of increase of unit labor costs, measured by the increase in compensation per hour adjusted for any offsetting increase in productivity. Since labor costs are the major expense in the production of most goods and in the provision of most services, this measure of the increase in unit labor costs provides a better estimate of the underlying inflationary pressure in the economy than does the more popular (but more variable) Consumer Price Index (CPI).

In the mid-1960s, inflation was running at a rate of just over 1 percent. When our involvement in Vietnam increased in the late 1960s, however, we had classical, old-fashioned "demand-pull" inflation—too much money chasing too few goods. This raised the core rate of inflation to something like 4 or 4½ percent. Once inflation ratcheted up, it appeared to be impervious to slack in the economy. We saw this happen often in the 1970s.

Then the economy was beset by the oil and food shocks of 1973–74. It was a classic case of Murphy's Law at work—whatever could go wrong did. OPEC contrived to produce an artificial shortage of oil and Mother Nature produced a real shortage of foodstuffs through poor grain harvests in North America and disastrous ones in the Soviet Union and sub-Saharan Africa. When even the Peruvian anchovy crop mysteriously disappeared (anchovies are a major source of protein), it appears that O'Toole's commentary had come into play. (It was O'Toole who suggested that "Murphy was an optimist.") Again, the inflation rate ratcheted up. The core rate hit the 6 to 6½ percent level—measured rates of inflation, such as the CPI, were even higher.

During the 1974–75 recession, while there were indeed big decreases in the measured rate of inflation as oil and food prices leveled off, the core rate of inflation stubbornly remained at about 6 percent. Then in 1978 and 1979, a combination of policy mistakes—leading to considerable excess demand in certain sectors—and another 125 percent increase in the price of oil kicked the inflation rate up again, taking with it wage costs and thus unit labor costs. The 1980 recession did not succeed in dampening the core rate of inflation either and it appeared that the core rate of inflation had risen to around 8 to 9 percent. The problem then was that from the mid-1960s to the early 1980s, the core rate of inflation steadily ratcheted upward. Each economic shock was built into the wage-cost structure and once a higher level of inflation became embedded in the system, there seemed to be no way of getting rid of it, at least with the unsustained doses of deflationary policies we were willing to accept in the 1970s.

The Agony of the Bond Investor

Because the inflation was unanticipated and allowance for it was not impounded into the prices of most paper assets, investors in bonds had disastrous results. For example, in 1966, 30-year long-term bonds offered a yield to maturity of about 6 percent. This provided protection against the going inflation rate of about 3 percent and an anticipated after-inflation real rate of return of 3 percent. Unfortunately, the actual rate of inflation over the 15-year period 1966–81 was well in excess of 6 percent, wiping out any positive real rate of returns. That's the good news part of this dreary story. The bad news was that there were capital losses. Who wanted to buy a bond yielding 6 percent in the late 1970s, when the rate of inflation was in double digits? No one! If you had to sell your bonds you sold at a loss so the new buyer could get a yield consonant with the higher rate of inflation. Yields rose even further as the risk premium on bonds rose to take into account their increased volatility.

Over some periods in the late 1970s and early 1980s, bond prices were actually more volatile than equity prices. This new drama in the bond market owed its existence to three main factors: First, the increased volatility of the inflation rate led to greater fluctuations in interest rates. Second, the deregulation of financial markets reduced the degree to which credit rationing could restrain the economy, leaving the entire job to interest rates. Finally, the operating procedures of the Federal Reserve, at least until mid-1982, placed more emphasis on the stability of the money supply and showed less concern for the stability of interest rates. To make matters worse, the tax system delivered the unkindest blow of all to bond investors. Even though bond investors often actually earned negative pre-tax rates of return, their bond coupons were taxed at regular income tax rates.

The Sorrow of the Stock Investor

Back in the days of the Neanderthals, defined by my thirteen-year-old as the days before he was born, it was widely believed that sensible investors should buy common stocks representing ownership claims on real property, for generous long-run returns and for protection against inflation. After all, in an era of inflation, factories, equipment, and inventories should rise in value along with all other prices.

Let's face it, though — during the 1970s, stock-market investing created a nouveau poor in the United States. The Dow Jones Industrial Average, which supposedly crossed the 1000 barrier "for good" in 1973, ended the 1970s languishing near the 800 level. Because this disastrous performance occurred at the same time the general price level increased about 70 percent, it became fashionable to believe that stocks were no longer an effective hedge against inflation (if they ever had been). In 1979, *Business Week* published a cover story on the death of equities. Institutional investors who did not believe in capital punishment rushed to the sidelines, and individuals were consistent net sellers of their equity mutual funds. As the 1980s began, few people were thanking Paine Webber, and even when E. F. Hutton talked, nobody listened.

Investors in the 1970s found little comfort in the satisfactory long-run performance record of common stocks. As was shown in Chapter Eight, over the long pull common stocks have produced an annual rate of return of about $9\frac{1}{2}$ percent — considerably above the long-run rate of inflation. But investors were well aware of Lord Keynes' admonition, "In the long run we are all dead"; and over the shorter run investors expect to enjoy themselves and earn satisfactory returns. Between 1968 and 1979, the annual rate of return on U.S. common stocks was a paltry 3.1 percent. The annual rate of return on gold and various objets d'art was more than six times as large. Robert S. Salomon, Jr., of the renowned investment firm of Salomon Brothers, plotted the 1968–79 investment records of several major assets. The results, shown in the following table, leave little doubt as to why money left the stock market in the 1970s.

In the eleven years 1968–79, common stocks actually underperformed long-term bonds, while gold, Chinese ceramics, stamps, and other nontraditional investments produced extraordinary returns.

Traditional vs. Nontraditional Investments, 1968–79

Investment	Compound Annual Growth in Value, 1968–79
Gold	19.4%
Chinese ceramics	19.1
Stamps	18.9
Rare books	15.7
Silver	13.7
Coins (U.S. nongold)	12.7
Old master paintings	12.5
Diamonds	11.8
Farmland	11.3
Single-family house	9.6
U.S. consumer price index	6.5
Foreign currencies[a]	6.4
High-grade corporate bonds	5.8
Common stocks	3.1

Source: Salomon Brothers.

[a] West German mark, Japanese yen, Swiss franc, and Dutch guilder.

Why Did Common Stocks Fail in the 1970s?— Some False Clues

The failure of bonds to protect investors against an *unanticipated* inflationary episode is hardly surprising. The common stock flop was something else. Since stocks represent claims on real assets that presumably rise in value with the price level, stock prices— according to this line of logic—should have risen also. It's like the story of the small boy on his first trip to an art museum. When told that a famous abstract painting was supposed to be a horse, the boy asked wisely, "Well, if it is supposed to be a horse, why isn't it a horse?" If common stocks were supposed to be an inflation hedge, then why weren't they?

Many different explanations involving faltering dividends and earnings growth have been offered that simply don't hold up under careful analysis. One common explanation was that inflation had caused corporate profits to shrink drastically, especially when reported figures were adjusted for inflation. Inflation was portrayed as a kind of financial neutron bomb, leaving the structure of corporate enterprise intact, but destroying the lifeblood of profits. Many saw the engine of capitalism as running out of control, so that a walk down Wall Street — random or otherwise — could prove extremely hazardous.

It used to be easy to measure profits. They were the excess of income over expenses. Not so in an era of inflation, when figuring out true profitability can be quite complex. The problem is that inflation tends to make reported profits appear misleadingly large. Inflation swells reported profits (as well as actual tax liabilities) through two fictitious elements — the overstatement of income (because of the inclusion of inventory profits) and the understatement of expenses (because depreciation charges are calculated on original rather than replacement costs).

Inventory profits provide the same kind of illusory benefits for a business firm that real estate gains provide for homeowners. Homeowners have paper capital gains from the rising values of their homes, but unless they obtain additional mortgages at high interest rates, they cannot use this wealth until they sell their homes. Even worse, as soon as their property is reassessed, property taxes go up. Similarly, inventory profits are not the benefit to a firm that they seem. As the firm disposes of its appreciated inventory, the goods must be replaced at higher prices. Thus, inventory profits provide no cash flow for the firm. Indeed, just the opposite is true, for these paper profits are taxed at regular income-tax rates.

Depreciation charges are another factor in the inflation-swollen profit picture. These are the expenses, charged against taxable income, for the wearing out of the firm's plant and equipment during the production process. The lower the charge, the more income (and profit) will be reported. Because depreciation charges are based on low original cost rather than higher current replacement cost, they are usually not as high as they should be. This makes the remaining income appear as healthy profit when it should be set aside to provide for the necessary replacement of the depreciating assets. Thus, we must be careful in looking at profits, to judge them as nearly as possible on a true economic basis.

The facts are, however, that after making all the necessary adjustments to reported profits, there is no evidence that true profits have been "sliding down a pole greased by cruel and inexorable inflation," as some in the financial community have believed. Over the long pull corporate profits, both in the aggregate and as a percentage of invested capital (figured at inflated replacement cost), have held up extremely well. Indeed, into the mid-1980s, thanks to lower inflation rates and the much higher depreciation allowances allowed by the tax law, enacted earlier in the decade, any inflation illusion to reported corporate profits has more than been wiped out. Indeed, in 1983 and 1984 reported profits were actually lower than true economic profits.

Perhaps, however, we are looking in the wrong place for a clue to the seventies slump. Remember the well-known story of the government bureaucrat searching on his hands and knees on Pennsylvania Avenue for some object during the midday rush?

"What are you looking for?" asked a passerby.

"My watch."

"Do you remember where you lost it?"

"Over on Connecticut Avenue."

"Then why are you looking here?"

"The light is better here."

There is much light placed on corporate earnings in the financial press; but perhaps the experts would be wiser to focus on dividends rather than earnings. Maybe the relevant question is not the amount of earnings—however adjusted—but rather what dividends U.S. corporations are able to pay. The acid test of whether true earning power is increasing is the ability of corporations to provide a stream of dividends whose growth will keep up with inflation. Let us, then, move our light over from earnings to dividends.

The following chart shows the progression of both dividends and the Consumers Price Index from 1960 through the mid-1980s. Dividends have more than held their own. Even during the stagflation period of the 1970s and the recession of the early 1980s, dividends rose by nearly the same rate as the CPI. An index of 28 major company growth stocks compiled by David Babson and Company has shown dividend growth far in excess of that for the S&P 500 and about four times the rate of growth of the CPI.* Clearly, then, the problem does not lie in inadequate dividend growth over the 25 years through the mid-80s.

Movie buffs may recall the marvelous final scene from *Casablanca*. Humphrey Bogart stands over the body of a Luftwaffe major, a smoking gun in his hand. Claude Rains, a captain in the French colonial police, turns his glance from Bogart to the smoking gun to the dead major and finally to his assistant, and says, "Major Strasser has been shot. Round up the usual suspects." We too have rounded up the usual suspects, but we have yet to find out who shot the stock market. Nor have we discovered a rational motive for the crime. Now let's look at the smoking gun.

The Smoking Gun: The P/E Crash of the 1970s

The major reason for the decline in equity prices was that the investor's evaluation of earnings—the number of dollars they were willing to pay for a dollar of earnings—fell by roughly half. Stocks failed to provide investors with protection against inflation not because earnings and dividends failed to grow with inflation, but rather because price-earnings multiples quite literally collapsed over the period.

*The names of the stocks in the Babson 28 Growth Stock Index are listed in the Appendix to this chapter.

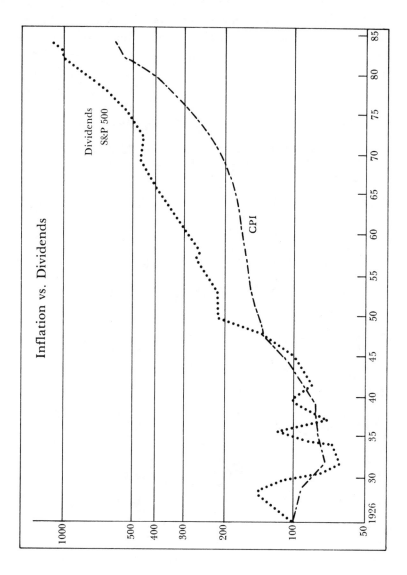

Inflation vs. Dividends

As the following figure shows, during the 1970s, the multiple for the S&P Index was cut by more than 50 percent. The multiples of growth stocks dropped even more drastically, falling by two-thirds. It was this decline in multiples that produced such extraordinarily poor returns for investors in the seventies and that prevented stock prices from reflecting the real underlying progress most companies made in earnings and dividend growth. Thus, the internationally respected financial economist Franco

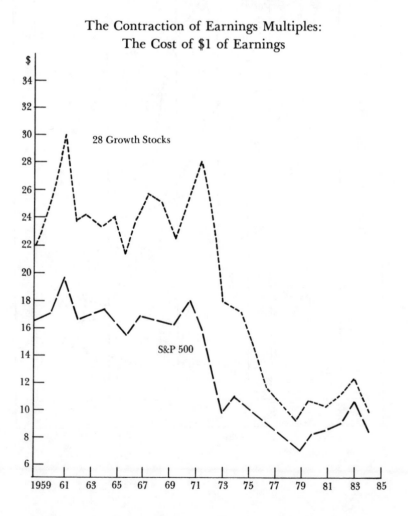

The Contraction of Earnings Multiples:
The Cost of $1 of Earnings

Modigliani (writing with Richard Cohn in the *Financial Analysts Journal*) has concluded that the market is simply irrational—it simply doesn't know how to capitalize earnings during an inflationary period.

It is, of course, quite possible that stock investors may have become irrationally pessimistic in the early 1980s, just as they were probably irrationally optimistic in the mid-1960s. But while I do not believe the market is always perfectly rational, if forced to choose between the stock market and the economics profession, I'd put my money on the stock market every time. I suspect that stock investors weren't irrational—they were just scared. In the mid-1960s, inflation was so modest as to be almost unnoticeable and investors were convinced that economists had found the cure for serious recessions—even mild downturns could be "fine-tuned" away. No one would have imagined in the 1960s that the economy could experience either double-digit unemployment or double-digit inflation, let alone that both could appear simultaneously. Clearly, we have learned that economic conditions are far less stable than had previously been imagined.

We also realize more fully that inflation is not a benign phenomenon, as it used to be described in some textbooks. When prices rise by 10 percent, all prices do not rise by the same amount. Rather, relative prices (and the relationship between input and output prices) are far more variable at higher levels of inflation. Furthermore, the higher the rate of inflation, the more variable and unpredictable inflation becomes. Thus, more volatile levels of real output and higher inflation rates, as well as the accompanying greater volatility of interest rates, have increased uncertainty throughout the economy. Equity securities (dare I say equity insecurities) are therefore considered riskier and deserving of higher risk compensation.*

---

*Economists often put the proposition in terms of the risk premium—that is, the extra return you can expect from an investment over and above the return from perfectly predictable short-term investments. According to this view, the risk premiums in the 1960s were very small—perhaps 1 or 2 percentage points. During the early 1980s risk premiums demanded by investors to hold both stocks and bonds expanded to a range of probably 4 to 6 percentage points, as I shall show below.

The market provides higher risk premiums through a drop in prices relative to earnings and dividends; this produces larger returns in the future consistent with the new riskier environment. Paradoxically, however, the same adjustments that produced very poor returns in the late 1960s and throughout the 1970s created some very attractive price levels early in the 1980s.

The 1980 Paper-Asset Thesis

Let me turn now to the thesis I presented in late 1980 that the decade of the 1980s would be the age of paper assets. I argued that both bonds and stocks had fully adjusted — and perhaps even overadjusted — to the changed economic environment. I suggested that stocks and bonds were priced not only to provide adequate protection against the likely rate of inflation, but also to give unusually generous real rates of return.

Let us consider the argument for the bond market first. In the early 1980s, this market was in disgrace. *The Bawl Street Journal*, in its 1981 annual comedy issue, wrote that "A bond is a fixed-rate instrument designed to fall in price." At the time, the yield on high-quality corporate bonds was 16 percent. The underlying rate of inflation (as measured by the growth of unit labor costs) was then about 8 percent. Thus, corporate bonds provided a prospective real rate of return of about 8 percent, a rate unusually generous by past historical standards. (According to Ibbotson and Sinquefield, the long-term real rate of return on corporate bonds was only 2 percent.) To be sure, bond prices had become volatile and, thus, it was reasonable to suppose that bonds ought to offer a somewhat larger risk premium than before. But I suggested then that panic-depressive institutional investors probably overdiscounted the risks of bond investments. Like generals fighting the last war, investors had been loathe to touch bonds because experience over the past 15 years had been so disastrous. But at some price, bonds are appropriately valued in the market and it was my thesis in 1980 that, because so many investors "would never buy a bond again," the market may even have overreacted. Even if inflation remained at its 1980–81 levels, bonds were a smart investment, particularly for tax-exempt investors (including Keogh and IRA participants).

What about stocks? It is possible to calculate the anticipated rate of return on stocks of the Dow Jones Industrial Average by adding the dividend yield of the average to the anticipated growth of dividends per share. As I will illustrate below, for a long-term holder of any security, this will be the realized rate of return. The calculations I performed during 1980 suggested a total expected rate of return from common stocks of 17 percent. This 17-percent rate was over 9 percentage points more than the core rate of inflation and was again very generous by historical standards.

Common stocks were also selling at unusually low multiples of cyclically depressed earnings and at prices that were only a fraction of the replacement value of the assets they represented. Small wonder we saw so many attempted takeovers in the early 1980s. Whenever assets can be bought in the stock market at less than the cost of acquiring them directly, there will be a tendency for firms to purchase the equities of other firms, as well as to buy back their own stocks. Thus, I argued that in the early 1980s we were presented with a market situation where paper assets had adjusted and perhaps overadjusted to inflation and the greater uncertainty associated with it. On the other hand, hard assets, despite their extraordinary performance during the 1970s, seemed fully priced. I concluded that the question was not how badly equity investors had done in the past — it was what investors may be kicking themselves about five years from now for not having bought today.

Realized Returns During the First Half of the 1980s

The stock and bond markets in the last half of 1982 and through 1983 finally reacted to what were apparently severely undervalued price levels of the earlier 1980s. During the last six

*"Let me put it this way. It's five years from now. What am I
kicking myself for not having bought?"*

Drawing by Whitney Darrow, Jr. © 1956 The New Yorker Magazine, Inc.

months of 1982 alone, common stocks appreciated by more than
28 percent as measured by the Dow Jones Industrial Average and
Standard & Poor's 500 Stock Index. Bonds performed even
better. In 1982, long-term taxable bonds had a banner year,
treating some investors to annual returns of close to 40 percent.
1983 was also a good year for paper assets, with stock prices
advancing further until mid-year and bond prices rising in the
early months of 1983 and falling later in the year to produce
small declines in capital values but reasonably generous total
returns.

While George Orwell was right and the first half of 1984 was something of a bummer for the securities markets, paper assets were the clear winners during the early years of the decade. Hard assets, such as gold, were left far behind. The following table, using data prepared by Robert Salomon, presents returns during the early 1980s for selected investment assets.

Traditional vs. Nontraditional Investment, 1980–84

Investment	Compound Annual Growth in Value 7/1/80–6/30/84
Common stocks	14.6%
High-grade corporate bonds	10.7
Chinese ceramics	8.8
U.S. consumer price index	6.2
Stamps	6.0
Housing	4.8
Farmland	3.7
Old master paintings	2.7
Silver	1.7
Diamonds	1.5
Foreign currencies[a]	−3.4
Coins (U.S. nongold)	−4.5
Gold	−6.6

Source: Salomon Brothers.
[a]West German mark, Japanese Yen, Swiss franc, and Dutch guilder.

Forward-looking Investments for the Remainder of the 1980s

While I remain convinced that no one can predict short-term movements in securities markets, I do believe it is possible to judge the long-run appropriateness of levels of stock prices and interest rates. Many factors suggest that paper assets seem fairly valued in the mid-1980s. Looking at the stock market, it is well to remember that the market has, like Alice in *Through the Looking Glass*, been on a treadmill—essentially selling at very near the same levels as in the mid-1960s. The chart below indicates that in "real" or inflation-adjusted terms, stocks in the mid-1980s were still selling at not much more than half of the level of the mid-1960s.

S&P 500 Stock Index—Inflation-Adjusted Level 1947–84

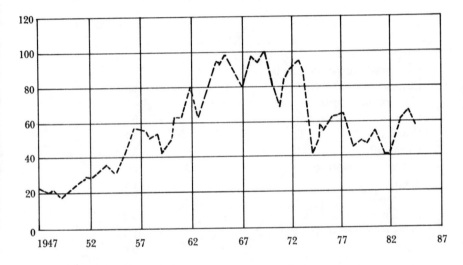

While the market is actually considerably lower in real terms, the earnings for the S&P and Dow were more than twice as high in 1984 as they were in 1966. Thus, referring back to the chart on page 303, we see that the P/E multiples for the S&P 500 and for the Babson 28 Growth Stock Index remain very modest. The P/E multiple for the S&P during mid-1984 was just under 9, while that for the Babson Growth Stock Index was just over 10. These multiples are substantially below the norms of the past thirty years.

Another indication that stocks are still reasonably valued by historical standards is that the total market value of the equities in the S&P 400 Industrial Stock Index is still substantially below the replacement values of the assets represented. Stocks have remained available at unusual discounts from the true worth of their assets.

Finally, let me update a simple example I used in 1980 to show that stocks still appear to provide very generous prospective returns. I will demonstrate that the prospective return from stocks can be estimated as the sum of the dividend yield plus the anticipated long-term growth rate of earnings and dividends. I believe that you can obtain a 15 percent return even on a stodgy stock like good old Exxon.

Exxon is not a spectacular investment, but it is a high-quality bellwether stock and very widely held by the public. Late in 1984, the basic investing measurements for an Exxon share were as shown below:

Price: $40.00

1985 Earnings (est.): $6.15

P/E Multiple: 6½

1985 Dividend (est.): $3.40

Yield: 8½%

Exxon's Late 1984 Investment Profile

We see that, for openers, an investor could expect an 8½ percent rate of return in 1985 just from a continuation of the $3.40 dividend. Exxon doesn't leap and bound, but it has been able to produce growing dividends. Even during the 1970s (a decade most equity investors would rather forget), the dividend grew at a rate of better than 10 percent. Let's be really cautious and suppose that during the remainder of the 1980s the dividend grows at only a 6½ percent rate (certainly a conservative assumption and actually somewhat below some estimates currently being made in Wall Street). Now we all know that when earnings and dividends grow at an average rate of, say, 6½ percent, we don't expect the growth to come in at exactly that rate of every year.

Prosperous years for the economy may bring much larger increases; recession years may even bring declines, especially in earnings. But let's suppose that 1986, for example, is an average year. We now have the picture shown below:

1986 Earnings (est.): $6.55
    ($6.15 + 6½%)

1986 Dividends (est.): $3.62
    ($3.40 + 6½%)

Exxon's 1986 Estimated Growth

Before we can project an Exxon investor's overall rate of return during 1985 — including both dividends and changes in the worth of a share — we need to project what the stock price will be at the end of 1985. Suppose we conservatively project that the market will be just as pessimistic at the end of 1985 as it was at the end of 1984. It's easier to get into a state of depression than to get out of it (like the old saw about making love to a gorilla: you don't quit when *you* get tired; you quit when the *gorilla* gets tired). With the same degree of pessimism prevailing at the end of 1985, the market will continue to assign a price-earnings multiple of 6½ and a dividend yield of 8½ percent to Exxon stock. Thus, it will sell at $42⅝ per share — 6½ times its estimated earnings of $6.55 — while still producing an 8½ percent yield with its then projected $3.62 dividend. We have now completed our investment profile.

Price: $42⅝ (6½ × 6.55 earnings)

1986 Earnings (est.): $6.55

P/E Multiple: 6½

1986 Dividend (est.): $3.62

Yield: 8½%
    ($3.62 dividend ÷ $42⅝ price)

Exxon's Late 1985 Estimated Investment Profile

Under these circumstances, the holder of Exxon stock can expect a yearly return of 15 percent—8½ percent from the dividend yield and 6½ percent from the growth of the company. The investor gets $3.40 in dividends and $2.62 in capital gains, for a total return of $6.02, which is 15 percent of the original $40 investment.

Purchase Price Late 1984: $40.00

Market Price Late 1985: $42.62

Capital Gain: $2.62

Dividend during Period Held: $3.40

$$\frac{\text{Total Return}}{\text{Purchase Price}} = \frac{\$6.02}{\$40.00} \approx 15\%$$

Returns to Holder of Exxon Stock
(12 Months, Late 1984 to Late 1985)

That seems almost too good to be true. And yet it's a conservative estimate. In general, the rule for finding the prospective rate of return on any stock is to add the expected growth rate of the company to its dividend yield. The rule works whenever there is no change in the general level of P/E multiples or yields.

Obviously, such neat calculations are not likely to work out year after year. Nevertheless, over longer periods of time results do average out so that total returns can well be approximated by adding the growth rate to the dividend yield. The moral is clear. Even a low-growth quality stock like Exxon was priced in late 1984 to provide a return of 15 percent.

What about the rest of the market? I've done similar calculations for the thirty stocks of the Dow Jones Industrial Average as of the end of 1984. When you add the dividend yields for each stock to the long-run growth rates, the prospective return is over 15 percent. (Growth rates are estimated by the *Value Line Investment Survey. Value Line* regularly provides information on growth prospects for a wide variety of companies, and while these estimates are subject to considerable error, the *Value Line* estimates have as good a record as any others). This average return of over 15 percent looks good not only now but also by historical equity standards, although, as I indicate below, bonds appear at least equally attractive.

The following figure plots prospective rates of return on common stocks (the Down Jones Industrial Average), calculated as above, since 1959. The chart shows that both expected stock returns and nominal bond yields (which are also plotted along with inflation rates) are still superb as of the mid-1980s. Expected stock returns of over 15 percent are still at near record levels in nominal terms and are especially high with respect to current rates of inflation. High-quality bond yields at over 14 percent are also at near record levels. But note that there has been a sharp drop in the inflation rate so that real interest rates are still at record high levels. While it is true that the core rate of inflation has not fallen as much as measured rates of inflation, wage behavior during the mid-1980s and productivity trends suggest a core inflation rate of not more than 5–6 percent, a considerable drop from the early eighties.

Thus, real interest rates on corporate bonds (nominal rates less the core inflation rates) are still abnormally high as this is written in the mid-1980s. Indeed, the bond market is at least as attractive as the stock market.

Could I Be Wrong?

The thesis presented here is that the bond and stock markets have fully or more than fully adjusted to the inflationary experience of the recent past and to the greater uncertainty that has been associated with it. Moreover, even though market prices are higher than at the start of the decade, the markets seem fairly priced on a long-term basis. A popular maxim warns, however, "If you can remain calm when everyone around you is panicked, perhaps you don't understand the problem." Could the problem be worse

Expected Total Return: Stocks and Bonds

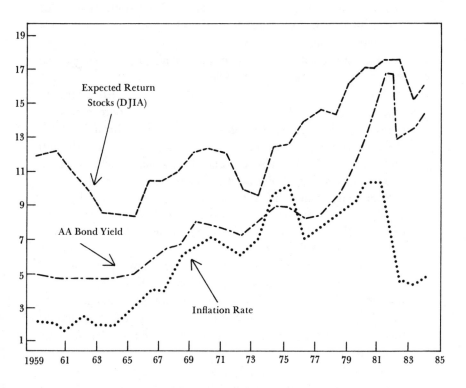

Expected Return
Stocks (DJIA)

AA Bond Yield

Inflation Rate

than I have described? Could the market actually be underestimating the long-run dangers to economic instability?

Is it possible that the upward ratcheting of the core rate of inflation I wrote about earlier in the chapter has just been halted temporarily? While current 14 percent yields give you an 8 percent return over a 6 percent core inflation rate, what if inflation soars back up to the double-digit level, as some investors fear? This is precisely the situation that would make my investment thesis wrong, at least as concerns long-term bonds. So the critical final question I must address is the likelihood that the current core inflation rate will remain at a restrained level.

While long-term forecasts of inflation are notoriously inaccurate, I would suggest that there are at least some reaons for optimism as well as some for concern. The most favorable part of the picture concerns the behavior of wage settlements during the first half of the 1980s. Average hourly earnings were rising at less than a 5 percent rate during 1984.

Of course, wage demands may well accelerate with continued economic growth. But over the longer term, there are some reasons to be sanguine. I think we have learned throughout the Western World that our economics do not work well with high and variable rates of inflation, and there is now a willingness to accept more stringent demand management policies than were previously thought politically feasible. This is true not only in the U.S., but also in all the European Economic Community countries, which have experienced unprecedented rate of unemployment during the mid-1980s.

Moreover, the high debt levels of the less developed countries should also restrain demand from this part of the world economy. It seems quite unlikely that the world economy will be characterized by excess demand over the next several years. This should moderate both wage demands and increases in the prices of basic commodities.

Also, U.S. labor clearly recognizes now that the U.S. economy has become sufficiently open to world trade that moderation in industrial wage demands and acceptance of changes in work rules are essential if we are to keep manufacturing employment from falling. Without restraint of industrial wage increases, the U.S. is in danger of becoming a service economy. An industry-by-industry analysis suggests that heightened competition pressures in both domestic and foreign markets (including substantially increased competition from developing countries such as Taiwan and South Korea) have significantly changed the wage-setting process. Moreover, the deregulation of such industries as airlines, trucking, and telephone service has also triggered increased wage competition. In addition, during the early 1980s U.S. tax policy made an abrupt turn in favor of savings and investment, which should encourage productivity growth. Finally, the tightening of controls throughout American industry and the increasing experience mix of our labor force augur well for a better productivity performance for the rest of the decade. While there are no guarantees, there are certainly reasons for optimism that the upward ratcheting of the core inflation rate has ended.

There is, however, one disturbing part of the picture that is a reason for concern: the huge U.S. federal budget deficit. It is this deficit, I believe, that has kept interest rates and economic uncertainty as high as they are. It is clear that a combination of increased tax revenues (preferably through tax reform), a slowdown in the rate of growth of military spending, and fundamental long-run reform of entitlements programs (for example, making increases to the retirement age for social security sooner than Congress has agreed to and tightening the Medicare reimbursement program) will be necessary to remove the legitimate fear that interest rates will continue to rise and that inflationary pressures will mount. Even if less progress is made than desirable, however, I still feel that paper assets — both stocks and bonds — are your best investment bets for the remainder of the 1980s.

It is also well to remember the lessons of the theories we examined in Part Two, which suggested that capital markets are at least reasonably efficient over the long pull. Fears about renewed inflation and economic instability are not reflected in stock and bond prices at some time in the future; they are reflected in the market now. If investors perceive that the investment risk of paper assets has increased, the financial pages reflect such thinking very quickly. In well-functioning financial markets, such as ours, investors are willing to buy only those assets that will provide the higher future rates of return sufficient to compensate them for added risk.

Does my expectation of an average return of 15 percent per

year on common stocks mean that I am predicting a bull-market rally during some specific period in the late 1980s? Not at all. As a random walker through Wall Street, I am skeptical that anyone can predict the course of short-term stock price movements, and perhaps we are better off for it. I am reminded of one of my favorite episodes from the marvelous old radio serial "I Love a Mystery." This mystery was about a greedy stock-market investor who wished that just once he would be allowed to see the paper, with its stock price changes, twenty-four hours in advance. By some occult twist his wish was granted, and early in the evening he received the late edition of the next morning's paper. He worked feverishly through the night planning early-morning purchases and late-afternoon sales which would guarantee him a killing in the market. Then, before his elation had diminished, he read through the remainder of the paper—and came upon his own obituary. His servant found him dead the next morning.

Since I, fortunately, do not have access to future newspapers, I cannot tell how stock and bond prices will behave in any particular period ahead. Nevertheless, I am convinced that bond and stock prices have fully adjusted to the increased economic uncertainty, and that they will produce generous real returns over the remainder of the 1980s. Investors will, I believe, be well served by putting their money where my mouth is and investing a substantial part of their wealth in paper assets.

Appendix: Babson 28 Growth Stocks

Air Products and Chemicals, Inc.
American Home Products Corp.
AMP, Inc.
Burroughs Corp.
Capital Holding Corp.
Citicorp
Coca-Cola Co.

Colgate-Palmolive Co. (Delaware)
Dow Chemical Co.
Eastman Kodak Co.
Exxon Corp.
Georgia-Pacific Corp.
Gillette Co.
Halliburton Co.
Hewlett-Packard Co.
International Business Machines Corp.
Johnson & Johnson
K mart Corp.
Marathon Oil Co.
Merck and Company, Inc.
Minnesota Mining and Manufacturing Co.
Pfizer, Inc.
Procter & Gamble
Provident Life and Accident Insurance Co.
Revlon, Inc.
Sears, Roebuck and Co.
Standard Brands, Inc.
Xerox Corp.

CHAPTER TWELVE

Three Giant Steps Down Wall Street

> Annual income twenty pounds, annual expenditure nineteen nineteen six, result happiness. Annual income twenty pounds, annual expenditure twenty pounds ought and six, result misery. —Charles Dickens, *David Copperfield*.

By now you have made sensible decisions on taxes, housing, insurance, and how to get the most out of your cash reserves. You have reviewed your objectives and risk tolerance and decided how much of your assets to put into the stock market. Now it is time for quick prayer at Trinity Church and then some bold steps forward, taking great care to avoid the graveyard on either side of you. In this chapter I'll present some sensible rules for buying stocks. These rules can help you to avoid costly mistakes and unnecessary sales charges and to increase your yield a mite without undo risk. I can't offer anything spectacular, but I do know that often a percent or two increase in the yield on your assets can mean the difference between misery and happiness.

How do you go about buying stocks? Basically, there are three ways: I call them the No-Brainer Step, the Deep Thinker Step, and the Substitute Player Step.

In the first case you simply buy a share of the market index through a so-called index fund. You're assured of the market's rate of return—a return that I believe will average 15 percent per year during the remainder of the 1980s. This method also has the virtue of being absolutely simple. Even if you have trouble chewing gum while walking randomly you can master it. You simply send one check, need make no further decisions, and are guaranteed the same yearly rate of return as the market, as measured by Standard & Poor's 500 Stock Index. The market, in effect, pulls you along with it.

Under the second system you jog down Wall Street, picking your own stocks and getting—in comparison with the yield obtained with the index fund—much higher or much lower rates of return. This involves work, but also, in the opinion of those who wouldn't play the game any other way, a lot of fun. To help tilt the odds of success a bit more in your favor, I've provided a series of rules to guide you in picking stocks.

Third, you can sit on a curb and choose a professional investment manager to do the walking down Wall Street for you. The only way investors of modest means can accomplish this is to purchase mutual funds, and I will present some helpful suggestions on how to go about picking the right fund for you.

Earlier editions of my book described a strategy called the Malkiel Step: buying closed-end investment company shares at a discount. Alas, that strategy was so successful that it is no longer available. The story of its demise is useful, however, in resolving the paradox careful readers will have noted throughout this book—namely, how markets can be both reasonably efficient and yet sometimes inefficient at the same time. The disappearance of the Malkiel Step is described at the end of the chapter.

The No-Brainer Step: Buying the Market

The Standard & Poor's 500 Stock Index, a composite that represents 70 percent of the value of all U.S. traded common stocks, beats most of the experts over the long pull. Buying a portfolio of all companies in this index would be an easy way to own stocks. I argued back in 1973 (in the first edition of this book) that the means to adopt this approach was sorely needed for the small investor:

> What we need is a no-load, minimum-management-fee mutual fund that simply buys the hundreds of stocks making up the broad stock-market averages and does no trading from security to security in an attempt to catch the winners. Whenever below average performance on the part of any mutual fund is noticed, fund spokesmen are quick to point out, "You can't buy the averages." It's time the public could.

Shorly after my book was published, the "index fund" idea caught on. At first only large pension clients were offered this investment opportunity. But one of the great virtues of capitalism is that when there is a need for a product, someone usually finds the will to produce it. In 1976, a fund was created that allowed the public to get into the act as well. The Vanguard Index Trust (also known as the "500 portfolio") is a mutual fund that is internally managed and therefore pays no investment advisory fee. The investments of the trust are the 500 stocks of the S&P 500, purchased in the same proportions as their weight in the index. Each investor shares proportionately in the net income and in the capital gains and losses of the fund's portfolio.

Since its inception, the Vanguard Index Trust has closely "tracked" the S&P 500. There are no so-called loading fees for buying the trust's shares. Management expenses (custodian fees, the costs of collecting and distributing dividends and preparing summary reports for investors, etc.) run at less than 0.3 percent of assets, far less than the expenses incurred by most mutual funds or bank trust departments. You can now buy the market conveniently and inexpensively.* In fact, if you own any of the 500 stocks of the S&P, Vanguard allows you to trade this stock in, without brokerage expense, for shares of the "500 portfolio."

The logic behind this strategy is the logic of the efficient-market theory. The above-average long-run performance of the S&P 500 compared with that of major institutional investors has been confirmed by Becker Securities Corporation, a firm specializing in compiling the track record of the experts managing corporate pension funds. For example, during the period 1965–79, the S&P 500 outperformed three-quarters of the institutional investors in the Becker sample; the average annual total return for the S&P 500 was approximately one percentage point better than that of the median fund in the Becker sample.

Similar data published in the *Pensions and Investments Performance Evaluation Report* analyze the investment returns of bank and insurance company pooled equity funds, revealing that the S&P 500 outperformed 95 of the 112 funds during the 1970s, as I reported in the 1981 edition. More up-to-date data continue to confirm the same results. The S&P beat two-thirds of professionally managed portfolios in the decade ending in 1982 and three-fourths of the pros in 1983.

Stock trading among institutional investors is like an isometric exercise: lots of energy is expended, but between one investment manager and another it all balances out, and the commissions the managers pay detract from performance. Like greyhounds at the dog track, professional money managers seem destined to lose their race with the mechanical rabbit. Small wonder that many institutional investors, including Exxon, Ford, American Telephone and Telegraph, Harvard University, and the New York State Teachers Association have put substantial portions of their assets into index funds. In 1977, $1 billion in

---

*A Vanguard Index Trust prospectus and application form can be obtained by writing to P.O. Box 1100, Valley Forge, PA 19482, or by calling 800/523-7025. I must remind the reader that I am a director of this fund.

assets were invested in index funds. By 1984, that amount had increased to $60 billion.

How about you? When you buy an index fund, you give up the chance of boasting at the golf club about the fantastic gains you've made by picking stock-market winners. Broad diversification rules out extraordinary losses relative to the whole market; it also, by definition, rules out extraordinary gains. Thus, many Wall Street critics refer to index-fund investing as "guaranteed mediocrity." But experience conclusively shows that index-fund buyers are likely to obtain results exceeding those of the typical fund manager, whose large advisory fees and substantial portfolio turnover tend to reduce investment yields. And index investors will *predictably* receive the market return. Of course, this strategy does not rule out risk: if the market goes down, your portfolio is guaranteed to follow suit. Many people will find the guarantee of playing the stock-market game at par every round a very attractive one—especially with the market priced to provide excellent returns in the late 1980s.

The index method of investment has other attractions for the small investor. It enables you to obtain very broad diversification with only a small investment. It also allows you to reduce brokerage charges. When an individual investor buys stocks, he or she pays a brokerage fee of almost a dollar a share on small trades (even if a discount broker is used). The index fund, by pooling the moneys of many investors, trades in larger blocks and can negotiate a brokerage fee below five cents a share on its transactions. The index fund does all the work of collecting the dividends from the 500 stocks it owns and sending you each quarter one check for all of your earnings (earnings which, incidentally, can be reinvested in the fund if you desire). In short, the index fund is a sensible, serviceable method for obtaining the market's rate of return with absolutely no effort and a minimal expense.

I have only a few quibbles with this easy way of index investing. First, while the S&P 500 represents 70 percent of U.S. stocks, the 30 percent it excludes may be precisely the kind of emerging growth companies that offer higher rewards (as well as higher risks). Recall that our discussion of the new investment technology pointed out that the S&P index is far from a perfect proxy for the market. It would be nice to have a fund available that bought an index of smaller companies—such as perhaps the American Stock Exchange or NASDAQ with their heavy weighting of younger growth companies and natural resource stocks. It would also be nice to have an international index fund. Second, being pulled through the market is very dull for a weak random walker. Those with speculative temperaments will undoubtedly prefer using their own steps (and wits) to pick winners. Third, there are a few professional investment managers who, at least in the past, have outdistanced the index and you may prefer to place your bets on them. I'll talk about them in Step Three below.

The Deep Thinker Step: Doing It Yourself

Having been smitten with the gambling urge since birth, I can well understand why many investors have not only a compulsion to pick the big winners on their own but also a total lack of interest in a system that promises results merely equivalent to those in the market as a whole. The problem is that it takes a lot of work to do it yourself, and as I've repeatedly shown, consistent winners are very rare. For those who regard investing as play, however, this section demonstrates how a sensible strategy can produce substantial rewards and, at the very least, minimize the risks in playing the stock-picking game.

Before putting my strategy to work, however, you need to know the sources of investment information and how to choose an appropriate broker. Most information sources can be obtained at public libraries. You should be an avid reader of the financial pages of daily newspapers, particularly the *New York Times* and the *Wall Street Journal*. Weeklies such as *Barron's*, the *Commercial and Financial Chronicle*, and the *Wall Street Transcript*, should also be on your "must read" list. Business magazines such as *Business Week, Fortune,* and *Forbes* are also valuable for gaining exposure to investment ideas. The major investment advisory services are also good. You should, for example, try to have access to Standard & Poor's *Outlook* and the *Value Line Investment Survey*. The first is a weekly publication which contains lists of recommendations; the second presents historical records, current reviews, and risk (beta) ratings of about 1700 securities, as well as weekly recommendations.

When choosing a broker, you may find that it does not pay to utilize the kind of discount firm recommended in Chapter Ten if you really do want help. The most important criterion for an investor who wants to be exposed to investment ideas is whether a brokerage firm can furnish investment information. The major question to ask is: Does your broker's firm have a large and well-respected research department? Does it produce comprehensive research reports—as opposed to one-page fly sheets—on the major investment alternatives? Also, the firm should be one that does a substantial amount of institutional business, insuring your contact with the ideas that are making the rounds of the investment community. While, on average, the value of these reports and ideas may be negligible, you've got to be exposed to them if you truly believe you are one of the rare individuals who can consistently win the game of guessing which idea is likely to catch on. Armed with solid information sources and a good broker, you can then begin the process of selecting individual stocks.

In the first edition of *A Random Walk Down Wall Street,* written in the early 1970s, I proposed four rules for successful stock selection. I find them just as serviceable today. Indeed, as I'll argue below, the stock-market environment of the later 1980s may be especially conducive to their success. In abridged form, the rules, some of which have been mentioned in earlier chapters, are as follows:

Rule 1: Confine stock purchases to companies that appear able to sustain above-average earnings growth for at least five years. As difficult as the job may be, picking stocks whose earnings grow is the name of the game. Consistent growth not only increases the earnings and dividends of the company but may also increase the multiple that the market is willing to pay for those earnings. This would further boost your gains. Thus, the purchaser of a stock whose earnings begin to grow rapidly has a potential double benefit—both the earnings and the multiple may increase.

Rule 2: Never pay more for a stock than can reasonably be justified by a firm foundation of value. While I am convinced that you can never judge the exact intrinsic value of a stock, I do feel that you can roughly gauge when a stock seems to be reasonably priced. The market price-earnings multiple is a good place to start: You should buy stocks selling at multiples in line with, or not very much above, this ratio. My strategy, then, is to look for growth situations that the market has not already recognized by bidding the stock's multiple to a large premium. As has been pointed out, if the growth actually takes place you will often get double bonus—both the earnings and the price-earnings multiple can rise, producing large gains. By the same token, beware of the stock with a very high multiple and many years of growth already discounted in the price. If earnings decline rather than grow, you will usually get double trouble—the multiple will drop along with the earnings, and heavy losses will result.*

Note that, while similar, this is not simply another endorsement of the currently popular "buy low P/E stocks" strategy. Under my rule it is perfectly all right to buy a stock with a P/E multiple slightly above the market average—as long as the company's growth prospects are substantially above average. You

---

*In 1973, I cautioned readers not to buy those premier growth stocks (the one decision Nifty Fifty stocks) whose multiples had soared in some cases to as much as sixty, seventy, and eighty times earnings, and I mentioned several of those stocks by name. Following Rule 2, therefore, could have enabled you to avoid one of the most notorious investment follies of the 1970s. It would also have kept you safe from the 1983 new-issue craze.

might call this an adjusted low P/E strategy. Buy stocks whose P/E's are low relative to their growth prospects. If you can be even reasonably accurate in picking companies that do indeed enjoy above-average growth, you will be rewarded with above-average returns.

Rule 3: It helps to buy stocks with the kinds of stories of antici-pated growth on which investors can build castles in the air. I stressed in Chapter Two the importance of psychological ele-ments in stock price determination. Individual and institutional investors are not computers that calculate warranted price-earnings multiples and then print out buy and sell decisions. They are emotional human beings—driven by greed, gambling instinct, hope, and fear in their stock-market decisions. This is why successful investing demands both intellectual and psycho-logical acuteness. Of course, the market is not totally subjective either; if a positive growth rate appears to be established, the stock is almost certain to develop some type of following. But stocks are like people—some have more attractive personalities than others, and the improvement in a stock's multiple may be smaller and slower to be realized if its story never catches on. The key to success is being where other investors will be, several months before they get there. So my advice is to ask yourself whether the story about your stock is one that is likely to catch the fancy of the crowd. Is it a story from which contagious dreams can be generated? It is a story on which investors can build castles in the air—but castles in the air that really rest on a firm foundation?

Rule 4: Trade as little as possible. I agree with the Wall Street maxim "Ride the winners and sell the losers," but not because I believe in technical analysis. Frequent switching accomplishes nothing but subsidizing your broker and increasing your tax burden when you do realize gains. I do not say, "Never sell a stock on which you have a gain." The circumstances that led you to buy the stock may change, and, especially when it gets to be tulip time in the market, many of your successful growth stocks may become way overpriced, as they did during the Nifty Fifty craze of the 1970s or the small company speculative bubble of 1983. But it is very difficult to recognize the proper time to sell, and heavy tax costs may be involved. My own philosophy leads me to minimize trading as much as possible. I am merciless with the losers, however. With few exceptions, I sell before the end of each calendar year any stocks on which I have a loss. The reason for this timing is that losses are deductible (up to certain amounts) for tax purposes, or can offset gains you may already have taken. Thus, taking losses can actually reduce the amount of loss. For example, if you are in the 50 percent tax bracket, have $1000 of short-term capital losses (that is, losses resulting from sales made within six months of the purchase), and have no other gains or losses, you can deduct the lost $1000 from your income and pay $500 less in taxes. I don't always take all losses. If the growth I expect begins to materialize and I am convinced my stock will work out a bit later, I may hold on for a while. But I do not recommend too much patience in losing situations, especially when prompt action can produce immediate tax benefits.

Do these rules work? They have for me, and they have for some of the few truly successful fund managers on the Street. But perhaps it might be instructive to revisit a couple whose investments were described in my last edition of *A Random Walk Down Wall Street*.

This couple, who prefer to hide behind the pseudonym of Smith, had undergone a dramatic change in life-style between that edition and this. They had become parents. Now, instead of perusing *Barron's*, they were powdering bottoms. It was not a situation conducive to extensive reading of investment information and they knew it. Still, investing can be an addictive activity and they found it hard to give up. The Smiths resorted to short cuts in finding investment opportunities.

One easy route was to look at my book. They had already read the first edition and had profited handsomely from following my rules. When the 1981 edition came out, they glanced at the tables and charts and were fascinated by what they saw.

The first eye-opener was a chart showing the decline in the

premium for growth stocks. In 1974, the P/E of these stocks was twice the market P/E; by 1979, it was barely 10 percent higher. Right across the page from this chart was a table showing the price-earnings multiples for IBM and for the market in general. That showed IBM's P/E going from 64 in 1961 to 9 in 1980, while the market P/E had dropped from 20 to 7. The numbers in that table told a dramatic story to the Smiths. As far as IBM was concerned, they felt investors had gone from floating castles in the air to digging deep dungeons in the ground.

The Smiths checked a number of investment sources. They learned that IBM had enjoyed rapid growth in earnings during the 1970s and that the 1980s looked even better. Growth in the computer market showed signs of accelerating rather than slackening and IBM's lead over its competition appeared to have widened. Rule 1 was clearly satisfied. As noted above, IBM's earnings multiple was little more than the multiple for the market as a whole and its dividend yield was higher than on a bank passbook account. The Smiths had no trouble convincing themselves that Rule 2 was met. Finally, there had been a spate of newspaper and magazine articles about enormous increases forecast in the speed and capability of computers as well as the many increased applications that were likely in the eighties. IBM looked like the kind of investment story on which people could build castles in the air.

The Smiths bought IBM at $55\frac{1}{2}$. A little over a year later — at the close of trading on December 31, 1981 — IBM was selling at a whopping $56\frac{7}{8}$! Were the Smiths discouraged? Well, to be honest, they were not overjoyed. But the Smiths resisted the temptation to break Rule 4 and sell out. Since nothing fundamental had gone wrong with IBM, the Smiths concluded that the market had not yet come to its senses. A year later, on December 31, 1982, the stock was selling at $96\frac{1}{4}$. It soon crossed 100 and, as this book goes to press, the Smiths were still holding and IBM had yet to fall below that price.

The Smiths also resorted to the boob tube to obtain investment ideas. Like millions of other television watchers, they enjoy the banter and appreciate the information given on *Wall Street Week*. Watching this show is an easy way to get investment advice; an expert names the stocks he or she likes and then gives the reasons for the stock pick. In 1983, one of the panelists on the show mentioned a stock named Snap-On Tools.

Snap-On Tools actually does what its name implies: it sells small tools, the majority to garage mechanics. The panelist felt the stock would ride along with the boom in new and used car sales and that the company's growth rate would be well above average. The Smiths thought this line of reasoning hit the nail on the head. They went to their public library and obtained information about the company from the *Value Line* and *Standard & Poor's* write-ups. They liked what they saw: Snap-On was well managed, had a sound financial position, and was a leader in a business that was really tooling up. There was one aspect about the company, however, that they felt could screw their investment: it had a P/E of 17, compared with a market P/E of 12. That was a bit more of a premium than they liked and there were some wrenching discussions in the Smith home as to whether they should buy or not. Because of Snap-On's above-average growth potential and the Smiths' feeling that *Wall Street Week* could be the beginning of increased recognition for the company, they believed the stock fit at least two of my rules quite well. They bought the stock at 29¾ in July 1983.

Market historians will immediately recognize that the Smiths' timing was off. They were buying just as the market was souring after a spectacular year-long binge. The Smiths' expectations for Snap-On Tools' earnings were right on target but the stock's P/E multiple decreased to little more than the market average and the stock price itself remained flat. Once again the Smiths' faith in the long-term efficiency of the market was tested, and once again they held on in the belief that the decreased P/E now meant that Snap-On satisfied all three of my rules. Sure enough, by September 1984, Snap-On was selling at 37 — a 20 percent annual increase when the broad market averages were eking out a 2 percent raise.

Paul Walsh, who likes to use his real name because he's a man who has nothing to hide, is a relative newcomer to the stock market. Rather than being fascinated with stock tables as I have always been, Walsh was intimidated. He firmly believed that stock investing was a complicated, number-crunching occupation that did not suit his creative talents as a writer. But Walsh did happen to read my book and found that the stock market could actually be interesting. He didn't know it at the time, but he had just been bitten by the investment bug.

One of the first things Walsh did was to go to his public library to take advantage of the information sources it had to offer: the financial pages of daily newspapers, a variety of business magazines, and—to Walsh most valuable of all—Standard & Poor's *Outlook* and the *Value Line Investment Survey*.

The chances are that if you went to Walsh's local library on a Saturday morning, you would find him there reading about stocks. And on Monday morning, you could hear him on the phone telling his discount broker to buy some. He loved it. Walsh would never put his money into an index fund. That would take the romance and whimsy out of investing. Why, if he had been content to invest in such a passive way, he would never have found Brooks Fashions.

Walsh came across this stock in his usual manner: turning the pages of the *Value Line Investment Survey* at the library. It was the name that first attracted him. Walsh's daughter, Brooks, is interested in fashion. "Wouldn't it be fun," he thought, "to buy a stock with such an auspicious name?" He then began a serious study of the company and he liked what he saw. Brooks Fashion Stores Inc. operates a chain of women's specialty stores and had been experiencing frenetic growth, which was expected to continue at a well above average rate for the next five years. Its P/E was about 10 times its estimated 1984 earnings, well within the range at which the general market was selling. Clearly, this was a stock that met my first and second rules. That was enough for Walsh: he bought it at $21 a share in May 1984. Would the market have eventually caught on to Brooks Fashions? We shall never know—for Dylex Ltd., Canada's largest fashion retailer, knew a good deal when they saw one and in July 1984 purchased Brooks at $32 a share. A loving father had made a 50 percent profit in three months.

The experience of these individuals illustrate the potential profits, pitfalls, and fun obtainable from employing my strategy. These are all success stories (losers, after all, rarely brag) but they did entail some nocturnal anxiety—for the Smiths especially—when they did not sleep well. Actually, in the Smiths' case, it was over a year before the market corrected itself with regard to IBM. As Paul Walsh's story illustrates, it also takes a lot of time and effort to invest wisely. The Smiths recognize this and they now have invested in one of the mutual funds I name in the next section. They realize the risk involved in not having a diversified portfolio and how one really disastrous investment could have wiped out a substantial part of their capital.

These small investors also felt a keen sense of ignorance in that they were not always sure they could trust earnings reports and they did not have the contacts and the up-to-the-minute information available to the "experts." They realized that once a story is out in the regular press, it's likely that the market has already taken account of the information, as the efficient-market theory supposes. Even today, they feel that they are neophytes in a very tricky business and agree with me that picking individual stocks is like breeding thoroughbred porcupines. You study and study and make up your mind, and then proceed very carefully. In the final analysis, as much as I hope their excellent record resulted from following my good advice, their success may have been mainly a matter of luck.

For all its hazards, picking individual stocks is a fascinating game. My rules do, I believe, tilt the odds in your favor while protecting you from the excessive risk involved in high-multiple stocks. The market environment during the mid-1980s remained particularly favorable for the successful application of my rules. Like the ends of a closing accordion, the price-earnings multiples of stocks with superior growth prospects and those of the more prosaic stocks had come together and stayed relatively close. Because recent speculative investment crazes involved the over-pricing of the premier growth stocks, an overreaction may even have set in, causing these stocks to be underpriced relative to the market. Recall the chart in Chapter Eleven, an earlier version of which had attracted the Smiths. The chart shows the contraction of the multiple of the Babson 28 Growth Stock Index relative to that of the S&P 500. While growth stocks tended to sell at more than double the multiple of the S&P at the height of the one-decision Nifty Fifty craze in 1973, they sold at only a 10 percent premium over more run-of-the-mill stocks during the mid-1980s. Precisely the most interesting stocks in the market — those whose earnings and dividends had been far outdistancing inflation — were selling at their most reasonable market valuations in years. Therefore, the mid-1980s could prove to be the ideal time to pick individual stocks on the basis of my rules. Unlike the early 1970s, it was not hard to find an abundant selection of strong companies that filled the bill.

But if you choose this course, remember that a large number of other investors — including the pros — are trying to play the same game. And the efficient-market theory suggests that the odds of anyone's consistently beating the market are pretty slim. Nevertheless, for many of us, trying to outguess the market is a game that is much too much fun to give up. Even if you were convinced you would not do any better than average, I'm sure that most of you with speculative temperaments would still want to keep on playing the game of selecting individual stocks. My rules, at least, permit you to do so in a way that significantly limits your exposure to risk.

The Substitute Player Step: Hire a Professional Wall-Street Walker

There's an easier way to gamble in your investment walk: instead of trying to pick the individual winners (stocks), pick the best coaches (investment managers). These "coaches" come in the form of mutual-fund managers, and there are over four hundred for you to pick from.

In addition to offering risk reduction through diversification, the mutual funds provide freedom from having to select stocks, and relief from paperwork and record-keeping for tax purposes. Most funds also offer a variety of special services, such as automatic reinvestment of dividends and regular cash-withdrawal plans. A mutual fund is particularly attractive as the investment vehicle for an Individual Retirement Account or Keogh plan, as described in Chapter Ten.

While some readers may well be disappointed that I do not name particular stocks in this book, they will find that I have absolutely no hesitation about citing mutual-fund managers who run their portfolios by following rules similar to mine and who have enjoyed perfectly splendid records. John Marks Templeton is one such person.

You may recall that in Part Two, when I was demonstrating how unreliable and temporary superior performance really is, one exception stood out: the Templeton Growth Fund not only was in the top twenty during the go-go year of 1968 but remained in the top twenty as it has during the most recent ten-year period, racking up a total gain of almost 500 percent.

The individual behind this exception to the rule is most unusual. A former Rhodes scholar, Templeton is fervently religious, believing in an omnipotent God who transcends narrow religious sects. Templeton starts each investment meeting with a prayer. He once told an interviewer, "We don't pray that our stocks will go up. We pray because it makes us think more clearly." He keeps a sense of detachment from the waves of euphoria and despair on Wall Street by running his portfolio from the quiet seclusion of Lyford Cay, in the Bahamas.

Templeton's basic technique is to search out low-multiple stocks that rest on the firmest foundation of value, and then to have patience while the market catches up to him. If the anticipated earnings growth materializes, he expects to be rewarded with substantial capital appreciation both from the earnings growth and from an increase in the earnings multiple. Templeton's ecumenism extends not only to religion but to the stock market as well. He seeks out the best bargains wherever they are to be found — however well known the company and whatever the country in which it is located. For example, following World War II, he invested heavily in Europe because the stocks were cheap and he felt European business would grow rapidly with the help of the Marshall Plan. Since then he has moved in and out of the Canadian and Japanese markets. It matters not whether the companies are in Seoul or Sandusky, Melbourne or Mexico City. Templeton's concern is that he own stocks whose selling prices are lowest in relationship to their "true" worth.

Early in the 1980s, Templeton believed that the U.S. market represented the best bargain in the world. He felt U.S. stocks were a better hedge against inflation than antiques, gold, or diamonds. He said, "Real estate is priced at twice what it was ten years ago, whereas common stocks are cheaper than they were then." He believed that investors would be attracted to U.S. common stocks to keep ahead of inflation just as they ran to gold and real estate. You can see why Templeton's style of management appeals to me.

One reasonable investment strategy is to bet that Templeton's outstanding record will continue. I have only two quibbles with this strategy: First, Templeton's fund is a load fund. A small investor has to pay an $8\frac{1}{2}$ percent service charge just to buy in, and it will therefore need a considerable period of above-average performance just to get back to even. Second, Templeton was born in 1912. While I am perfectly willing to believe that God is in fact on his side and will remain so, even Moses didn't live forever.

A younger version of John Templeton is the brillant portfolio manager for the Windsor Fund, John Neff. Neff's track record is not as long as Templeton's but during recent periods it was almost as fast. During 1975 and 1976, Windsor outperformed every fund in the nation with assets over $100 million. Neff's record over longer periods is also exceptional. Like Templeton, he is an inveterate bargain hunter. His motto: "Get 'em while they're cold." His philosophy: "At Windsor we court the downtrodden and misunderstood and overlooked." His nickname: The Contrarian.

Neff is particularly fond of what he calls "lesser recognized" or "secondary growth stocks"—stocks with growth characteristics but nongrowth multiples. He uses a handy rule of thumb for stock selection: "I take current yield plus the earnings growth rate [this is what I called "prospective return" in Chapter Eleven] and divide it by the current price-earnings ratio. This means I am dividing what I am getting by what I am paying. If the answer is two or more, it's a buy."

It used to be hard to find stocks that met the test. But in the mid-1980s even venerable Exxon was a buy under Neff's system. Recall that the prospective return (dividend yield plus growth) was about 15 percent while the earnings multiple was 6½. Neff is often able to include in his portfolio many stocks with a prospective return of over three times the earnings multiple. If stocks are in the doghouse, Neff says, "Fine—then it's time to buy dogs." "I'm not smart enough to call the bottom," said Neff in 1980, "but I don't need to be with all the outstanding bargains around."

So Neff's system is to look for good value in terms of prospective return, combined with a low multiple. Then he patiently waits for Wall Street (or would-be acquirers) to pick up the scent. The key to success is, in his own words, "Have guts and be right." John Neff certainly has guts, and thus far he has usually been right.

Has Neff ever been wrong? Yes, in 1972 Neff was dead wrong on the market and found himself in the bottom half of the performance derby. But it is that performance in 1972 that makes me especially fond of Neff as a portfolio manager. For 1972 was the year of the rush to the one-decision stock (as described in Part One), and the only issues that were doing well were those recognized growth stocks with multiples rising to 50, 60, 70, or more. Neff was quoted in *Forbes* in early 1973 as follows:

"My problem," Neff says, "is that up to last July almost all the market advance has come from growth stocks with silly multiples, stocks that I won't touch at these prices.

"Okay, you may say, 'You dummy, you, why aren't you there where the action is?' and I say, 'The hell with it. I won't take the risk.'"

It's this contrarian philosophy that lets Windsor Fund shareholders sleep well at night while still enjoying excellent long-run performance.

Dean Francis LeBaron, president of Batterymarch Financial Management, is similar to Neff and Templeton in many respects. While LeBaron calls himself a modified random walker and believes that market prices are generally correct, he is convinced that the majority opinion is not always fully rational. Taking advantage of these times is the path to superior investment performance. Thus, like Neff and Templeton, LeBaron is fundamentally a contrarian who buys securities that are out of favor with traditional Wall Street analysts. "Wrong is right" says a clipping prominently displayed on his office wall. He seems to follow its advice. For example, conventional wisdom has it that companies with six consecutive declines in earnings should be avoided at any price. Not so for LeBaron. These are the kinds of companies, he says, that "can benefit from favorable earnings surprises and not be hurt by unfavorable surprises." Traditional managers will often sell such stocks because they could be an embarrassment on the manager's next quarterly report. LeBaron is more likely to regard them as an excellent bargain.

While LeBaron is a consummate value-oriented investor, his similarity to other contrarians ends there. For LeBaron's method of portfolio selection would make Neff's and Templeton's hair stand on end. While Neff dutifully calculates prospective returns and Templeton prays for clarity of mind, LeBaron flips on the computer. The Batterymarch method is to pick a few broad investment strategies (e.g., invest in large companies with highest yields) and then let the computer make all buy and sell decisions strictly by the numbers. LeBaron's fascination with the computer is in line with his lifelong avocation as a gadget buff. He has owned an amphibious car, motorized draperies, an electronic driveway that melts snow, a working flight simulator (he tried to get around the no-car rule at Phillips Exeter by keeping a plane), and — much to the affront of serious golfers — an adjustable golf club.

An absent-minded professor type, LeBaron wears rumpled suits and stained raincoats. His weight has fluctuated widely — at one point he lost forty pounds in three months and his trousers had to be taken in so much that their back pockets nearly touched. His reading ranges from *The Dancing Wu Li Masters* to *Zen and Creative Management*. (Zen teaches him to relax about things.) LeBaron may seem flaky, but he has produced excellent investment results. Over the 14 years to 1984, the total rate of return for funds managed by Batterymarch has exceeded the S&P 500 by six percentage points, and assets under his management grew to over 11 billion dollars.

Here are some of the broad strategies LeBaron has told his computer to use in selecting what stocks to hold. Earlier in the 1980s, LeBaron believed that the market had become so paranoid with fear over the viability of many U.S. corporations that companies seemingly on the brink of bankruptcy were very attractive. He instructed his computer programmers to set up a "corporate recovery" database and from this exercise he bought Chrysler and Manville at prices between $5 and $10. Over a 12-month period these investments returned over 100 percent. At another time, believing that corporations which decided to buy back their own stock might know things not reflected in the market, he developed a "financial cannibals" strategy. Other strategies have included low P/E stocks, high-yield stocks, small companies, asset-rich companies, and high-growth firms specializing in consumer products. One new strategy, initiated at the end of 1984, involved the purchase of stocks for which security analysts had particularly pessimistic forecasts of future earnings growth and thus whole market prices were depressed. Recalling the rather poor accuracy of the analysts' forecasts we reviewed in Chapter Seven it is easy to see why Batterymarch believes that such stocks are far more likely to be the beneficiaries of positive surprises than are the current institutional favorites. Once the strategy is set, the computer spits out the buy orders. The whole investment operation is on automatic pilot.

Humanists will be pleased to know that the computer has laid an egg or two. As part of a high-yield strategy, Batterymarch spent close to $40 million to buy a 5 percent stake in Continental Illinois Bank during the early 1980s. By late 1984 the shares were worth well under 10 million dollars, indicating a loss of about 30 million dollars. Batterymarch had never examined Continental's finances in any detail beyond what was listed in the computer tapes. Overall, however, despite some hiccups in 1984, the record has been an excellent one.

I did not recommend LeBaron in previous editions because his services were available only to an elite corps of institutional investors who could invest at least $10 million. Now, however, LeBaron has formed a mutual fund that is available to the public. With a terribly maladroit name "Trustees Commingled Fund"—that sounds like it was spit out by the computer—it has both a domestic and a foreign portfolio available for investors.

The table on pages 342 and 343 presents data on six mutual funds, each with an outstanding long-term record.* The clear lesson of Part Two is that you can't count on these outstanding results persisting. But unlike the majority of the top-performing funds of 1968, these six funds have not achieved their records by being on the bandwagon of a popular fad. They do not take on excessive risk—indeed, their volatility (beta) ratings are (except in one instance) lower than that for Standard & Poor's 500 Stock Index. All these funds have a philosophy of hunting for value. While you have no guarantee that the managers will continue to beat the market, at least you know that they did not achieve their records by building castles in the air. I may be a mostly random

---

*No long-term record is available for Trustees Commingled Fund because it has only recently been formed. An excellent long-term record has been recorded by Batterymarch, the fund's investment manager, as indicated in the text.

walker, but I am also a gambling man, and there is much to be said for placing one's bets on these funds rather than on the market as a whole.

The Demise of the Malkiel Step

In previous editions I highly recommended a strategy of buying shares in a special type of mutual fund called a closed-end fund (officially, a closed-end investment company). Closed-end funds differ from open-end mutual funds (the kind discussed in the previous section) in that they neither issue nor redeem shares after the initial offering. To buy or sell shares, you have to go to the market—generally the New York Stock Exchange.

The price of the shares depends on what other investors are willing to pay for them and, unlike the price of shares in an open-end fund, is not necessarily related to net asset value. Thus, a closed-end fund can sell at a premium above or at a discount from its net asset value. During much of the 1970s and at the start of the 1980s, these funds were selling at substantial discounts from their net asset value. Closed-end funds hire professional managers, and their expenses are no higher than those of ordinary mutual funds. So for those who believe in professional investment management, here was a way to buy it a discount and I told my readers so. One of the closed-end funds I recommended was run by John Neff.

A small proportion of the discounts on closed-end funds could be explained by rational considerations. Some funds had a substantial amount of unrealized capital gains in their portfolios that could affect the timing of an individual's tax liabilities. Other funds had substantial holdings of "letter stock," the sale of which was restricted and whose market prices might not have been accurate reflections of their true value. But these considerations could at best explain only a minor proportion of the discounts that ran as high as 40 percent during the late 1970s. My own explanation for the discounts ran in terms of an

Selected Mutual Funds with Good Performance Records

Fund	Sales Charge (%)	Year Organized	Minimum Amount, Initial Purchase ($)	Minimum Amount, Subsequent Purchases ($)	Expense Ratio (%) (1983)	Total Net Assets ($ Millions) (6/29/84)	% Change in Net Assets per Share with Capital Gains and Income Dividends Reinvested Accepted in Shares (to 6/29/84) 5½ Years	% Change ... 10½ Years	Rate of Portfolio Turnover (% of Average Assets, 1983)	% Yield Last 12 Months (6/29/84)	Risk Level (Beta Coefficient)	Payroll Deduction or Bank Draft Payment Plan Available	Keogh Plan Available	Individual Retirement Account Available
Fidelity Equity Income Fund 82 Devonshire Street Boston, MA 02109 800/225-6190	2.0	1966	1,000	250	0.83	837.2	211.8	512.1	118	6.8	0.82	No	Yes	Yes
Mutual Shares Corporation 26 Broadway New York, NY 10004 212/908-4048	None	1949	1,000	None	0.78	370.3	202.2	828.9	70	2.0	0.62	No	Yes	Yes

Templeton Growth Fund 44 Victoria St. Toronto, M5C 182 Canada 800/237-0738	8.5[b]	1954	500	25	0.75	842.9	120.8	462.5	10	1.9	0.89	Yes	No	No
Trustee Commingled Fund-U.S. Equity Portfolio[a] P.O. Box 2600 Valley Forge, PA 19482 800/523-7025 (800/362-0530 in PA)	None	1980	25,000	1,000	0.50	237.5	N/A	N/A	30	4.6	0.99	Yes	Yes	Yes
20th Century Investors Growth Fund P.O. Box 200 Kansas City, MO 64141 816/531-5575	None	1957	None	None	1.02	616.4	224.2	764.0	98	0.4	1.35	Yes	Yes	Yes
Windsor Fund[a] P.O. Box 2600 Valley Forge, PA 19482 800/523-7025 (800/362-0530 in PA)	None	1958	1,500	100	0.67	1,887.3	172.2	462.6	48	5.9	0.85	Yes	Yes	Yes

Source: Wiesenberger, Investment Companies Service.

[a] I am a director of this fund.

[b] Actually ranging from 8.5%, depending on amount of purchase.

unexploited market inefficiency and I urged investors to take full advantage of the opportunity for as long as it lasted.

The beauty of buying these highly discounted closed-end funds was that, even if the discounts remained at high levels, investors would still reap extraordinary rewards from their purchase. If you could buy shares at a 25 percent discount, you would have 4 dollars of asset value on which dividends could be earned for every 3 dollars you invested. So even if the funds just equaled the market return, as believers in the random walk would expect, you would beat the averages.

It was like having a $100 savings account paying 5 percent interest. You deposit $100 and earn $5 interest each year. Only this savings account could be bought at a 25 percent discount; in other words, for $75. You still got $5 interest (5 percent of $100), but since you paid only $75 for the account, your rate of return was 6.67 percent (5 ÷ 75). Note that this increase in yield was in no way predicated on the discount narrowing. Even if you got only $75 back when you cashed in, you would still have received a big bonus in extra returns while holding the account. The discount on closed-end funds provided a similar bonus. You got your share of dividends from $1 worth of assets, even though you paid only 75¢.

I also recommended a number of special-purpose closed-end funds called the capital shares of dual-purpose funds. The details of these funds need not concern us here except to note that for these funds the discount was guaranteed to be eliminated at a specified maturity date during the early 1980s, when the shares could either be redeemed at net asset value or left invested with a regular open-end fund. The table on the following page lists the funds I recommend in the 1981 edition, together with the discounts existing at that time.

The strategy worked even better than expected. Discounts were eliminated for the special purpose funds noted above, and either disappeared or narrowed significantly on the regular funds. This is indicated in the last column of the table. While the publicity given closed-end fund in my books may have helped to

Closed-end Funds Recommended in 1980

Regular Funds

Fund	Discount from Net Asset Value (Jan. 1980)	Average Discount Preceding 15 Years	Discount (Aug. 1984)[a]
Baker Fentress	33.8%	Not available for 15 years	10.1
Lehman	20.4	8	1.1 p
General American Investors	20.1	10	0.1 p
Madison	19.2	4.5	0
Niagara Shares	17.5	6	0.6 p
Tri Continental Corp.	23.1	16	2.6
U.S. & Foreign Securities	23.4	20	0
Adams Express	18.5	11	8.8

Dual-Purpose Funds

Fund	Discount from Net Asset Value (Jan. 1980)	Average Discount Inception of Fund to 1980	Discount (Aug. 1984)[a]
Income and Capital	22.3%	23%	0
Gemini	13.5	19	1.2
Leverage	16.1	22	0
Putnam Duo-Fund	18.2	22	0
Scudder Duo-Vest	15.0	25	0

Source: *Wall Street Journal* for discounts. Past discounts were calculated from Wiesenberger Financial Services, *Investment Companies and Their Securities*, 1980.

[a]p indicates premium; 0 indicates the fund has liquidated or now operates as an open-end fund.

eliminate the discounts, I think the fundamental reason for the narrowing is that our capital markets are reasonably efficient. The market may misvalue assets from time to time creating temporary inefficiencies. But if there is *truly* some area of pricing inefficiency that can be discovered by the market and dependably exploited, then value-seeking investors will take advantage of these opportunities and thereby eliminate them. Pricing irregularities may well exist and even persist for periods of time, but the financial laws of gravity will eventually take hold and true value will out.

I mentioned in previous editions that I gave my son, Jonathan, the royalties from the first edition of this book. Practicing what I preached, I invested them in a portfolio of closed-end and dual-purpose funds selling at substantial discounts. The investments were made mainly at the end of 1973 (near a peak in the market and thus a terrible time to invest) and near the end of 1974 (after the market had suffered a very sharp decline). The table on the facing page shows how Jonathan's investments have appreciated between the time they were made and the middle of 1984. The strategy has significantly outperformed the market and was an inflation beater even during the dismal markets of the 1970s. The narrowing of the discounts helped to produce quite spectacular returns. The strategy required courage, however. The 1973 investments, made when the market was very high, were under a good deal of water at the end of 1974.* Fortunately, new royalty checks came in at that time and more shares were bought for Jonathan, and the overall results have been more than satisfactory.

A Paradox

With their discounts just about dried up at the time this edition goes to press, closed-end funds are no longer an attractive

---

*According to my Rule 4 I might have switched to other closed-end funds to gain some tax advantages in 1974. However, Jonathan's tax situation did not warrant incurring the brokerage charges to effect such a switch.

Jonathan's Portfolio

	Price			Compounded Rate of Return, Including Dividends and Capital Gains	
	12/31/73	12/31/74	6/30/84	End 73 to Mid-84	End 74 to Mid-84
Regular Closed-End Funds					
Baker Fentress	8½ bid[a]	5¼ bid[a]	29¾ bid	16.8%	25.5%
Former Dual-Purpose Funds					
Putnam Capital Fund	4¼ bid	2¼ bid	7.21	12.7	25.6
Scudder Capital Growth Fund	2[a]	1¼[a]	13.97	10.8	17.6
Standard & Poor's 500 Stock Index	97.55	68.56	153.18	8.3	12.9

[a] Adjusted for subsequent splits.

investment opportunity. I have discussed them in some detail, however, because they illustrate an important paradox about investment advice, as well as the maxim that true values do eventually prevail in the market. There is a fundamental paradox about the usefulness of investment advice concerning specific securities. If the advice reaches enough people and they act on it, knowledge of the advice destroys its usefulness. If everyone knows about a "good buy" and they all rush in to buy, the price of the "good buy" will rise until it is no longer particularly attractive for investment. Indeed, there will be pressure on the price to rise as long as it is still a good buy.

This is the main logical pillar on which the efficient-market theory rests. If the spread of news is unimpeded prices will react quickly so that they reflect all that is known about the particular situation. This led me to predict in the 1981 edition that such favorable discounts would not always be available. I wrote, "I would be very surprised to see the early-1980s levels of discounts perpetuate themselves indefinitely." For the same reason, I am skeptical that very simple currently popular rules such as "buy low P/E stocks" or "buy small company stocks" will perpetually produce unusually high risk-adjusted returns.

There is a well-known academic story about the random walk of a finance professor and two of his students. The finance professor, a proponent of the strongest form of the random walk theory, was convinced that markets were always perfectly efficient. When he and the students spotted a $10 bill lying on the street, he told them to ignore it. "If it was really a $10 bill, he reasoned out loud, someone would have already picked it up." Fortunately, the students were skeptical, not only of Wall Street professionals, but also of learned professors, and so they picked up the $10 bill.

Clearly, there is considerable logic to the finance professor's position. In markets where intelligent people are searching for value, it is unlikely that people will perpetually leave $10 bills around ready for the taking. But history tells us that unexploited opportunities do exist from time to time, as do periods of speculative excess pricing. We know of Dutchmen paying astronomical prices for tulip bulbs, of Englishmen splurging on the most improbable bubbles, and of modern institutional fund managers who convinced themselves that some stocks were so "nifty" that any price was reasonable. And while investors were building castles in the air, real fundamental investment opportunities such as closed-end funds were passed by. Yet eventually excessive valuations were corrected and eventually investors did snatch up the bargain closed-end funds. Perhaps the finance professor's advice should have been, "You had better pick that $10 bill up quickly because if it's really there, someone else will surely pick it up." It is in this sense that I consider myself a random walker. I am convinced that true value will out, but from time to time it doesn't surprise me that anomalies do exist. There may be some $10 bills around at times and I'll certainly interrupt my random walk to purposefully stoop and pick them up.

Some Last Reflections on Our Walk

We are now at the end of our walk. Let's look back for a moment and see where we have been. It is clear that the ability to beat the average consistently is most rare. Neither fundamental analysis of a stock's firm foundation of value nor technical analysis of the market's propensity for building castles in the air can produce reliably superior results. Even the pros must hide their heads in shame when they compare their results with those obtained by the dart-board method of picking stocks. The only way to achieve above-average returns in an efficient market is to assume greater risk. But as Part Three showed, risk is far from a simple concept and neither beta nor any other single risk measure is likely to be adequate.

Sensible investment policies for individuals must then be developed in two steps. First, it is crucially important to under-stand the risk-return tradeoffs that are available and to tailor your choice of securities to your temper and requirements.

Chapter Ten provided a careful guide for this part of the walk, including a number of warm-up exercises concerning everything from tax planning to the management of reserve funds.

Chapter Eleven argued the case for paper assets as the cornerstone of most portfolios. This chapter has covered the major part of our walk down Wall Street — three important steps for buying common stocks. I began by suggesting sensible strategies that are consistent with the existence of efficient markets. I recognized, however, that most investors will not be convinced that the random-walk theory is valid. Telling an investor there is no hope of beating the averages is like telling a six-year-old there is no Santa Claus. It takes the zing out of life.

For those of you, incurably smitten with the speculative bug, who insist on picking individual stocks in an attempt to beat the market, I offered four rules. The odds are really stacked against you, but you may just get lucky and win big. I also suggested that you might want to place your bets on the few rare investment managers who, at least in the past, have shown some talent for finding those rare $10 bills lying around in the marketplace.

Investing is a bit like lovemaking. Ultimately it is really an art requiring a certain talent and the presence of a mysterious force called luck. Indeed, luck may be 99 percent responsible for the success of the very few people who have beaten the averages. "Although men flatter themselves with their great actions," La Rochefoucauld wrote, "they are not so often the result of great design as of chance."

The game of investing is like lovemaking in another important respect, too. It's much too much fun to give up. If you have the talent to recognize stocks that have good value, and the art to recognize a story that will catch the fancy of others, it's a great feeling to see the market vindicate you. Even if you are not so lucky, my rules will help you limit your risks and avoid much of the pain that is sometimes involved in the playing. If you know you will either win or at least lose not too much, you will be able to play the game with more satisfaction. At the very least, I hope this book makes the game all the more enjoyable.

Bibliography

I have suppressed my academic proclivity for sprinkling each page with footnotes to learned references showing who said what on particular issues. I do hope, however, that this bibliography indicates clearly the sources of the studies I have discussed and provides useful additional readings for those interested in particular points. The references are grouped by chapter, and in some cases (especially for Chapters Six and Seven), notation is made of what the sources contain. Where certain references are cited throughout this book, they are listed only in the first chapter for which they were used.

Part One

CHAPTER ONE

Bernard Baruch, *My Own Story*. Holt, 1957.

Jess H. Chua and Richard S. Woodward, "J. M. Keynes's Investment Performance: A Note." *The Journal of Finance*, March 1983.

Irving Fisher, *The Theory of Interest*. Kelley, 1961.

Benjamin Graham and David L. Dodd, *Security Analysis*. 1st ed. McGraw-Hill, 1934.

Samuel Eliot Guild, *Stock Growth and Discount Tables*, Financial Publishers, 1931.

John M. Keynes, *The General Theory of Employment Interest and Money*. Harcourt, 1936.

Oskar Morgenstern and Clive William John Granger, *Predictability of Stock Market Prices*. Heath Lexington, 1970.

"Adam Smith," *The Money Game*. Random House, 1968.

John Von Neuman and Oskar Morgenstern, *Theory of Games and Economic Behavior*. Princeton University Press, 1941.

John Burr Williams, The Theory of Investment Value. Harvard University Press, 1938.

CHAPTER TWO

Frederick L. Allen, *Only Yesterday*. Harper, 1931.

Edward Angly, *Oh Yeah?* Viking, 1931.

Walter Bagehot, *Lombard Street*. London: Murray, 1922.

Bruce Barton, *The Man Nobody Knows*. Bobbs-Merrill, 1925.

John N. Brooks, *Once in Golconda*. Harper & Row, 1969.

———, *The Seven Fat Years*. Harper, 1958.

John Carswell, *The South Sea Bubble*. London: Cresset Press, 1960.

Lester V. Chandler, *America's Greatest Depression 1929–1941*. Harper & Row, 1970.

William Cobbett, *The Parliamentary History of England*, Volume VII. London: Hansard, 1811.

Cedric B. Cowing, *Populists, Plungers, and Progressives*. Princeton University Press, 1965.

Charles Amos Dice, *New Levels in the Stock Market*. McGraw-Hill, 1929.

John Kenneth Galbraith, *The Great Crash, 1929*. Houghton Mifflin, 1955.

Gustave Le Bon, *The Crowd: A Study of the Popular Mind*. Woking and London: Unwin Bros., 1895.

Charles Mackay, *Memoirs of Extraordinary Popular Delusions*, Volume I. Lindsay, 1850.

(My discussions of the tulip-bulb craze and the South Sea Bubble rely heavily on Mackay's description.)

Cabell Phillips, *The New York Times Chronicle of American Life: From the Crash to the Blitz, 1929–1939*. Macmillan, 1969.

Nicolaas W. Posthumus, *Inquiry into the History of Prices in Holland*. Leiden: Brill, 1964.

Jelle C. Riemersma, *Religious Factors in Early Dutch Capitalism 1550–1650*. The Hague: Mouton, 1967.

Lionel Robbins, *The Great Depression*. Loudon: Macmillan, 1935.

Robert Sobel, *Panic on Wall Street*. Macmillan, 1968.

Dana L. Thomas, *The Plungers and the Peacocks*. Putnam, 1967.

Twentieth Century Fund, *The Security Markets*. 1935.

CHAPTER THREE

Bill Adler, ed., *The Wall Street Reader*. World, 1970.

David L. Babson and Company, Inc., "Wall Street 'Discovers' Investment Quality." *Weekly Staff Letter*, August 6, 1970.

Hurd Baruch, *Wall Street: Security Risk*. Acropolis, 1971.

Murray Teigh Bloom, *Rogues to Riches*. Putnam, 1971.

John Brooks, *Business Adventures*. Weybright and Talley, 1969.

McGeorge Bundy, President's Review in *The Ford Foundation Annual Report 1966*. February 1, 1967.

Christopher Elias, *Fleecing the Lambs*. Regnery, 1971.

John G. Fuller, *The Money Changers*. Dial, 1962.

William W. Helman, *Conglomerates— What Happened?* Smith, Barney & Co., September 24, 1969.

Sidney K. Margolius, *The Innocent Investor and the Shaky Ground Floor*, Trident, 1971.

Martin Mayer, *New Breed on Wall Street*. Macmillan, 1969.

——, *Wall Street: Men and Money*. Harper, 1955.

Securities and Exchange Commission, *Special Study of Securities Market*. House Document No. 95, 88th Congress. U.S. Government Printing Office, 1963.

Robert Sobel, *The Big Board*. Free Press, 1965.

"So Long As It's Electronic," *Forbes*, February 15, 1959.

Andrew Tobias, *The Funny Money Game*. Playboy Press, 1971.

John Wall, "Want to Get Rich Quick?" *Barron's*, February 5, 1968.

CHAPTER FOUR

Burton G. Malkiel and John G. Cragg, "Expectations and the Structure of Share Prices." *American Economic Review*, September 1970. (This is a formal empirical study documenting the changing valuation standards of the market over time. It is the study referred to in the text.)

J. Peter Williamson, *Investments*. Praeger, 1971.

Part Two

CHAPTER FIVE

Benjamin Graham, *The Intelligent Investor*. Harper & Row, 1965.
Albert Haas, Jr. and Don D. Jackson, M.D., *Bulbs, Bears and Dr. Freud*. World, 1967.
Gerald M. Loeb, *The Battle for Investment Survival*. Simon & Schuster, 1965.
John Magee and Robert Davis Edwards, *Technical Analysis of Stock Trends*. Stock Trend Service, 1954.
Fred Schwed, Jr., *Where Are the Customers' Yachts?* Simon & Schuster, 1940.

CHAPTER SIX

The following are general works summarizing parts of the academic literature on the efficacy of technical analysis:
Fischer Black, "Implications of the Random Walk Hypothesis for Portfolio Management." *Financial Analysts Journal*, March–April 1971.
   (A layman's survey of a number of studies.)
Richard A. Brealey, *An Introduction to Risk and Return from Common Stocks*. M.I.T. Press, 1969.
   (Only slightly mathematical.)
——, *Security Prices in a Competitive Market: More About Risk and Return from Common Stocks*. M.I.T. Press, 1971.
   (Only slightly mathematical.)
—— and Stewart Myers, *Principles of Corporate Finance*. McGraw-Hill, 1981.
Paul Cootner, ed., *The Random Character of Stock Market Prices*. M.I.T. Press, 1964.
   (A compendium of mathematical articles.)
Eugene F. Fama, "Efficient Capital Markets: A Review of Theory and Empirical Work," *Journal of Finance*, May 1970.
   (An excellent but highly mathematical summary of empirical research on the random-walk theory.)
James H. Lorie and Mary T. Hamilton, *The Stock Market: Theories and Evidence*. Irwin, 1975.
   (Only slightly mathematical.)
—— and Richard A. Brealey, eds., *Modern Developments in Investment Management: A Book of Readings*. Praeger, 1972.

Specific studies of technical systems follow:

Sidney S. Alexander, "Price Movements in Speculative Markets: Trends or Random Walks." *Industrial Management Review*, May 1961.

Louis Bachelier, *Théorie de la Spéculation*. Paris: Gauthier-Villars, 1900.

Paul Cootner, "Stock Prices: Random vs. Systematic Changes." *Industrial Management Review*, Spring 1962.

John L. Evans, "The Random Walk Hypothesis, Portfolio Analysis and the Buy-and-Hold Criterion." *Journal of Financial and Quantitative Analysis*, September 1968.

Eugene F. Fama, "Mandelbrot and the Stable Paretian Hypothesis" *Journal of Business*, October 1963.

——, "Tomorrow on the New York Stock Exchange." *Journal of Business*, July 1965.

—— and Marshall E. Blume, "Filter Rules and Stock-Market Trading." *Journal of Business*, January 1966.

——, Lawrence Fisher, Michael C. Jensen, and Richard Roll, "The Adjustment of Stock Prices to New Information." *International Economic Review*, February 1969.

Michael D. Godfrey, C.W.J. Granger, and O. Morgenstern, "The Random-Walk Hypothesis of Stock Market Behavior." *Kyklos*, 1964.

C.W.J. Granger and O. Morgenstern, "Spectral Analysis of New York Stock Market Prices." *Kyklos*, 1963.

F.E. James, Jr., "Monthly Moving Averages—An Effective Investment Tool?" *Journal of Financial and Quantitative Analysis*, September 1968.

Michael C. Jensen, "Random Walks: Reality or Myth—Comment." *Financial Analysts Journal*, November–December 1967.

—— and George A. Benington, "Random Walks and Technical Theories: Some Additional Evidence." *Journal of Finance*, May 1970.

Charles P. Jones and Robert H. Litzenberger, "Quarterly Earnings Reports and Intermediate Stock Price Trends." *Journal of Finance*, March 1970.

Maurice G. Kendall, "The Analysis of Economic Time-Series, Part I: Prices." *Journal of the Royal Statistical Society*, 1953.

Thomas J. Kewley and Richard A. Stevenson, "The Odd-Lot Theory as Revealed by Purchase and Sale Statistics for Individual Stocks." *Financial Analysts Journal*, September–October 1967.

Robert A. Levy, "Random Walks: Reality or Myth." *Financial Analysts Journal*, November–December 1967.

——, "Relative Strength as a Criterion for Investment Selection." *Journal of Finance*, December 1967.

——, "The Predictive Significance of Five-Point Chart Patterns." *Journal of Business*, July 1971.

Benoit Mandelbrot, "Forecasts of Future Prices, Unbiased Markets, and 'Martingale' Models." *Journal of Business*, Special Supplement, January 1966.

—— and Howard M. Taylor, "On the Distribution of Stock Price Differences." *Operations Research*, November–December 1967.

Victor Niederhoffer and M.F.M. Osborne, "Market Making and Reversal on the Stock Exchange." *Journal of the American Statistical Association*, December 1966.

M.F.M. Osborne, "Brownian Motion in the Stock Market." *Operations Research*, March–April 1959.

——, "Periodic Structure in the Brownian Motion of Stock Prices." *Operations Research*, May–June 1962.

Harry V. Roberts, "Stock Market 'Patterns' and Financial Analysis: Methodological Suggestions." *Journal of Finance*, March 1959.

Paul A. Samuelson, "Proof that Properly Anticipated Prices Fluctuate Randomly." *Industrial Management Review*, Spring 1965.

Alan Seelenfreund, George G. C. Parker, and James C. Van Horne, "Stock Price Behavior and Trading." *Journal of Financial and Quantitative Analysis*, September 1968.

Seymour Smidt, "A New Look at the Random Walk Hypothesis." *Journal of Financial and Quantitative Analysis*, September 1968.

H. Theil and C. T. Leenders, "Tomorrow on the Amsterdam Stock Exchange." *Journal of Business*, July 1965.

James C. Van Horne and George G. C. Parker, "The Random-Walk Theory: An Empirical Test." *Financial Analysts Journal*, November–December 1967.

Charles C. Ying, "Stock Market Prices and Volumes of Sales." *Econometrica*, July 1966.

Alan J. Zakon and James C. Pennypacker, "An Analysis of the Advance Decline Line as a Stock Market Indicator." *Journal of Financial and Quantitative Analysis*, September 1968.

Other works cited:

Ira Cobleigh, *Happiness Is a Stock That Doubles in a Year*. Geis, 1967.

——, "Bull Markets and Bare Knees." In *The Wall Street Reader*, Bill Adler, ed., World, 1970.

Nicholas Darvas, *How I Made Two Million Dollars in the Stock Market*. American Research Council, 1960.

Garfield A. Drew, "The Misunderstood Odd-Lotter." *Barron's*, June 25, 1962.

——, "A Clarification of the Odd Lot Theory." *Financial Analysts Journal*, September–October 1967.

Ralph A. Rotnem, "Measuring Mass Opinion in the Stock Market." *AIC* (American International College) *Journal*, Winter 1972.

Michael Sivvy, "Joe Granville: Messiah or Menace?" *Financial World*, June 15, 1980.

John Slatter, "Lambs in the Street." *Barron's*, January 31, 1966.

Edward O. Thorp, *Beat the Dealer*. Random House, 1966.

CHAPTER SEVEN

The following are general works summarizing parts of the academic literature on the efficacy of fundamental analysis:

Irwin Friend, Marshall Blume and Jean Crockett, *Mutual Funds and Other Institutional Investors*, McGraw-Hill, 1970.

(A nonmathematical and very readable report on the performance of mutual funds.)

Michael C. Jensen, "Capital Markets: Theory and Evidence." *Bell Journal of Economics and Management Science*, Autumn 1972.

(An excellent but highly mathematical summary of findings on the broad form of the random walk theory.)

Specific studies of fundamental analysis follow:

Fred D. Arditti, "Another Look at Mutual Fund Performance." *Journal of Financial and Quantitative Analysis*, June 1971.

Marshall E. Blume, "The Measurement of Investment Performance." *Wall Street Transcript*, July 26, 1971.

Robert S. Carlson, "Aggregate Performance of Mutual Funds, 1948-1967." *Journal of Financial and Quantitative Analysis*, March 1970.

Kalman J. Cohen and Jerry A. Pogue, "Some Comments Concerning Mutual Fund Versus Random Portfolio Performance." *Journal of Business*, April, 1968.

Irwin Friend, F. E. Brown, Edward S. Herman, and Douglas Vickers, *A Study of Mutual Funds*. 87th Congress, House Report No. 2274. U.S. Government Printing Office, 1962.

Irwin Friend and Douglas Vickers, "Portfolio Selection and Investment Performance." *Journal of Finance*, September 1965.

Ira Horowitz, "The 'Reward-to-Variability' Ratio and Mutual Fund Performance." *Journal of Business*, October 1966.

——, "The Varying (?) Quality of Investment Trust Management." *Journal of the American Statisitical Association*, December 1963.

Michael C. Jensen, "The Performance of Mutual Funds in the Period 1945-64." *Journal of Finance*, May 1968.

——, "Risk, the Pricing of Capital Assets, and the Evaluation of Investment Portfolios." *Journal of Business*, April 1969.

Robert A. Levy, "Fund Managers Are Better Than Dart Throwers." *Institutional Investor*, April 1971.

I.M.D. Little, "Higgledy Piggledy Growth." In the *Bulletin of the Oxford University Institute of Economics and Statistics*, November 1962.

Burton G. Malkiel and John G. Cragg, *Expectations and the Valuation of Shares.* National Bureau of Economic Research, Working Paper No. 471, April 1980.

Harry Markowitz, *Portfolio Selection: Efficient Diversification of Investments.* Wiley, 1959.

Everett Mattlin, "Are the Days of the Numbers Games Numbered? *Institutional Investor*, November 1971.

"Portfolio Management: U.S. Senate Style." *Institutional Investor*, October 1957.

D. L. Rosenhan, "On Being Sane in Insane Places." *Science*, January 1973.

Paul A. Samuelson, Statement before *Committee on Banking and Currency*, U.S. Senate, August 2, 1967, re Mutual Fund Legislation of 1967.

G. William Schwert, "Size and Stock Returns, and Other Empirical Regularities." *The Journal of Financial Economics*, June 1983.

William F. Sharpe, "Mutual Fund Performance." *Journal of Business*, Special Supplement, January 1966.

———, *Portfolio Theory and Capital Markets*. McGraw-Hill, 1970.

———, "Risk-Aversion in the Stock Market: Some Empirical Evidence." *Journal of Finance*, September 1965.

John P. Shelton, "The Value Line Contest: A Test of the Predictability of Stock-Price Changes." *Journal of Business*, 1967.

Robert J. Shiller, "Do Stock Prices Move Too Much to be Justified by Subsequent Changes in Dividends?" *American Economic Review*, June 1981.

Jack L. Treymor, "How to Rate Management of Investment Funds." *Harvard Business Review*. January–February 1965.

Oldrich Vasicek and John A. McQuown, "The Efficient Market Model." *Financial Analysts Journal*, September–October 1972.

Henry C. Wallich, "What Really Is the Value of Investment Advice?" *Institutional Investor*, August 1967.

———, "What Does the Random Walk Hypothesis Mean to Security Analysts?" *Financial Analysts Journal*, March–April 1968.

Richard R. West, "Mutual Fund Performance and the Theory of Capital Asset Pricing: Some Comments." *Journal of Business*, April 1968.

Part Three

CHAPTER EIGHT

The following are general discussions of capital-asset pricing theory arranged in increasing order of difficulty:

James H. Lorie and Mary T. Hamilton, *The Stock Market: Theories and Evidence*. Irwin, 1975, Chapters 10–12.

Franco Modigliani and Gerald A. Pogue, "An Introduction to Risk and Return, I." *Financial Analysts Journal*, March–April 1974.

——, "An Introduction to Risk and Return, II." *Financial Analysts Journal*, May–June 1974.

Michael C. Jensen, "Capital Markets, Theory and Evidence." *Bell Journal of Economics and Management Science*, Autumn 1972.

A number of more specific and technical studies follow:

William J. Baumol, "Mathematical Analysis of Portfolio Selection." *Financial Analysts Journal*, September–October 1966.

Fischer Black, Michael C. Jensen, and Myron Scholes, "The Capital Asset Pricing Model: Some Empirical Tests." In *Studies in the Theory of Capital Markets*, Michael C. Jensen, ed., Praeger, 1972.

Murray T. Bloom, *Rogues to Riches*. Putnam, 1971.

Eugene F. Fama and James D. MacBeth, "Risk, Return and Equilibrium: Empirical Tests." Unpublished Working Paper No. 7237, University of Chicago, Graduate School of Business, August 1972.

William L. Fouse, William W. Jahnke and Barr Rosenberg, "Is Beta Phlogiston?" *Financial Analysts Journal*, January–February 1974.

Roger G. Ibbotson and Rex A. Sinquefield, *Stocks, Bonds, Bills, and Inflation: Historical Returns*. The Financial Analysts Research Foundation, University of Virginia, 1979, 1984.

Institutional Investors and Corporate Stock. U.S. Securities and Exchange Commission Institutional Investors Study Report, Raymond W. Goldsmith, ed., National Bureau of Economic Research, 1973.

Gerald D. Levitz, "Market Risk and the Management of Institutional Equity Portfolios." *Financial Analysts Journal*, January–February 1974.

Robert A. Levy, "Beta Coefficients as Predictors of Return." *Financial Analysts Journal*, January–February 1974.

Harry Markowitz, *Portfolio Selection: Efficient Diversification of Investments*. Wiley, 1959.

William F. Sharpe, *Portfolio Theory and Capital Markets*. McGraw-Hill, 1970.

——, "Risk, Market Sensitivity and Diversification." *Financial Analysts Journal*, January–February 1972.

—— and Guy M. Cooper, "Risk-Return Classes of New York Stock Exchange Common Stocks, 1931–1967." *Financial Analysts Journal*, March–April 1972.

Bruno H. Solnik, "The International Pricing of Risk: An Empirical Investigation of the World Capital Market Structure." *Journal of Finance*, May 1974.

"The Strange News About Risk and Return." *Fortune*, June 1973.

Chris Welles, "The Beta Revolution: Learning to Live With Risk." *Institutional Investor*, September 1971.

CHAPTER NINE

Marshall E. Blume, "On the Assessment of Risk." *Journal of Finance*, March 1971.

Vladimir P. Chernik, *The Consumer's Guide to Insurance Buying*, Sherbourne, 1970.

John G. Cragg and Burton G. Malkiel, *Expectations and the Structure of Share Prices*, The University of Chicago Press, 1982.

Max Fogiel, *How to Pay Lots Less for Life Insurance*. Research and Education Association, 1971.

Pennsylvania Insurance Department. *A Shoppers' Guide to Life Insurance*, 1972.

Richard Roll, "A Critique of the Asset Pricing Theory's Tests: Part 1: On Past and Potential Testability of the Theory." *Journal of Financial Economics*, March 1977.

S. A. Ross, "The Arbitrage Theory of Capital Asset Pricing." *Journal of Economic Theory*, December 1976.

Anise Wallace, "Is Beta Dead?" *Institutional Investor*, July 1980.

Part Four

CHAPTER TEN

David L. Babson and Company, Inc., *Weekly Staff Letter*. March 4, 1971.

Zvi Bodie, *Purchasing-Power Annuities: Financial Innovation for Stable Real Retirement Income in an Inflationary Environment*. National Bureau of Economic Research Working Paper No. 442, February 1980.

George E. Pinches, "The Random Walk Hypothesis and Technical Analysis." *Financial Analysts Journal*, March–April 1970.

Wiesenberger Financial Services, *Investment Companies and Their Securities*, 1980.

CHAPTER ELEVEN

Franco Modigliani and Richard Cohn, "Inflation and the Stock Market, *Financial Analysts Journal*, March–April 1979.

Lawrence Fisher, "Outcomes for 'Random' Investments in Common Stocks Listed on the New York Stock Exchange." *Journal of Business*, April 1965.

—— and James H. Lorie, "Rates of Return on Investments in Common Stocks." *Journal of Business*, January 1964.

CHAPTER TWELVE

David Dreman, *The New Contrarian Investment Strategy*, Random House, 1982.

Barry Feldman, *An Economic Analysis of Constant Purchasing Power Bonds*. Unpublished Senior Thesis, Princeton University, 1972.

Robert Frank, *Successful Investing Through Mutual Funds*. Hart, 1969.

Burton G. Malkiel, "The Valuation of Closed-End Investment-Company Shares." *Journal of Finance*, June 1977.

Eugene Pratt, "Myths Associated with Closed-End Investment Company Discounts." *Financial Analysts Journal*, July–August 1966.

Ralph Lee Smith, *The Grim Truth About Mutual Funds*. Putnam, 1963.

John A. Straley, *What About Mutual Funds?* 2nd rev. ed., Harper & Row, 1967.

Rex Thompson, *Capital Market Efficiency and the Information Content of Discounts and Premiums on Closed-End Fund Shares: An Empirical Analysis*. Graduate School of Industrial Administration, Carnegie-Mellon University, Working Paper No. 30, February 1978.

Index